21 世纪全国应用型本科电子通信系列实用规划教材

信息与通信工程专业英语

（第 2 版）

主　编　韩定定　李明明

参　编　赵菊敏　史健婷　董自健

王　锦　陈　趣

北京大学出版社

PEKING UNIVERSITY PRESS

内 容 简 介

本书旨在进一步提高读者英语阅读及翻译的水平，锻炼科技论文写作能力。本书所选的资料多是从国外书刊、杂志和科学文献中精选而来，在选材上注重科学性、知识性、趣味性和文体语言的规范化及时间性。本书不仅从理论上概述了英语翻译的主要技巧和写作的基本技巧，而且辅以大量的例句及实践性练习，通过不断训练，培养学生对这类技巧和方法灵活运用的能力。

全书共分为 3 章：第 1 章介绍科技英语的翻译理论及方法，包括科技专业词汇的翻译方法和疑难句子、科技文体的翻译技巧及翻译要求；第 2 章介绍科技英语文献的阅读及翻译，所选文章的编排和选材根据电路与系统、信息处理技术、现代通信技术及网络应用等分成相应的 10 个部分；第 3 章介绍科技论文写作的基础知识。

本书可作为本科电子信息工程和通信工程专业三、四年级的专业英语教材，也可供研究生及广大工程技术人员使用。

图书在版编目(CIP)数据

信息与通信工程专业英语/韩定定，李明明主编. —2 版. —北京：北京大学出版社，2012.8
(21 世纪全国应用型本科电子通信系列实用规划教材)
ISBN 978-7-301-19318-1

Ⅰ. ①信… Ⅱ. ①韩…②李… Ⅲ. ①信息技术—英语—高等学校—教材②通信工程—英语—高等学校—教材 Ⅳ. ①H31

中国版本图书馆 CIP 数据核字(2011)第 154891 号

书　　　　名：	信息与通信工程专业英语(第 2 版)	
著作责任者：	韩定定　李明明　主编	
策 划 编 辑：	程志强　姜晓楠	
责 任 编 辑：	程志强	
标 准 书 号：	ISBN 978-7-301-19318-1/TN·0074	
出 版 者：	北京大学出版社	
地　　　　址：	北京市海淀区成府路 205 号　　100871	
网　　　　址：	http://www.pup.cn　　http://www.pup6.cn	
电　　　　话：	邮购部 62752015　发行部 62750672　编辑部 62750667　出版部 62754962	
电 子 邮 箱：	pup_6@163.com	
印 刷 者：	河北滦县鑫华书刊印刷厂	
发 行 者：	北京大学出版社	
经 销 者：	新华书店	

787mm×1092mm　16 开本　16.75 印张　390 千字
2006 年 8 月第 1 版　2012 年 8 月第 2 版　2012 年 8 月第 1 次印刷

定　　　　价：32.00 元

第 2 版前言

本书第 1 版自 2006 年出版以来，在各兄弟院校师生和广大读者的关注下，至今已成为信息与通信领域中深受喜爱的教材和参考资料。在这段时间内，编者一方面收到了各方的建议；另一方面通过几年的教学实践，认识到书中有些内容已不能适应当前教学改革形势的需要。本次修订的第 2 版将在总结经验、改正错误的基础上，力求能在以下几个方面有所完善。

(1) 为了提高翻译技巧方法的理论性和完整性，对第 1 章的"科技术语翻译"、"处理词汇现象的技巧"等内容进行了修订补充，使之具有更强的理论性，实际案例也更丰富。

(2) 为了体现适合信息与通信领域发展的先进性，对第 2 章的课文阅读进行了较大篇幅的改动。删除了过时的文章，结合最新发展成果选取了一些先进的技术成果，如设计模式、密码学、复杂网络、云计算等。而且，每篇课文的篇幅都控制在 4～5 页，以便课堂教学的安排，在内容上又不失完整性。

(3) 为了便于学生自学和老师教学，本书增加了"参考译文"部分。

本书第 2 版中的 1.3～1.5 节由太原理工大学赵菊敏完成；第 2 章由华东师范大学韩定定、西安科技大学李明明、太原理工大学赵菊敏、黑龙江科技学院史健婷、天津工程师范学院王锦等共同完成。其中韩定定完成了第 3 课、第 6 课、第 9 课内容的编写；赵菊敏完成了第 2 课参考译文的编写；李明明完成了第 1 课、第 4 课、第 8 课课文的编写和参考译文的编写；史健婷编写了第 5 课和第 8 课的参考译文；王锦对第 10 课的课文和参考译文进行了补充；淮海工学院董自健和华东师范大学陈趣参加了编写工作。韩定定和李明明任本书主编，负责组织各章节的内容及定稿。本书是针对第 1 版教材使用中所出现的问题加以修改而成的。在此谨向这些提出批评意见和建议的读者表示衷心的感谢！

信息与通信技术在不断地发展，专业英语教学改革任重道远，编者的能力与这两方面的发展所提出的要求相比还存在很大差距。恳请读者一如既往地对书中的不足之处多加指正，以使编者不断改进。

编　者

2012 年 5 月 20 日

目　　录

第1章 翻译理论与方法

1.1 翻译的概念

人类社会的发展和进步是从古至今不同文化的民族之间沟通和交流的结果，而不同文化间的交流离不开翻译。翻译是人类社会发展和进步的需要，正如 Steiner 和张培基所说的那样：Translating it is that openeth the window, to let in the light; that breaketh the shell, that we may eat the kernel.(Steiner)；翻译是沟通各族人民的思想，促进政治、经济、文化、科学、技术交流的重要手段，也是进行国际斗争的必要武器。翻译是学习好外语的重要手段之一，也是探讨两种语言对应关系的一门学科(张培基等)。

"翻译是一项对语言进行操作的工作，即用一种语言文本来替代另一种语言文本的过程。"(J.C.卡特福德，1994)；"翻译是把一种语言的言语产物在保持内容方面，也就是意义不变的情况下，改变为另一种语言的言语产物的过程。"(巴尔胡达罗夫，1985)；"翻译是在接受语中寻找和原语信息尽可能接近自然的对等话语，首先是意义上的对等，其次才是风格上的对等。"(E.A.奈达，1969)；"翻译乃是与语言行为抉择密切相关的一种语际信息传递的特殊方式。"(沃尔夫拉姆·威尔斯，1982)；"翻译是一种跨文化的信息交流与交换的活动，其本质是传播。"(吕俊，1997)。Translating consists in reproducing in the receptor language the closest natural equivalent of the source language message, first in terms of meaning and secondly in terms of style. (Nida)；翻译是一种创造性的工作，好的翻译等于创作，甚至还可能超过创作。(郭沫若)；…translation is first a science, which entails the knowledge and verification of the facts and the language that describes themhere, what is wrong, mistakes of truth, can be identified; secondly, it is a skill, which calls for appropriate language and acceptable usage; thirdly, an art, which distinguishes good from undistinguished writing and is the creative, the intuitive, sometimes the inspired, level of the translation; lastly, a matter of taste, where argument ceases, preferences are expressed, and the variety of meritorious translation is the reflection of individual differences. (Newmark)

翻译是一门综合性的学科，因为它集语言学、文学、社会学、教育学、心理学、人类学、信息理论等学科之特点于一身，在长期的社会实践中已经拥有了它自己的一套抽象的理论、原则和具体方法，形成了它自己独立的体系，而且在相当一部分的语言材料中这些方法正在逐渐模式化。由此可见，视角的不同可以导致对翻译性质认识的差异。

在以上众多定义中，哪种更准确、更贴切？要回答这个问题，先来看看翻译活动本身。

翻译的具体形式很多，有口译、笔译、机器翻译等，从翻译的物质形态来说，它表现为各类符号系统的选择组合，具体可分为4类。

(1) 有声语言符号，即自然语言的口头语言，其表现形式为电话通信、内外谈判和接待外宾等。

(2) 无声语言符号，包括了文字符号和图像符号，其表现形式为谈判决议、社交书信、电文、通信及各种文学作品等印刷品。

(3) 有声非语言符号，即传播过程中所谓的有声而不分音节的"类语言"符号，其常见方式为：说话时的特殊重读、语调变化、笑声和掌声，这类符号无具体的音节可分，语义也不是固定不变的，其信息是在一定的语言环境中得以传播的。例如，笑声可能是负载着正信息，也可能负载着负信息，又如掌声可以传播欢迎、赞成、高兴等信息，也可以是传递一种礼貌的否定等。

(4) 无声非语言符号，即各种人体语言符号，表现为人的动作、表情和服饰等无声伴随语言符号，这类符号具有鲜明的民族文化性，例如，人的有些动作，在不同的民族文化中所表示的语义信息完全不同，不仅如此，它还能强化有声语言的传播效果。例如，在交谈时，如果伴有适当的人体语言，会明显增强口头语言的表达效果。

这四大类符号既可以表达翻译的原码，也可以表达翻译出的译码，它们即可以单独作为原码或译码的物质载体，也可以由两种、三种、四种共同组成译码或原码的载体。

从翻译的运作程序上看，实际包括了理解、转换、表达3个环节。理解是分析原码，准确地掌握原码所表达的信息；转换是运用多种方法，如口译或笔译的形式，各类符号系统的选择、组合，引申、浓缩等翻译技巧的运用等，将原码所表达的信息转换成译码中的等值信息；表达是用一种新的语言系统进行准确的表达。

翻译的形式和内容如此纷繁复杂，从中抽象出一个具有哲学高度的翻译的定义也是一项非常艰难的重任，国内外的众多学者对此做出了许多努力，仁者见仁，智者见智，从不同的角度对翻译活动做出了概括和总结。

在众多的定义中，有些学者(如，吕俊，1997)将翻译纳入传播学的研究范围，将翻译学视为传播学的一个分支，这给人们以有益的启迪：它更明确了翻译学是一个开放的动态系统，它充分注意了在信息传递过程中有影响作用的其他诸多因素，如传播方式、传播渠道、传播目的、传播的不同对象等，它可以更广泛地借鉴其他学科的研究成果或对其他学科的研究起到影响和指导的作用。

在上文的诸多翻译形式中可以归纳为一点，翻译实际上是一种特殊形式的信息传播。整个翻译活动实际上表现为一种社会信息的传递，表现为传播者、传播渠道、受者之间的一系列互动关系。与普通传播过程不同的是，翻译是在两种文化之间进行的，操纵者所选择的符号不再是原来的符号系统，而是产生了文化换码，但其原理却是与普通传播相同的。

要做好翻译工作，一是要具备良好的政治素质，二是要具备良好的业务素质。政治素质包括译者对党和国家大政方针政策的正确了解和贯彻执行、严肃认真的工作态度和一丝不苟的工作作风；良好的业务素质指的是扎实的语言功底、出色的写作技能、丰富的文化知识以及过硬的翻译理论知识和熟练应用翻译技巧的能力。

1.2　中西方文化、思维差异与英汉语对比

既然翻译要涉及两种语言的相互转换，而语言是与文化和民族思维休戚相关的。所以，要掌握有效的翻译方法，必须先了解语言之间的差异，了解引起语言差异的中西方在文化、

思维等方面的差异。本节通过对比词汇在中、英两种语言文化背景下，反映在含义、日常生活、称呼、社交礼节、性别、感情色彩等方面的差异来探讨英语翻译中如何融文化知识于语言中，以导入文化的适度性。

词是语句的基本单位，通常所说的话都是由一个个词构成。如果只是把单词按字面意义串起来，而丝毫不懂有关文化背景知识，在实际运用中是行不通的。例如下述两句。

(1) 英语中 green with envy 是什么意思？人们忌妒或羡慕时脸色真的变绿或发青吗？

(2) 英语中说 Paul was in blue mood; Paul(保罗)是什么情绪？高兴、激动、悲哀，还是什么？

在上述两句中，green(绿)和 blue(蓝)都不是指颜色，两个词都有别的意思——某种文化方面的联想，从字面上看这种意思不明显。在词典中，green 这个词有"(脸色)变绿"的意思，但 green with envy 是个固定词组，不过表示"十分妒忌"而已。 blue 这个词与 mood 之类的词连用表现某种情绪时，表示"沮丧的"、"忧郁的"，例(2)之意为"保罗情绪低落"。以上两个例子都涉及词的字面意义和联想内涵意义，这就是语言文化差异问题，在翻译过程中许多在理解目的语(target language)时，遇到的障碍并非语言知识造成，而是由文化差异导致的。由此可见，加强语言文化因素的对比显得尤为重要。

1. 语言与文化

学语言的目的是为了交流。人类的交际不单是一种语言现象，也是一种跨文化现象。要对两种交际文化进行对比，首先要从文化谈起。

文化 culture 一词是一个含义极其广泛的词语。它狭义上是指文学、音乐、美术等，而广义上讲是一个社会学术语。按照社会学家和人类学家对"文化"所下的定义，人们所说的"文化"是指一个社会所具有的独特的信仰、习惯、制度、目标和技术的总模式。语言是文化的一部分，又是文化的载体和折射镜。透过一个民族的语言，可以窥见该民族绚丽多姿的文化形态。英语词汇作为英语中最活跃、最具生命力的组成部分，最能反映英美文化独特的魅力和内涵。学习英语，实际上也是学习西方文化。对于在母语环境下学英语的中国人来说，应该了解在中西方不同文化背景影响下，英汉词语之间所存在的差异；从另一方面来看，语言又受文化的影响，反映文化。可以说语言反映一个民族的特征，它不仅包含着该民族的历史和文化背景，而且蕴藏着该民族对人生的看法、生活方式和思维方式。

汉语的文化氛围中，"东风"即是"春天的风"；夏天常与酷暑炎热联系在一起，"赤日炎炎似火烧"、"骄阳似火"是常被用来描述夏天的词语。而英国地处西半球，北温带、海洋性气候，报告春天消息的却是西风，英国著名诗人雪莱的"西风颂"正是对春的讴歌。英国的夏季正是温馨宜人的季节，常与"可爱"、"温和"、"美好"相连。莎士比亚在他的一首十四行诗中把爱人比作夏天，Shall I compare thee to a summer's day?/Thou art more lovely and more temperate，能体会到莎翁的"爱"吗？

关于英汉习俗差异，最典型的莫过于在对狗这种动物的态度上。狗在汉语中是一种卑微的动物。汉语中与狗有关的习语大都含有贬义："狐朋狗党"、"狗急跳墙"、"狼心狗肺"、"狗腿子"等，尽管近些年来养宠物狗的人数大大增加，狗的"地位"似乎有所改变，但狗的贬义形象却深深地留在了汉语言文化中。而在西方英语国家，狗被认为是人类最忠诚的朋友。英语中有关狗的习语除了一部分因受其他语言的影响而含有贬义外，大部分都没有贬义。如 You are a lucky dog(你是一个幸运儿)。Every dog has his day(凡人皆有得意日)。Old dog will not learn new tricks(老人学不了新东西)等。又如形容人"病得厉害"用 as sick as a dog;"累极了"是 dog-tired。与此相反,中国人十分喜爱猫,用"馋猫"比喻人贪嘴,常有亲昵的成分,而在西方文化中,"猫"被用来比喻"包藏祸心的女人"。

与宗教信仰有关的习语也大量地出现在英汉语言中。佛教传入中国已有一千多年的历史,人们相信有"佛祖"在左右着人世间的一切,与此有关的习语很多,如"借花献佛"、"闲时不烧香,临时抱佛脚"等。在许多西方国家,特别是在英美,人们信奉基督教,相关的习语如 God helps those who help themselves(上帝帮助自助的人),也有 Go to hell(下地狱去)这样的诅咒。

英语属于印欧语系(Indo-Europeanlanguages),包含着印度、西亚和欧洲的语言。目前使用的英语单词中,有不少是从非印欧语系"拿来"的,这在狭义上,就是英语中的外来语。这些白皮黄心的"鸡蛋词",无须向"英语世界"做额外解释,就能被顺利地理解、沟通。脱胎于汉语的"鸡蛋词",早就默默地影响全世界了。除了"孔夫子(Confucious)"、"中国功夫(kungfu)"、"麻将(mahjong)"或者"豆腐(tofu)"之类绝无仅有的称谓,"silk"的发音,显然是汉语"丝绸"的音译,茶 ——tea 是英国人从拗口的闽南话里拿走的,世外桃源——Shangrila 出自西藏的传说之地——香格里拉;点心——dimsum,一听发音,就知道,这个略带小资情调的词儿,来自闽粤。走狗——running dogs,纸老虎——paper tiger,大款、巨亨——tycoon 这种称呼是近些年才流行街巷的,指有钱有势的商人或者企业家,中国传统的叫法是"大掌柜",被英语拿走,又是闽粤之地的音译。

2. 字面意义和含义

字面意义就是基本的或明显的意义。词的含义是词的隐含或附加意义。如"peasant"一词,是"农民"之义,但外国人眼里不是"农民"之意。英语中的 peasant 与汉语中的"农民"所体现的意义并不完全相同,可能有不同的含义,英语中的 peasant 是贬义。《美国传统词典》给 peasant 下定义:"乡下人、庄稼人、乡巴佬","教养不好的人、粗鲁的人"。《新编韦氏大学词典》:"一般指未受过教育的、社会地位低下的人"。在汉语中,"农民"指直接从事农业生产劳动的人,无论在革命斗争中或是在社会主义建设中都是一支重要的力量,丝毫无贬义,所以一般应把"农民"译成 farmer。再如,politician 和 statesman 这两个英语词。Politician 是"政治家"吗?反过来说,汉语中的"政治家"这个词应该怎样译成英语呢?有些略懂英语的学生译作 politician,这是不合适的。Politician 这个词在美国英语中,往往有很强烈的贬义色彩,引起别人的蔑视。它只为谋取个人私利而搞政治、耍手腕的人。这个词还有"精明圆滑的人"(smooth-operator)之义,指一个人做事和说话时,信心十足,非常老练。汉语"政治家"这个词应译为 statesman,在英国英语和美国英语中都很贴切,statesman 主要表示善于管理国家的明知之士;人们通常把有威望的高级政府官员称为 statesman。

事实上,汉英两种语言在字面意义和含义上有以下的关系。

1) 字面意义与含义相同或相似

(1) Look before you leap.三思而后行。

(2) Burn one's boat.破釜沉舟。

(3) Strike while the iron is hot.趁热打铁。

(4) An eye for an eye, a tooth for a tooth.以眼还眼，以牙还牙。

(5) To lose one's face, to save one's face.丢面子，保面子。

2) 含义相似，字面意义不同

(1) The grass is always greener on the other side of the fence.这山望着那山高。

(2) Nothing ventured, nothing gained.不入虎穴，焉得虎子。

(3) That's a piece of cake.那是小菜一碟。

(4) As poor as a church mouse.一贫如洗。

(5) Let sleeping dogs lie.切勿打草惊蛇。

3) 含义不同，字面意义相似

(1) To fish in muddy water.(英语：形容多管闲事，自讨没趣)浑水摸鱼。

(2) To make one's hair stand on end.(英语：令人毛骨悚然)令人发指。

(3) To blow one's own horn.(英语：自我炫耀，自吹自播)各吹各的号。

(4) To lock the stable gate after the horse has bolted.(英语意思是"太迟了")亡羊补牢。

4) 含义与字面意义都不同

(1) Modest dogs miss much meat.(英语：谦虚的狗没肉吃。)满招损，谦受益。

(2) Where there is fear there is modesty.(原为拉丁语格言：谦虚源于胆怯。)老王卖瓜，自卖自夸(反讽)。

(3) An excess of modesty obstructs the tongue.(英语：谦虚过分束缚舌头。)自知之明(赞誉)。

3. 日常谈话中的文化区别

中国人在吃饭前后打招呼时常用："吃(饭)了吗？"，而美国人则用"Hello"或"Hi"等。如果不理解其含义，美国人会认为，这种打招呼是说："没有吃的话，我正要请你到我家去呢。"总之，这样打招呼在西方有时意味着邀请对方去吃饭。

再如，汉语中的"上哪去啊？"以及"到哪儿去啊？"这样打招呼的话直译成英语就是 Where are you going? 和 Where have you been? 而大部分讲英语的人听了会不高兴，他们对此的反应很可能是：It's none of your business! (你管得着吗？)

所以，英语国家人打招呼通常以天气、健康状况、交通、体育以及兴趣爱好为话题。

4. 其他社交礼节上的不同

以 please "请"为例，在某些场所却不宜用英语 please。让别人先进门或先上车时，不说 please，一般说：After you。但是初学英语的人常用 You go first，这是不对的。在餐桌上请人吃饭、喝酒、或者请人抽烟时，一般用 Help yourself(to something)，也不用 please。

一般来说，中国人在家庭成员之间很少用"谢谢"。如果用了，听起来会很怪，或相互关系上有了距离。而在英语国家"Thank you"几乎用于一切场合，所有人之间，即使父母与子女，兄弟姐妹之间也不例外。送上一瓶饮料，准备一桌美餐，对方都会说一声"Thank you"。公共场合，不管别人帮你什么忙，你都要道一声"Thank you"，这是最起码的礼节。当别人问是否要吃点或喝点什么时(Would you like something to eat/drink?)，人们通常习惯于客气一番，回答："不用了"、"别麻烦了"等。按照英语国家的习惯，你若想要，就不必推辞，说声"Yes，please"，若不想要，只要说"No，thanks"就行了。这也充分体现了中国人的含蓄和英语国家人坦荡直率的不同风格。

在英语国家，赞美也常用来作为交谈的引子。赞美的内容主要有个人的外貌、外表、新买的东西、个人财物、个人在某方面出色的工作等。通常称赞别人的外表时只称赞她努力(打扮)的结果，而不是她的天生丽质。因此赞美别人发型的很多，赞美别人漂亮头发的很少。对别人的赞美，最普通的回答是："Thank you"如下所述。

A：Your skirt looks nice.

B：Thank you.

中国人初次见面问及年龄、婚姻、收入表示关心，而英语国家人却对此比较反感，认为这些都涉及个人隐私。如在 JEFC Book 1 Lesson 16 中有这样的对话："How old are you, Mrs. Read？""Ah， it's a secret！"。为什么 Mrs. Read 不肯说出自己的年龄呢？因为英语国家人都希望自己在对方眼中显得精力充沛、青春永驻，对自己实际年龄秘而不宣，妇女更是如此。再如中国人表示关心的"你去哪儿？"(Where are you going？)和"你在干什么？"(What are you doing？)，在英语中就成为刺探别人隐私的审问或监视别人的话语而不受欢迎。

中国和英语国家的文化差异还显著地表现在节日方面。在节日里，对于别人送来的礼物，中国人和英语国家的人也表现出不同的态度。中国人往往要推辞一番，表现得无可奈何地接受，接受后一般也不当面打开。如果当面打开并喜形于色，可能招致"贪财"的嫌疑。而在英语文化中，人们对别人送的礼品，一般都要当面打开称赞一番，并且欣然道谢。

总之，文化差异现象的根源主要由于概念意义的差异和联想意义的差异。概念意义即基本意义。它是客观事物在人们意识中的反映和概括。在中西方不同文化背景下，客观事物本身存在差异，人们对客观事物的反应和概括便会留下深刻的文化烙印，因此，英汉词汇在概念意义上常具有不同的内涵，如西方饮食中的 sandwich、hamburger、salad，中国人既未看过，也未吃过，只好音译为"三明治"、"汉堡包"、"色拉"，美国人生活中特有的 drugstore，汉语中还没有一个词语能贴切地表达其内涵，也只能以注释性的文字说明它是"出售药物、糖果、饮料及其他日用杂品的店铺"。同样，汉语里的一些词，如"天干"、"地支"、"楷书"、"普通话"、"太极拳"等，在英语中也找不到对应词。

联想意义是人们在概括自己对客观世界的感性认识和情感体验之后，通过联系、类比等手段赋予词汇一定的象征意义。联想意义是词汇内涵的重要组成部分，同样植根于文化的土壤之中。正如上文所述，英汉颜色词，从物理学角度讲是没有区别的，但在语言交流中，它们却各具不同的联想意义，此时的颜色不再是自然色彩，而是象征色彩。例如，黄色(yellow)在中国文化中象征至高无上的权力或色情淫秽，人们常说"黄袍加身"、"黄色书刊"、"黄色录像"等，但在美国，yellow 没有这种特定的内涵，人们常用蓝色(blue)来指代色情(如 a blue movie)。再如，绿色(green)在汉语中象征春天、新生的希望，但一提到它，英美人却会由此想到嫉妒(green eyed)与缺乏经验(green hand)。

要使译文在功能上与原文对等，翻译时译者除了在语言层面(音韵、词法、句法、修辞等)有效再现原文特征外，还要充分考虑双语间的文化及民族心理差异等因素。美国的 Coca Cola 之所以在中国如此畅销，恐怕与"可口可乐"这一完美的译名不无关系；而美国杂志"play boy"在国内几乎难觅其踪影，这与其译名"花花公子"具有"衣着华丽、只会吃喝玩乐、不务正业的富家子弟"之意是有一定关系的。由此可见广告翻译中充分考虑文化差异及民族心理差异的重要性。

1.3 科技术语的主要翻译方法

1.3.1 概述

翻译标准或原则的共同特点是：翻译既要"忠实"又要"通顺"，即译文必须既要考虑到原作者又要考虑到译文的读者。用张培基等人的话说就是：

"所谓忠实，首先指忠实于原作的内容。译者必须把原作的内容完整而准确地表达出来，不得有任何篡改、歪曲、遗漏阉割或任意增删的现象。……忠实还指保持原作的风格——即原作的民族风格、时代风格、语体风格、作者个人的语言风格等译者对原作的风格不能任意破坏和改变，不能以译者的风格代替原作的风格。……所谓通顺，指译文语言必须通顺易懂，符合规范。译文必须是明白晓畅的现代语言，没有逐词死译、硬译的现象，没有语言晦涩难懂、佶屈聱牙的现象，没有文理不通、结构混乱、逻辑不清的现象……"(《英汉翻译教程》)

翻译过程主要包括理解、表达和校核 3 个方面。下面重点对"理解"进行说明。

理解可分为广义理解和狭义理解。广义理解指对原文作者的个人、原文产生的时代背景、作品的内容以及原文读者对该作品的反映。狭义的理解仅指对原作文本的理解。这种理解主要包括语法分析、语义分析、语体分析和语篇分析(grammatical analysis、semantic analysis、stylistic analysis and text analysis)。理解是翻译成功与否的先决条件和重要步骤，务必正确可靠，杜绝谬误。

表达是理解后能否保证译文成功的又一个关键步骤，是理解的深化和体现。在此过程中，译者要注意恰到好处地再现原文的思想内容和语体色彩，使译文既忠实于原作又符合译入语的语法和表达习惯。要做到这一点，译者就必须在选词用字、组词成句、组句成篇上下工夫，在技巧运用上下工夫。能直译时尽可能地直译，不能直译时则可考虑意译，灵活运用翻译技巧。例如下述例子。

The winds of November were like summer breezes to him, and his face glowed with the pleasant cold. His cheeks were flushed and his eyes glistened; his vitality was intense, shining out upon others with almost a material warmth.十一月的寒风，对他就像夏天吹拂的凉风一样。舒适的冷空气使他容光焕发、两颊通红、两眼闪光。他生气勃勃，让别人感到是一团炙手的火。(英语 material warmth 字面意思是"物质的温暖"，这里具体译作"一团炙手的火"言明意清，让人一看就懂。)

My dear girls, I am ambitious for you, but not to have you make a dash in the world—marry rich men merely because they are rich, or have splendid houses, which are not homes because love is wanting…亲爱的姑娘们，我对你们期望很高，可并不是叫你们在世上出人头地——要你们去嫁给富人，仅仅因为他们有钱，有奢华的住房，缺少爱情的话，豪华的住房算不上家。(英语 ambitious 既可表示"雄心壮志的"意思，也可表示"野心勃勃的"意思，这里选用褒义词"期望很高"翻译比较妥当。)

It was morning, and the new sun sparkled gold across the ripples of gentle sea.清晨，初升的太阳照着平静的海面，微波荡漾，闪耀着金色的光芒。(英语 the ripples of the gentle sea 译

成汉语时在结构上做了调整，这样译文念起来意思清楚，行文漂亮。)

The sea was wonderfully calm and now it was rich with all the color of the setting sun. In the sky already a solitary star twinkled.大海平静得出奇，晚霞映照的绚丽多彩，天空已有孤星闪烁。(英语原文两句译成汉语合为一句。)

表达时还应注意避免翻译腔、过分表达和欠表达。所谓翻译腔，就是指译文不符合汉语语法和表达习惯，佶屈聱牙，晦涩难懂。例如下面的表达。

To appease their thirst, its readers drank deeper than before, until they were seized with a kind of delirium. 为了解渴，读者比以前越饮越深，直到陷入了昏迷状态。

这个句子的译文死抠原文形式，死抠字典释义，翻译腔严重，让人难以明白其意思，可改译为：读者为了满足自己的渴望，越读越想读，直到进入了如痴如醉的状态。

所谓过分表达，就是指译文画蛇添足，增加了原文没有的东西；而欠表达则是省略或删节原文的内容。翻译时均应避免这类错误。

校核是对理解和表达质量的全面检查，是纠正错误、改进译文的极好时机，切不可认为是多余之举。优秀的译者总是十分重视校核的作用，总是利用这一良机来克服自己可能犯下的错误，初学翻译的人就更应该如此了。

1.3.2 科技英语的翻译

科技英语(English for Science and Technology)诞生于 20 世纪 50 年代，是第二次世界大战后科学技术迅猛发展的产物。20 世纪 70 年代以来，科技英语在国际上引起了广泛的关注和研究，目前已经发展成为一种重要的英语文体。科技英语泛指一切论及或谈及科学技术的书面语和口语，其中包括：科技著述、科技论文和报告、实验报告和方案；各类科技情报和文字资料；科技实用手册的结构描述和操作规程；有关科技问题的会谈、会议、交谈用语；有关科技的影片、录像、光盘等有声资料的解说词等。

术语是表示某一专门概念的词语，科技术语就是在科技方面表示某一专门概念的词语。因此翻译时要十分注意，不能疏忽。英语科技术语的特点是词义繁多，专业性强，翻译时必须根据专业内容谨慎处理，稍不注意就会造成很大的错误。如有的人把"the newly developed picture tub"错译为"新近被发展了画面管"，但正确的翻译应该是："最新研制成功的显像管"。因为这里的 picture tub 应该意译为"显像管"。又有人把"a unique instant-picture system"错译为"独特的图像系统"，但正确的翻译应该是："独特的瞬时显像装置"。再以"cassette"这个术语为例，它除了其他方面的意思之外，在录音磁带方面也还有两个意思：一为"装填式磁带盒"，一为"盒式磁带"。究竟应译为哪个意思，要从上下文的具体意思去分析判断。如进口的收录两用机的使用说明书上有"checking the cassette"和"to insert cassette"两个小标题，究竟应当怎么译呢？看来分别将其译为"检查盒式磁带"和"装上盒式磁带"，要比分别译为"检查磁带盒"和"装上磁带盒"更好一些。

随着当今世界科学技术的迅速发展，新的科技术语不断涌现。因此，统一科技术语对科学知识的跨国传播、新学科的开拓、新理论的建立等方面都是不可缺少的，更是当前信息时代的紧迫要求。然而科技术语的准确翻译不仅是个学术问题，同样也是伴随科技进步后需要经常研讨的永恒课题。本文基于一些典型科技术语翻译实例的各种疑难表现，结合有关翻译原则和特点，针对性地提出了一些问题的解决办法。

1.3.3 合成科技术语的语义分析

科技翻译不仅仅是词汇、语法、修辞等语言问题，还涉及许多非语言方面的因素。逻辑便是其中最活跃、最重要的因素。苏联语言学家巴尔胡达罗夫曾举过这样一个例子："John is in the pen"，任何人也不会把句中的 "pen" 译为笔，而只能译为 "牲口圈"，因为 "人在钢笔里" 是不合事理的。这说明在翻译中常常会碰到需要运用逻辑来判断和解决一些似乎不合逻辑的语言现象，这里说的逻辑判断，主要是指对原文语言思维逻辑的判断和译文的技术逻辑的判断。

就科技英语而论，理解原文的过程，在多数情况下，是一个语义辨认、语法分析和逻辑分析 3 方面交互作用的过程。

无论是理解原文的过程，还是寻求适当的汉语表达形式的过程，都是跟判断分析打交道的过程。科技英语因其专业特点及其相关背景知识，逻辑判断、语义分析在我们进行译文处理时，显得尤其重要。语言具有民族的特点，而判断则具有全人类的性质。

逻辑判断、语义分析中常见的错误有以下几种。

1. 判断中的相关概念搭配不当

判断可以看成是表达概念间的关系的。判断所表达的概念之间的关系必须符合客观事物之间的真实关系，否则就会导致判断错误或判断不当。如下所述。

The subject of computers, which also began its development at that time, began to grow and become a separate subject itself.

原译：计算机这一项目也是在那时开始研制、发展并成为一个独立的学科的。

分析：如果 "计算机这项目" 是指作为机械的计算机本身，则可以说 "研制"，但不能说 "成为一个学科"；如果 "计算机这项目" 是指作为科学分支的 "学科"，则可以说 "成为一个学科"，但不能说 "研制"，众所周知，"学科" 是不能研制的。

译文：计算机这一学科也是在那个时候开始兴起，逐渐发展成为一门独立的学科的。

2. 判断反映的思想自相矛盾

True eccentrics never deliberately set out to draw attention to themselves. They disregard social conventions without being conscious that they are doing anything extraordinary. This invariably wins them love and respect of others…

原译：真正的怪人从不有意做些什么怪事来引人注目。他们玩世不恭，却并未意识到他们自己的所作所为与众不同。他们因此总是赢得尊敬和爱慕……

分析：他们 "玩世不恭"，居然还能 "赢得尊敬和爱慕"，这不是有点矛盾吗？把 disregard social conventions 译为 "蔑视社会习俗"，便可避免这一逻辑错误。

译文：真正的怪人从不有意做些什么怪事来引人注目。他们蔑视社会习俗，却并未意识到他们自己的所作所为与众不同。因此他们总是赢得尊敬和爱慕……

3. 判断不严密

如果一个判断有明显的不严密之处，那么这往往是由于译者误解原文所致，请看下面的句子及其译文。

Some other factors which may influence reasoning are (a) faulty analogizing; (b) the inhibiting effect on further research of concepts which have been widely accepted as satisfactory…

原译：其他会影响推理的一些因素是：(a)错误的类比；(b)对一些概念进一步研究的抑制性影响，而这些概念是被广泛认为满意的……

分析：什么是"抑制性影响"，是什么东西的抑制性影响？"抑制性影响"怎么会成为影响推理的因素？所有这些都是不明确的，因而，这个判断很不严密。一查原文，发现译文果然有误。从译文看，译者把介词短语 of concepts 看成是 research 这个动作名词的逻辑上的宾语了。实际上，介词短语 of concepts 在语法上是 the effect 的宾语，而在逻辑上则表示施动性的主语。句中的关键结构是 the effect A (up) on B of A，它的意义是：A 对 B 的作用，或者 A 对 B 的影响。由此可见，the inhibiting effect on further research of concepts…并不是"对一些概念进一步研究的抑制性影响"，而是"某些被公认正确的概念对进一步研究的阻碍作用"。

译文：影响推理的一些其他因素：(a)错误的类比；(b)某些被公认为正确的概念对进一步研究的阻碍作用……

4. 判断之间缺乏逻辑联系

前面用实例探讨了某些成分由于句子本身的内容而不允许分译的情形，下面再用实例探讨一下它们由于上下文的逻辑联系而不允许分译的情形。

Before these metals in their natural state can be converted into useful forms to be of service to man, they must be separated from the other elements or substances with which they are combined. Chemists, who are well acquainted with the properties of metals, have been able to develop processes for separating metals from substances with which they are combined in nature…

原译：处于天然状态的金属在转换成为人类服务有用形式之前，必须从和它结合在一起的其他元素或物质中分离出来。化学家们十分熟悉金属的性能。他们已能创造出一些方法，把金属从和它在自然界中结合在一起的物质中分离出来……

分析：这里引用的两个句子，虽然很长，但从上下文的联系来看，是一气呵成、前后连贯的。译文将定语从句"who…metals"拆译成独立的句子，插在两个句子中间，显得很突兀，不仅破坏了前后两个句子之间的紧密的逻辑联系，而且也使语气无法连贯下去。再者，从概念上说，并不是任何化学家都十分熟悉金属的性能。

译文：……分离出来。熟悉金属性能的化学家们已经研究出来一些方法，能够……

1.3.4 科技术语构词中的前缀和后缀

让我们了解一下英语缀合词的构词要素，即：前缀、后缀、词根。

1. 前缀

前缀(Prefixes)是加在词根或单词前面的部分，具有一定的意义。相同词根前加以不同前缀会有不同的意义，构成新词。在许多单词中，只有一个前缀，但也有一些单词有两个前缀，甚至有多个前缀。例如，incompatible(不兼容的)，其中前缀 in 表示"不"。前缀 com

表示"共同，一起"，词根 pat 表示"忍受，忍耐"，后缀-ible 表示"可……的"。前缀一般不改变词性，只改变原来单词的意思。例如，load 与 unload 的词意不同，词性相同如下所列。

(1) milli-，表示毫，千分之一：

volt 伏——millivolt(毫伏)   liter 升——milliliter(毫升)

gram 克——milligram(毫克)

(2) mis-，表示误，错，坏：

fortune 运气——misfortune(不幸)   lead 引导——mislead(误导)

understand 理解——misunderstand(误解)

(3) mono-，表示单，一：

tone 音调——monotone(单音，单调)   chrome 铬，铬合金——monochrome(单色)

(4) multi-，表示多：

color 颜色——multicolor(多色的)   program 程序——multiprogram(多程序)

form 形式——multiform(多形的，多样的)

(5) non-，表示非，不，无：

stop 停——nonstop(直达，中途不停)   metal 金属——nonmetal(非金属)

conductor 导体——nonconductor(绝缘体)

(6) over-，表示过分，在……上面；超过；压倒；额外：

load 负载——overload(过载)   current 电流——overcurrent(过电流)

exposure 曝光——overexposure(曝光过度)

有的前缀含义狭窄，有的含义广泛。前者大都意义明显，后者则较为隐晦。

2. 后缀

后缀(Suffixes)是加在词根或单词后面的部分。后缀不仅改变原来单词的意思，而且可以改变单词的词性，实现词类转变。因此，给单词加后缀是构成新词，尤其是不同类型词类的常用方法。例如：work 是动词，表示"工作"的意思，加-er 构成名词 worker，表示"工人"的意思；加-able 构成动词 workable，表示"可加工的"的意思，可见加不同后缀构成的单词，其词性不同。根据后缀构成单词的词性，通常把后缀分为名词后缀、动词后缀、形容词后缀及副词后缀等。

每一后缀都有一定的含义。有的后缀只有单一的意思，有的后缀有多种意思。同时，同一个意思又可以由不同的后缀表示。使用后缀的单词可以只有一个后缀，也可以有两个后缀，甚至有多个后缀。例如，geosynchronous 表示"与地球同步的"；interchangeably 表示"可以交换地"。

(1) 名词后缀有许多种，使一个非名词成为名词的后缀，如下所列。

表示人	-er: worker(工人)	-ist: artist(艺术家)	
表示物	-or: tractor(拖拉机)	-ant: disinfectant(消毒剂)	
抽象名词	-hood: childhood(童年)	-ship: friendship(友谊)	
集合名词	-ry: peasantry(农民总称)	-age: mileage(英里数)	
场所地点	-ery: piggery(养猪场)	-arium: planetarium(天文馆)	
表示小	-let: streamlet(小溪)	-ock: hillock(小丘)	
	-et: floweret(小花)		

表示阴性	-ine: heroine(女英雄)	-ess: lioness(母狮)
	-enne: comedienne(女喜剧演员)	
表示疾病	-ome: trachome(沙眼)	-it is: bronchitis(支气管炎)
	-ism: rheumatism(风湿)	
表示行为	-ade: blockade(封锁)	-ation: visitation(访问)
	-ism: criticism(批评)	
化学名词	-ane: methane(甲烷)	-ide: oxide(氧化物)
	-one: acetone(丙酮)	
身份地位	-age: pupliage(学生身份)	-cy: captaincy(船长职位)
	-dom: serfdom(农奴地位)	
……学	-logy: zoology(动物学)	-ics: electronics(电子学)
	-ry: forestry(林学)	

(2) 形容词后缀,表示一种事物具有或属于某种性质或状态。意义是……的、似……的、具有……的、多……的、关于……的、有……性质的;等等,如下所列。

-ic: atomic(原子的)　　　　　　　　　-al: digital(数字的)

-ful: powerful(有力的)　　　　　　　　-y: hilly(多山的)

(3) 动词后缀,表示使成为……、致使、做……化、变成……,如下所列。

-fy: glorify(使光荣)　　　　　　　　　-ize: modernize(现代化)

-en: lengthen(加长)　　　　　　　　　ate: hyphenate(加连字符)

(4) 副词后缀,表示状态、方式、方向等,如下所列。

-wise: clockwise(顺时针地)　　　　　　-ways: crossways(交叉地)

-wards: southwards(向南)　　　　　　　-ly: hourly(每小时地)

-s: outdoors(户外地)

3. 词根

词根(Root)是一个单词的根本部分,表示单词的根本意义,是同根词可以辨认出来的部分。词根是组成单词的最主要元素。一个单词可以没有前缀,也可以没有后缀,但不能没有词根。由相同词根构成的一系列单词叫做"同根词"。

大部分词根都是单音节的,只包含一个元音,如 part。但是,还有一些词根是双音节的,包含两个元音,如 laser。还有少量的词根由多音节构成,包含两个以上的元音,如 algebra。随着技术的发展,原来一些单词变成了词根。例如,atom 表示"原子",它是由前缀 a(表示"不"),与词根 tom,(表示"切割")组成的单词,现在已经成为词根了。同时,由于计算机技术的发展,也出现了一些新的词根,如 cyber 表示"与计算机有关的"。

如:eulogize(称赞)　　　　　　　　　　prologue(序言)

　　monologue(独语)　　　　　　　　　dialogue(对话)

　　epilogue(结束语)　　　　　　　　　apologize(道歉)

　　logogram(语标)　　　　　　　　　　neologism(新语)

以上例子都有一个共同的部分"log",它们表示一个共同的意思——"言","log"就是这些单词的词根。一个词根可以派生出许多新词。

词根大部分是单音节的，小部分是多音节的。有的词根可以单独成词,如 act、man、work 等。

前缀和后缀原来也是独立的词或词根，由于经常缀在别的词上辅助中心意义，就逐渐失去其独立性，成为附加成分。

1.3.5 类比构词及其翻译

类比构词(Word-Formation by Analogy)是英语中一种有趣而又实用的构词方式。其构词特点是：以某个同类词为模式，在语义上进行联想类比，替换其中某个词素，构造出与之对应或类似的新词来。例如，workaholic(工作迷)是仿 alcoholic(嗜酒者)而造，而 seajack(海上劫持)和 skyjack(空中劫持)则是类比 hijack(拦路抢劫)而成的，故都属类比词。

从原形词与类比词的联系来看，英语类比构词大致可分以下 3 类。

1. 数字、色彩类比

先看数字类比，例如，"美国总统夫人"，在英语中称 First Lady(第一夫人)，通过该词美国人又联想类比出 Fist Family(第一家庭)，First Mother(第一母亲)等词。就连总统的爱犬也身价倍增，获得了 First Dog(第一狗)的殊荣，可谓一人得道，鸡犬升天。

再看色彩类比，例如，Black Power(黑人权力)最初是美国黑人在争取自身权力斗争中提出的政治口号，后为美国其他少数族裔所借用，为了反歧视争平等。印第安人提出 Red Power，美籍墨西哥人也提出了 Brown Power。另外，老年人为维护自身权益则提出 Gray Power。美国英语中还因美元为绿色钞票而类比出 green power 一词，借指"金钱的力量"。green power 虽与上述种种 Power 风马牛不相及，但同属色彩类比，甚是有趣，亦含幽默。再看一例，较早出现的 blue-collar(蓝领阶层的)和 white-collar(白领阶层的)分别指"体力工作者的"和"脑力工作者的"，稍后产生的 pink-collar(粉领阶层的)和 gray-collar(灰领阶层的)，则分别指"典型女性职业工作者的"和"维修保养行业工作者的"。近年来，又有两个新的英语类比词问世，即 gold-collar(金领阶层的)和 bright-collar(亮领阶层的)，分别表示"高级专业人士的"和"计算机及通信专业人士的"。

2. 反义、对义类比

这方面英语类比词数目不少，俯拾可得，如下所列。

brain-gain(人才流入)	brain-drain(人才流失)
flash-forward(超前叙述)	flashback(倒叙)
low-tech(低技术的)	high- tech(高技术的)

在这方面，有些类比词来得有趣，仿造奇特。如 man Friday 源于小说《鲁宾逊漂流记》，指主人公于星期五救出的一个土人，后成其忠仆，故名。该词进入英语词汇后泛指"忠实的仆人"或"得力的助手"。后来出现的 girl Friday 一词系仿此而造，专指"忠实的女仆"或"得力的女助手"。又如，boycott(联合抵制)一词的来历可追溯到 19 世纪末。当年在爱尔兰的梅奥郡有个地主名叫 Charles Cunnigham Boycott，他压榨佃农，灾年拒不减租，结果激起公愤。全郡居民联合行动，拒绝与他往来，迫使他逃离本地。此事成了报刊上的头号新闻，Boycott 姓氏不胫而走，成为"联合抵制"的代用语，并为法语、德语、西班牙语等

欧洲语言所借用。最为有趣的是，人们将本为姓氏的 boycott 中的"boy"视为与 girl 相对应的 boy(男子)一词，故意加以错误类比，仿造出 girlcott 一词，作为"妇女界联合抵制"之意。

3. 近似情形类比

在英语类比词中，这部分词为数最多。

Olympiad(奥运会)	Asiad(亚运会),
baby-sit(临时代人照看孩子)	house-sit(临时代人照看房子)
escalator(自动扶手电梯)	ravolator(设在机场等处的自动人行道)
chain-smoke(一支接一支地抽烟)	chain-drink(一杯接一杯地喝酒或饮料)
human rights(人权)	animal rights(动物权)
hunger strike (绝食罢工或抗议)	sleep strike(绝眠罢工或抗议)
boat people (乘船出逃的难民)	land people(陆路出逃的难民)

有时英语里还发生连锁类比现象，以某原形词为模式仿造出一系列类比词来，令人叹为观止。例如，从 marathon(马拉松赛跑)一词中类比出的新词就有好几个。

walkathon(步行马拉松)	alkathon(马拉松式冗长演说)
telethon(马拉松式电视节目)	sellathon (马拉松式推销)

又如，以 racism(种族歧视)为模式类比出的新词为数也不少。

sexism(性别歧视)	ageism(对老年人的歧视)
ableism(对残疾人的歧视)	fattism(对胖子的歧视)

alphabetism(对姓氏按首字母顺序排列在后面的人的歧视)。-ism 实际已成为表示歧视之义的后缀。再如，hamburger(汉堡包)这个词的类比也很有趣，它用作食物名本源于地名，但人们有意进行错误类比，将该词中的"ham"理解为"火腿"，并据此仿造出一系列新词，用以指称类似汉堡包，夹有各种馅子的食品，如 fishburger、cheeseburger、nutburger、beefburger、soyburger 等。

在现代英语中，类比构词一直很活跃。由于它合乎人们思维习惯，操作简便，故在百姓口语、报刊文章里均有运用,加之构词范围广，因而新词语不断涌现，层出不穷。

科技的发展常产生新的英语类比词。例如，EQ(情商)是当前颇流行的心理学新概念，该词系仿 IQ(智商)而造，指一个人控制自己情绪、承受外来压力、保持心理平衡的能力。航天技术的发展也为英语增添了一些类比词，如下所列。

sunrise(日出)	earthrise(地出)
earthquake(地震)	moonquake(月震)
starquake(星震)	youthquake(青年动乱)

有趣的是，在后一组词的类比过程中，人们从地球联想到太空，然后思路一转，又回到地球上的美国社会。

政治运动及社会生活也是英语类比构词的另一重要来源。20 世纪 60 年代时，美国黑人曾掀起大规模的反种族隔离运动。当时黑人举行的室内静坐示威叫 sit-in。随着运动的深入与扩大，黑人纷纷进入原先严禁他们入内的各种公共场所表示抗议，以 verb+in 为模式仿造的新词随之大量出现。黑人与白人同乘一车叫 ride-in，到白人游泳池游泳叫 swim-in，进白人图书馆阅读叫 read-in，入白人教堂做礼拜叫 pray-in。后来，-in 的含义又扩展到其他内容或方式的抗议示威活动上。如下所列。

camp-in(露营示威)	sign-in(签名示威)
talk-in(演讲示威)	mail-in(邮寄示威)
lie-in(卧街示威)	lock-in(占驻示威)
laugh-in(哄笑示威)	stall-in(阻塞交通示威)

turn-in(退还征兵令示威)。

凡此种种，不一而足，英语类比构词的活跃性和创造性，由此可见一斑。

直译加注指直译原文，并附加解释性注释。注释可长可短，既可采用文中注释，也可采用脚注，还可二者合用。如下所列。

big apple 大苹果(纽约的别称)

mad-cow disease 疯牛病(牛海绵状脑病)

oval office 椭圆形办公室(美国白宫总统办公室)

desert storm 沙漠风暴(1991 年美国领导的多国部队对伊拉克实施的军事打击行动)

1.3.6 音译及形译

由于英汉文化存在着许多差异，因此英语中某些文化词语在汉语中根本就没有对等词，形成了词义上的空缺。在这种情况下，英译汉时常常要采用加注法来弥补空缺。加注通常可以用来补充诸如背景材料、词语起源等相关信息，便于读者理解。加注法可分为音译加注和直译加注两种。

1. 音译

音译是翻译英语专业名词的一种常用方法，就是根据英语单词的发音译成读音与原词大致相同的汉字。科技英语中某些由专有名词构成的术语、单位名称、新型材料的名称等，在翻译时都可采用音译法。考虑到译名的规范化和通用性，用词要大众化，读音应以普通话的语音为标准。

例如：

(1) 新发现的自然现象或物质名称。例如：gene 基因；quark 夸克。

(2) 计量单位名称一般用音译。例如：hertz(Hz) 赫兹(频率单位)；bit 比特(度量信息的单位，二进制位)；calorie 卡路里(热量单位)；var 乏(无功功率单位)。

(3) 新型材料的名称，一般采用音译。例如：celluloid 赛璐珞；nylon 尼龙。

(4) 专有名词：cartoon 卡通片；hamburger 汉堡包；benz 奔驰车

音译加注指音译后附加解释性注释。注释可长可短，可采用文中注释，也可采用脚注，还可二者合用。

如下所列。

clone 克隆(一种无性繁殖方法)

sauna 桑拿浴(源于芬兰的一种蒸汽浴)

hacker 黑客(在信息空间中主动出击，对他人的计算机或网络系统进行诸如窥探、篡改或盗窃保密数据及程序的过程，并可能由此造成混乱和破坏的计算机迷)

El Niño 厄尔尼诺(现象)(指严重影响全球气候的太平洋热带海域的大风及海水的大规模移动)

Bunsen 本生灯(一种煤气灯)

AIDS 艾滋病(获得性免疫缺损综合症)

一般来说，音译比意译容易，但不如意译能够明确地表达新术语的含义。因此，有些音译词经过一段时间后又被意译词所取代，或者同时使用。如下所列。

valve 凡尔→阀门   motor 马达→电动机

washer 华司→垫   engine 引擎→发动机

laser 莱塞→激光   vitamin 维他命→维生素

penicillin 盘尼西林→青霉素   telephone 德律风→电话

2. 形译

用英语常用字母的形象来为形状相似的物体定名。翻译这类术语时，一般采用形译法。常用的形译法又分为下列 3 种情况。

(1) 选用能够表达原字母形象的汉语词来译。

T- square 丁字尺   I-column 工字柱

U-bend 马蹄弯头   V-slot 三角形槽

(2) 保留原字母不译，在该字母后加 "形" 字，这种译法更为普遍。

A-bedplate A 形底座   D-valve D 形阀

C-network C 形网络   M-wing M 形机翼

(3) 保留原字母不译，以字母代表一种概念。

X-ray X 光   α-iron α 铁

Y-ray Y 射线   p-n-p junction p-n-p 结

1.4 处理词汇现象的技巧

1.4.1 选择和确定词义

英汉两种语言都有一词多类、一词多义的现象。一词多类指的是一个词属于不同的词类，具有几个不同的意义。一词多义就是说同一个词在同一个词类中又有几个不同的词义。

在翻译的过程中，在弄清原句的结构后，要善于选择和确定原句中关键词的词义。选择和确定词义通常可以从以下两个方面入手。

1. 根据词在句中的词类来选择和确定词义

选择某个词的词义，首先要判明这个词在原句中应属于哪一种词类，然后再进一步确定其含义。

eg.1 <u>Like</u> charges repel；<u>unlike</u> charges attract.

译文：<u>同性</u>电荷相斥，<u>异性</u>电荷相吸引。

这句话中的 "like" 是 "charges" 的定语，用做形容词，它与汉语相对应的含义应当是 "同性的"，同样 "unlike" 也是形容词性，含义为 "异性的"。

但在以下各句中 like 又分别属于其他几个不同词类。

eg.2　Servers are computers exactly <u>like</u> the W.S.

译文：服务器是与 W.S.(工作站)非常<u>相似</u>的计算机。

这里的 like 是介词，可译为"相似，像"。

eg.3　Never do <u>the like</u> again.

译文：不要再做<u>这样</u>的事了。

这句话中的 like 与定冠词 the 组合成名词性词组，相当于汉语中的"形似的人或事物"。

eg.4　Some theorems <u>like</u> regarding noise as Gaussian white noise.

译文：许多理论<u>倾向</u>于将噪声看做高斯白噪声。

这里的 like 用作动词，表示"喜欢"。

又如：

eg.5　The <u>sampling</u> theorem shows that all values of a signal can be determined by sampling the signal at a rate equal to at least twice the bandwidth .

译文：抽样定理表明信号的<u>抽样</u>频率至少为信号频率的两倍时，信号才能全部恢复。

这里"sampling"显然是动词的现在分词，作"theorem" 的定语，它与汉语相对应的词义应当是"抽样"。

eg.6　Air oxidation is accelerated by <u>light</u> (n.) and catalysis.

译文：<u>光</u>和催化剂加速空气氧化。

eg.7　This instrument is <u>light</u> (adj.) in weight and simple to operate.

译文：这台机器<u>轻</u>而且操作简单。

以上两个例句中的 light，也反映出不同的词类有不同的含义。

2. 根据上下文的联系以及在句中的搭配关系，来选择和确定词义

英语中的同一个词、同一类词，在不同的场合往往也有不同的含义，必须根据上下文的联系以及词的搭配关系或句型来判断和确定某个词在特定场合下的具体词义。

eg.1　Most DSPs are based on the so-called Harvard <u>architecture</u>, where the data path (including the <u>bus</u> and memory units) is made distinct from the program path, allowing an instruction search to be performed simultaneously with another instruction execution and other tasks .

译文：大部分的 DSP 是采用所谓的 Harvard <u>结构</u>，这种结构的数据线(包括<u>总线</u>和存储单元)与程序线相互独立，这样就能在执行某个指令或任务的同时接受其他指令的执行请求。

这里"architecture"的含义应该是"结构"，"bus" 的含义应该是"总线"，也就是说在专业英语中一些词汇的含义会有特殊的含义。

eg.2　Chips require much less space and power and are cheaper to manufacture than an equivalent circuit built by employing <u>individual</u> transistors.

译文：与使用<u>分立</u>的三极管构造的等效电路相比，芯片需要的空间更小，功率更低，更便宜。

"individual"译作"分立"比译作"独立"、"个人"更合适。

eg.3　An electric charge will flow for a short time and accumulate on <u>the plate</u> .

译文：一个电荷在很短的时间内移动并到达<u>负极</u>。

"the plate"在该句中应指"负极"，故可以将该词的所指范围确定为"负极"。

eg.4　When a current passes through the <u>coil</u>, a magnetic field is set up around it .

译文：当电流流过<u>线圈</u>时，就会在线圈周围产生磁场。

由于原文是介绍电磁场产生的原理，句中的"coil"的含义很明确，指的是"线圈"。

eg.5　In practice, a relationship is used in which the received <u>power</u> is related to the transmitted <u>power</u> by a factor which depends on the fourth <u>power</u> of the inverse of the distance.

译文：实际上，在接收<u>功率</u>和发送<u>功率</u>之间有一个关系是由距离的倒数的 4 次<u>幂</u>这个因素所决定的。

句中前两个"power"都是功率的含义，第三个"power"是幂，即乘方的含义。

eg.6　Few of these <u>charge</u> carriers combine with the <u>charge</u> (positive in NPN, negative in PNP) in the base.

译文：<u>载流子</u>中很少一部分与基区中(NPN 结的正电荷，PNP 结的负电荷)的<u>电荷</u>结合。

第一个"charge"指的是"载流子"；第二个"charge"是电荷的含义。

eg.7　The motor can <u>feed</u> several machines.

译文：这部电动机可以给几部机器<u>供应</u>动力。

eg.8　The roller press <u>feeds</u> the existing grinding plant depending on the circulating load of the mill.

译文：辊压机按照现有破碎系统的循环破碎能力<u>供料</u>。

1.4.2　词量的改变：增词和减词

由于表达习惯的不同，在专业英语的翻译过程中，有时需要将英语原文中省略的词语在译文中添加进来，即增词；有时又需要原文中多次重复的词在翻译时省略，即减词。这样使得译文更加符合汉语表达的习惯。

1. 增词

增词法就是在翻译时按意义上和句法上的需要增加一些词来更忠实、自然、通顺地表达原文的内容。一般而言，增词法的情况有两种。一种是根据意义上或修辞的需要，如增加表示时态意义的词，增加英语不及物动词隐含的宾语意义的词。另一种是根据句法上的需要，把原文中省略的句子成分补充进去，使译文的句子具有完整的意思。

eg.1　Three symbols are used to represent the three types of bus, <u>the symbols</u> for data bus is D.B., for address　bus A.B., for control bus C.B..

译文：我们用 3 种符号来表示 3 种总线，用<u>符号</u> D.B.表示数据总线，用<u>符号</u> A.B.表示地址总线，用<u>符号</u> C.B.表示控制总线。

这个句子的原文中两处省略了"the symbols"，尽管英语表达含义非常清楚，但是汉语的表达习惯却不做这样的省略，故需要增词。

eg.2　When being negative, grid repels electrons, and only a fraction of the electrons emitted by the cathode can reach the anode .

译文：当栅极为负时，就会排斥电子，此时只有一小部分由阴极发射的电子可以到达阳极。

这个句子省略了一个 grid。因为当从句的逻辑主语与主句一致时从句的主语可以省去。但在中文翻译时需将省略的词翻译出来。

eg.3　The classical Greek civilization knew of seven metals: gold, silver, copperm, iron, tin, lead and mercury.

译文：古希腊文化时期，人们已经知道使用金、银、铜、铁、锡、铅和汞 7 种金属。

很明显，为了使译文更加符合汉语的语法习惯，译文的最后增加了"使用"，并对句子的顺序进行了调整，即把"seven metals"的翻译由句中放到句末的位置。

eg.4　The leakage current of a capacitor is an important measure of its quality.

译文：电容器漏电流的大小，是衡量电容器质量好坏的重要尺度。

此句在增加了或补充了"大小"、"好坏"和"衡量"几个词之后，译文质量就大为改善。

2. 减词

减词法指的是原文中的有些词在译文中不翻译，原因是译文中尽管没有译出这个词但已经包含了其含义，或者这个词所表达的含义是不言而喻的。也就是说减词就是将英语表达方式中习惯使用的一些词而汉语表达方式中却不必使用的词在翻译时不予翻译。

eg.1　If you know the frequency, you can find the wave length.

译文：如果知道频率，就可求出波长。

这里省略了两个"you"，译文简洁明了。

eg.2　If we should select some sample function n(t), we could not predict the value attained by that same sample function at the time $t+\tau$ with the help of n(t).

译文：如果我们选定某样本函数 n(t)，则它在 t 时刻的值不能有助于预测相同样本函数在 $t+\tau$ 时刻的值。

这里主从句中都有"we"，在翻译时若将二者都译出，则显重复。故在翻译时只译"if"从句中的"we"。

eg.3　Throughout this text we shall assume that the random processes with which we shall have occasion to deal are ergodic.

译文：在整篇文章中，我们假定要研究的随机过程均为各态历经过程。

本句中介词"with"引导的宾语从句中重复使用了"we"，为了表述逻辑清晰，译文中省略了第二个"we"的翻译。

eg.4　The jammer covers an operating frequency range from 20～500MHz.

译文：干扰机的工作频段为 20～500MHz。

此句省略了"覆盖"一词，但意思一样完整。

eg.5　Stainless steels possess good hardness and high strength.

译文：不锈钢硬度大、强度高。

"possess"是"占有"、"拥有"的意思，如将该词直译放在译文中，则其表达不符合汉语的习惯，故省略。

eg.6　The mechanical energy can be changed back into electrical energy by means of a generator or dynamo.

译文：用发电机能把机械能转变成电能。

译文省略了"by means of"，原因是"generator or dynamo."就是实现机械能与电能转换具体的工具。如果将"by means of"翻译出来，表达就会有些啰嗦。

总之，为了能够更加清楚地表达原文的含义，在进行翻译的过程中，要首先弄清原文，再根据汉语的语法习惯进行适当的"增词"和"减词"，但增词、减词不能影响对原文含义的理解。

1.4.3 词义的引申

在阅读的过程中，人们会遇到这样一些词语，辞典上给出的这些词语的词义放在句子中都不能够清楚地表达原文的含义，而如果硬要把辞典中的意思直接套进译文中，就会使得译文生硬晦涩，不能确切表达原意，甚至让读者误解原文。在这种情况下，就要根据上下文以及逻辑关系，进而从这个词的基本含义出发做一定的引申，选择比较恰当的汉语词汇来表达。

eg.1　To achieve its function, a video amplifier must operate over a wide band and amplify all frequencies equally and with low distortion.

译文：为了实现这一功能，视频放大器就必须在宽频带且能够对所有频率进行同样放大并且失真很小的环境下运行。

"achieve"的原意是"达到"，在这里引申为"实现"，是为了和后面的"功能"相搭配。

eg.2　Oscillators are used to produce audio and radio signals <u>for a wide variety of purposes</u>.

译文：振荡器用于产生音频和视频信号，<u>用途广泛</u>。

"purposes"是"目的"的意思，这里引申为"用途"更为贴切。

eg.3　This CD-ROM feature over 100 applets for you to learn from the <u>master</u>.

译文：此光盘提供了一百多个程序，供你向<u>专家</u>学习。

"master"的原意是"主人"，这里指为版权所有者，译为"专家"。

eg.4　The instrument is used to <u>determine</u> how fully the batteries are charged.

译文：这种仪表用来<u>测定</u>电瓶充电的程度。

本句中的"*determine*"一词译作"确定"不符合专业规范，而应译为"测定"。

eg.5　Then hundreds of years from now, billions and billions of miles away, the embryos will be thawed and their hearts will start beating. These <u>space-farers</u> of the future will not grow inside a mother's body but will be incubated in a machine.

译文：几百年后，在距离地球数十亿英里处，冷冻的胚胎将会解冻，胎儿的心脏便开始跳动。这些未来的<u>太空旅人</u>，并非在母体内孕育，而是在机器中孵育。

本句中的"space-farers"一词在《英汉大词典》中的释义是：宇航员，宇宙飞行员。但将其直接译为"宇航员"，似值得商榷。而"宇宙旅行者"又略显生硬。farer 一词是由 fare 派生而来，而 fare 用做动词时，表示"行走，旅行"，《英汉大词典》特别注明【诗】。这个【诗】提醒译者：fare 是一个语体高雅之词。这样人们可以把其译得文绉绉些，令驰骋想象的行文顿显庄重：太空旅人。

eg.6　The <u>pure scientists</u> study phenomena in the universe.

译文：<u>从事理论研究的科学家</u>研究宇宙中的各种现象。

不可译为"纯的科学家"。

eg.7　The major <u>contributors</u> in component technology have been in the semi-conductors.

译文：电子元件中起主要<u>作用</u>的是半导体元件。

查阅词典，contributors 的意思是"贡献者"，表示具体的人，但逐字翻译不符合汉语的语言习惯，只能根据实际含义，将"主要贡献者"作抽象化引申，译为"起主要作用"。

1.4.4　词类的转换

在专业英语的翻译过程中，有些句子可以逐词翻译，有些句子则由于英汉两种语言表达方式的不同，就不能一个词接一个词地简单罗列。实际上在翻译的过程中有些词需要进行转换才能使译文通顺自然。

eg.1　The process of quantization leads to <u>unavoidable</u> error.

译文：量化过程<u>不可避免地</u>产生误差。(形容词转化为副词)

eg.2　Taking the former view gives a good <u>insight</u> into the behavior of the quantization error .

译文：经过前面的讲解使我们更好地<u>理解</u>量化误差的特性。(名词转化为动词)

eg.3　Most satellites are <u>designed</u> to burn up themselves after completing mission.

译文：按照<u>设计</u>大部分卫星在完成任务后自行燃烧。(动词转化为名词)

eg.4　He has no <u>knowledge</u> of how electricity is generated.

译文：他不<u>知道</u>电是如何产生的。(名词转化为动词)

eg.5　The salts of some organic acid are <u>capable of</u> <u>fluorescing</u> while the free acid are not .

译文：有些有机酸盐能<u>发荧光</u>，而其游离酸则不能。(形容词转化为动词)

eg.6　The electron <u>weighs</u> about 1/1850 as much as atom of hydrogen.

译文：电子的<u>重量</u>约为氢原子的 1/1850。(动词转化为名词)

eg.7　Alloy steel is <u>stronger and harder</u> than carbon steel .

译文：合金钢的<u>强度和硬度</u>比碳钢大。(形容词转化为名词)

eg.8　It's well - known that neutrons <u>act</u> differently from protons.

译文：大家知道，中子的<u>作用</u>与质子不同。(动词转化为名词)

eg.9　In certain cases frictions is an absolute <u>necessity</u>.

译文：在一定场合下摩擦是绝对<u>必要的。</u>(名词转化为形容词)

eg.10　The <u>acquaintance</u> of science means mastering the law of nature.

译文：<u>认识</u>科学意味着掌握自然规律。(名词转化为动词)

1.4.5　词汇的重复

重复法实际上也是一种增词法，所增加的词是上文刚刚出现过的词。尽管翻译和写作的要求相同应当力求精练，尽量省略一些可有可无的词，但有时为了明确强调某个事件或表达生动，就需要将一些关键词加以重复。在专业英语的阅读中，往往会对某些关键性的词进行重复，这样才能给读者留下较为深刻的印象，在翻译过程中也需要采用相同的重复手段。

eg.1　Both CW and pulse modulation may be classed as analog modulation.

译文：连续波调制和脉冲调制都归类于模拟调制。

这里 modulation 被重复多次。

eg.2　I had experienced oxygen and /or engine trouble.

译文：我曾碰到过，不是氧气设备出故障，就是引擎出故障，或两者都出故障(这些情况)。

英文原文的表述中，能够清楚地由"trouble"这一个词将"麻烦"表达清楚，而在翻译过程中，为了能够将译文含义描述清晰，就多次重复了"故障"。但不觉得译文拖沓，烦琐。

eg.3　Under ordinary conditions of pressure, water becomes ice at 0°C and steam at 100°C.

译文：在常压下，水在摄氏零度时变成冰，在摄氏一百度时变成蒸汽。

增加了动词"变成"，使句子的含义更加明确。

eg.4　While stars and nebulae look like specks or small patches of light, they are really enormous bodies.

译文：星星和星云看起来只是斑斑点点，或者是小片的光，但它们确实是巨大的天体。

用"斑斑点点"来描述"天体"的小，更符合汉语的思维。

1.4.6　动词时态的翻译

由于科技英语文体本身的特点和专业性，动词时态的翻译不仅要注意动词时态的语法结构，还要考虑所含有的专业含义，才能在某一特定的专业领域达到译文的准确无误。

1. 动词时态的翻译

在科技文章中，英汉两种语言在很多情况下的时态从字面看并不一致。这是由于英汉两种语言的不同特点决定的，但两者表达的概念、条理、逻辑的要求是一致的，例如，Since the middle of the century oil has been in the fore of energy resources 可译为"本世纪石油一直是最重要的能源之一"。这样英译汉时,为了符合汉语的表达习惯,就要进行时态转换。科技英语翻译中常见的时态转换有以下几种。

(1) 英语的一般现在时译为汉语的将来时、进行时或过去时。

eg.1　The cancer reverses completely thanks to early treatment.

译文：治疗及时的话，癌症是可以完全治愈的(将来时)。

eg.2　The electronic computer plays an important part in science and technology.

译文：电子计算机在科学和技术方面起着重要的作用(进行时)。

eg.3　These substances further speed up the decay process.

译文：这些物质进一步加速了衰变过程(过去时)。

(2) 英语动词的进行时可译成汉语的将来时。

eg4.　Knowing severe winter is coming would enable squirrel to store plenty of food.

译文：严冬将至，松鼠会储藏大量的食物。

(3) 英语动词的完成时翻译成汉语的过去时。

eg5.　The sales of industrial electronic products have multiplied six times.

译文：工业电子产品销售值增长了 5 倍。

2. 非限定性动词的翻译

作为科技英语中广泛使用的非限定性动词(即分词、不定式和动名词)在句子中扮演着各种成分，英译汉时也要根据它所具有的语法意义和在科技英语中暗含的科技含义转换为适当的汉语词汇意义，必要时还要进行词的增补。

(1) 汉语中没有限定动词和非限定动词的分类，非限定性动词相当于汉语中的动词，而且英语语言主要依据形态表意。汉语主要依据词汇表意，英译汉时为了准确表达出它的科技含义，最为常见的是对词的增补和意译。 如下所述。

① 增补英语中省略的词。

eg6　radio telescope to be used
译文：将要交付使用的射电望远镜

eg.7　modulated voltage
译文：已调制电压

eg.8　a canning tomato
译文：一种供做罐头的西红柿

② 增加关联词语。

eg.9　Heated, water will change to vapour.
译文：如水受热，就会气化。

③ 修饰加词，语气连贯。

eg.10　Heat from the sun stirs up the atmosphere, generating winds.
译文：太阳发出的热能搅动大气，于是产生了风。

按照事件发生的逻辑顺序，译文中自然增加了"于是"使句子结构更完整。

(2) 在翻译的过程中，当非限定性动词的概念难以用汉语的动词表达时，也可转换成汉语的其他词类。

eg.11　Momentum is defined as the product of the velocity and a quantity called the mass of the body.
译文：动量的定义是速度和物体质量的乘积(转换成名词)。

eg.12　There are ten factories of varying sizes in this district.
译文：这个地区有大小 10 家工厂(译成形容词)。

1.4.7　名词化结构的翻译

名词化结构用词简洁、结构紧凑、表意具体、表达客观，而且整个句子的结构便于写作修辞，词句负载信息的容量得到了增加，有利于达到交际的目的。经常使用的名词化结构有以下几种。

1. 名词/(行为名词)+介词+名词

在此结构中，若"介词+名词"构成的介词短语在逻辑上是行为名词的动作对象或动作的发出者，行为名词的含义在深层中转换或变异，使原来的名词变为动词，构成了动宾或主谓的关系，那么在翻译时可以译成汉语的动宾结构或主谓结构。

eg.1　<u>The flow of electrons</u> is from the negative zinc plate to the positive copper plate.

译文：电子从负的锌板流向正的铜板。

eg.2　Again in the case of all motor vehicles, friction is essential in <u>the operation of the brake</u>.

译文：还有，所有机动车辆的制动器工作时都需要摩擦。

eg.3　They are the employers of managers, as much as they are <u>the employers of work people</u>.

译文：他们不仅雇用工人也雇用经理。

eg.4　Television is the transmission and reception of moving objects image by radio waves.

译文：电视通过无线电波发射和接收活动物体的图像。

eg.5　Farm tractors are <u>big users of diesel power</u>.

译文：农用拖拉机也大多以柴油机为动力。

2. 介词+名词(行为名词)

在此结构中，往往因行为名词的动作意义相对完整，与它同句中的其他部分之间存在着一定的逻辑关系，能起到时间状语、原因状语、条件状语和让步状语等作用，因此在翻译时可以用这种介词短语来代替各种状语从句。

eg.6　<u>Before germination</u>, the seed is watered.

译文：在发芽前给种子浇水。

eg.7　A soluble crystalline solid may be separated from a solution <u>by evaporation</u> .

译文：可溶性晶体可以通过蒸发从溶液中分离出来。

3. 中性名词+行为名词(介词短语)

此结构可以将宾语(介词宾语) 转换成谓语。

eg.8　Rockets have found application for the exploration of the universe.

译文：火箭已经用来探索宇宙。

eg.9　Curved rails offer resistance to the movement of the train .

译文：弯曲的钢轨阻碍火车运行。

4. 与动词构成固定搭配

名词化结构与动词构成固定搭配的常用形式为：动词名词化结构/动词+介词名词化结构。这种搭配大量地以动词短语的形式出现，约定俗成。

eg.10　call attention to　　　　　　　　注意

draw a distinction between　　　　区分

lay emphasis on　　　　　　　　　强调

take possession of　　　　　　　　拥有

5. 行为名词+短语/从句

在此结构中行为名词可以译成动词，与后面的成分一起构成汉语的动宾结构。

eg.11   I have a doubt whether the news is true.

译文：我怀疑这消息是否真实。

6. 名词+名词(行为名词)

在此结构中，名词在表层结构上是前置定语，但在翻译过程中，其深层结构的内在含义可以译成动宾词组，行为名词转换成谓语。

eg.12   power generation   发电

hail prevention   防冰雹

1.5　句子的主要翻译方法

1.5.1　英汉句式比较及常见的翻译方法

翻译英语句子时，有时可以把原文的句子结构整个保存下来或只稍加改变即可，也就是通常所说的直译。

eg.1.   Thus for a fixed signal power and in the presence of white Gaussian noise the channel capacity approaches an upper limit.

译文：因此，对于一定的信号功率，且存在白高斯噪声时，信道容量将趋近于上限值。

eg.2   The pulses are of the same form but have random amplitudes.

译文：这些脉冲形状相同，但幅度随机。

eg.3   Only by studying such cases of human intelligence with all the details and by comparing the results of exact investigation with the solutions of AI (Artificial Intelligence) usually given in the elementary books on computer science can a computer engineer acquire a thorough understanding of theory and method in AI, develop intelligent computer programs that work in a human-like way, and apply them to solving more complex and difficult problems that present computer can't .

译文：只有很详细地研究这些人类智能情况，并将实际研究得出的结果与基础计算机科学书上给出的人工智能结论相比较，计算机工程师才能彻底地了解人工智能的理论和方法，开发出具有人类智能的计算机程序，并将其用于解决目前计算机不能解决的更复杂和更难的问题。

eg.4   Moving around the nucleus are extremely tiny particles, called electrons, which revolve around the nucleus in much the same way as the nine planets do around the sun.

译文：围绕着原子核运动的是一些极其微小的粒子，称为电子，这些电子围绕着原子核旋转，正像九大行星围绕着太阳旋转一样。

eg.5   The development of industrial technology largely strengthens human physical capabilities, enabling people to harness more energy, process and shape materials more easily, travel faster, and so on, while the development of microelectronics extends mental capabilities, enabling electronic "intelligence" to be closely related to a wide range of products and processes.

译文：工业技术的发展大大增强了人的能力，使人们能更广泛地利用能源，更方便地对材料进行加工和成形，更快地旅行等；而微电子学的发展则增强了人的智力，使电子"智能"用于各种各样的产品和过程。

然而，由于英语和汉语的语法习惯不同，在多数情况需要对原文中的句子进行调整。这里从以下几个方面进行说明。

1. 句子顺序的调整

eg.1　The presence or absence(or, alternatively, the sign) of pulses in a group of pulses is made to depend, in a some what arbitrary manner, on message samples.

译文：从属性的角度来说，每组脉冲中脉冲符号的存在或消失都取决于消息样本。

eg.2　Electronic amplifiers are used mainly to increase the voltage、current or power of a signal.

译文：电子放大器主要用于对信号的电压、电流及功率进行放大。

eg.3　A linear amplifier provides signal amplification with little or no distortion, so that the output is proportional to the input.

译文：线性放大器可以在失真很小或没有失真的情况下放大信号，这样输出信号就与输入信号成正比例变化。

eg.4　DPCM works well with data that is reasonably continuous and exhibits small gradual changes such as photographs with smooth tone transitions.

译文：DPCM 适用于比较连续且变化缓慢的数据，如经过平滑处理后的图片。

eg.5　This university has 6 newly-established faculties, namely Electronic Computer, High Energy Physics, Laser, Geo-physics, Remote Sensing and Genetic Engineering.

译文：这所大学现在有电子计算机、高能物理、激光、地球物理、遥感技术、基因工程 6 个新建的专业。

eg.6　The structure of an atom can be accurately described though we cannot see it.
译文：虽然我们看不见原子结构，但能准确地描述它。(被动句倒译成主动句)

eg.7　These data will be of some value in our research work .
译文：这些资料对于我们的研究工作有些价值。

eg.8　This wavelength division multiplexed operation, particularly with dense packing of the optical wavelengths (or, essentially, fine frequency spacing), offers the potential for a fiber information-carrying capacity which is many orders of magnitude in excess of that obtained using copper cables or a wideband radio system.

译文：应用波分复用(技术)，尤其是密集波分复用(或者说，实质上的精细频分复用)，使光纤的信息载容量能超过电缆或宽带无线系统好多个数量级。

eg.9　In particular, it has to be possible to provide extension telephone service on the same channel as it exists in homes today, to communicate between an ISDN telephone and a PSTN telephone, and to send data between an ISDN terminal, with its direct digital connection to the ISDN, and a terminal - modem combination communicating data through a PSTN voice channel.

译文：特别的是，目前家庭使用的同一个信道上提供扩展的电话业务，在 ISDN 电话和 PSTN 电话之间进行通信，在直接用数字连接的 ISDN 终端与通过 PSTN 语音信道进行数据通信的终端——调制解调器组合之间传达数据应该是可能的。

eg.10 On the other hand, the detained decomposition gas might become the cause of reducing the purity of the metal oxide coating adhered to the ribbon glass in the case the aforementioned decomposition gas is not thoroughly removed from the spraying locale.

译文：从另一方面来说，如果上面提到的分解气体在喷射处没有被彻底地清除掉的话，那么，留下来的分解气体就会使黏附在带状玻璃表面上的金属氧化膜的纯度降低。

eg.11 It may be economically sound, in the long run, to subsidize their initial production, even at prices above the projected marked for natural hydrocarbon fluids, in order to accelerate the deduction of dependence on oil imports.

译文：从长远的观点来看，资助开发气体等燃料，既使价格高于自然炭氢化合液的市场价格，但为了加快减少对进口石油的依赖，这在经济上可能还是合算的。

由以上的例句可以看到，英语的语法习惯跟汉语是有着明显的差别的。在英语的表达中能够较为灵活地将原因放到结果之后进行表述，并且将做状语的介词短语放在句子中间，突出了句子的主题。而在译文中，可以看到汉语的语法表述，尤其在科技文章中是很讲究逻辑关系的。

2. 简单句译成复合句

eg.12 Operational amplifiers (op-amps), built with integrated circuits and consisting of DC-coupled, multistage, linear amplifiers are popular for audio amplifiers.

译文：运算放大器的内部结构是直流耦合的多级线性放大器组成的集成电路，该元件在音频放大器中经常用到。

eg.13 An integrated circuit (IC) consists of many circuit elements such as transistors and resistors fabricated on a single piece of silicon or other semi-conducting material.

译文：集成电路包含大量的电子元件，如晶体管和电阻，它们是被加工在一个硅晶体上或其他半导体材料上的。

eg.14 The signal handled by the amplifier becomes the visual information presented on the television screen, with the signal amplitude regulating the brightness of the spot forming the image on the screen.

译文：经过放大器处理后的信号就成为可视信息在电视屏幕上显示出来，图像每个像素的亮度由信号的幅度进行调整。

3. 复合句译成简单句

eg.15 For example, the largest early computers occupied a volume of hundreds of cubic meters and required many tens of kilowatts of electrical power and a sizable air conditioning installation to allow this amount of energy to be dissipated without raising the room temperature to unbearable values.

译文：例如，早期最大的计算机要占据数百立方米的空间，需要几十千瓦的电源和一个相当大的空调设备来消除大量的热，从而避免室温超过允许值。

eg.16 The resulting coded wideband speech not only sounds better than telephone bandwidth speech, but is also more intelligible for humans and works well with modern speech recognition system.

译文：得到的宽带编码语音不仅听起来比电话带宽的语音好，而且更清晰，适用于现代语音识别系统。

eg.17 The porous wall acts as a kind of seine for separating molecules.

译文：多孔壁的作用就像一把筛子，它把不同质量的分子分开。

eg.18 This body of knowledge is customarily divided for convenience of study into the classifications: mechanics, heat, light, electricity and sound.

译文：为便于研究起见，通常将这门学科分为力学、热学、光学、电学和声学。

eg.19 Crossbar switching was carried out by a special circuit called a marker, which provide common control of number entry and line selection for calls.

译文：纵横制交换由一个称为标志器的特定电路控制，标志器提供整个号码的公共控制并选择所有呼叫的路由。

eg.20 It will mediate human-machine interactions that are inseparable parts of many customer applications, and pull together the scattered resources, some belonging to the network and some not, to create communications sessions that might invoke a multiplicity of connections and computer applications.

译文：它将协调与客户应用密切相关的人机交互作用，并将分散的资源集中在一起。这些资源有些属于网络，有些则不是，这就可以建立进行多种连接和计算机应用的通信业务了。

eg.21 Computer simulation results show that, with an antenna spacing as low as 1m, a DF error of less than 1° can be obtained on a signal with a bandwidth of 100MHz at a received power level lower than -100dBm, using an integration time of a few milliseconds.

译文：计算机模拟结果表明，当天线间距短到 1m 时，可以在接收功率电平低于 -100dBm 时，仅用几个毫秒的积分时间，对带宽为 100MHz 的信号进行测向，其测向误差小于1°。

1.5.2 一些英语特别句式的翻译

1. 被动语态的译法

由于专业英语的客观性，决定了其所用非人称的表达方式和常用句型为一般现在时时态及被动语态，这主要是因为不需要明确动作的执行者是谁，或者不必关心谁是动作的执行者。例如：Two problems are considered…一般不写成 We consider two problems…。在阅读和翻译的过程中要将这类句子进行适当的转化。

eg.1 MATLAB is originally written to provide easy access to matrix software developed by the LINPACK and EISPACK projects.

译文：MATLAB 是为了方便使用由 LINPACK 和 EISPACK 项目组开发的矩阵软件而编写的。

eg.2　The signals which fall outside the channel bandwidth are attenuated by filters so that they will not interfere with other signals.

译文：滤波器将销弱信道带宽以外的信号，因此这些信号就不会干扰其他信号。

这里将原句的主语译为宾语。

eg.3　Computers may be classified as analog and digital.

译文：计算机可分为模拟计算机和数字计算机两种。

eg.4　The switching time of the new-type transistor is shortened three times.

译文：新型晶体管的开关时间(比原来)缩短了三分之二。(或缩短为原来的三分之一)

eg.5　This steel alloy is believed to be the best available here .

译文：人们认为这种合金钢是这里能提供的最好的合金钢。

eg.6　Attention must be paid to the working temperature of the machine.

译文：应当注意机器的工作温度。

eg.7　Today different measures are taken to prevent corrosion.

译文：今天，为预防腐蚀人们采取了各种措施。

eg.8　Virtual leaks should be paid attention to.

译文：应该注意假性渗漏。

2. 句式为 It...结构

专业英语中的表达常用到非人称的语气和态度，尤其常见的句式为"It..."结构。对于以 it 作为形式主语的句子而言，在译文中常要改成主动形式，有时需要加主语，有时则可加不确定主语，如"有人"、"大家"、"人们"、"我们"等。

eg.9　It can be shown that a system using a three-level code must have a signal-to-noise ratio of 8.5dB, or 3.7dB greater, for equal performance in the same channel.

译文：这表明对于相同的信道特性，使用三级编码的系统信噪比为 8.5 分贝，或高于 3.7 分贝。

eg.10　It is evident that a well lubricated bearing turns more easily than a dry one.

译文：显然，润滑好的轴承，比没润滑的轴承容易转动。

eg.11　It seems that these two branches of science are mutually dependent and interacting.

译文：看来这两个科学分支是相互依存，相互作用的。

eg.12　It has been proved that induced voltage causes a current to flow in opposition to the force producing it.

译文：已经证明，感应电压使电流的方向与产生电流的磁场力方向相反。

eg.13　It is thus essential for the carbonaceous materials to be decomposed and returned to the atmosphere in order for higher organisms to continue to thrive.

译文：因此，为了使高等生物能继续茁壮成长，含碳物质就必须分解并回归到大气中去。

另外，常见的这类表达方式还有以下几种。

It is hoped that …	希望
It is reported that…	据报
It is said that…	据说

It must be admitted that …	必须承认
It must be pointed out that …	必须指出
It will be seen from this that …	由此可见
It is asserted that …	有人主张
It is believed that …	有人认为
It is well known that …	众所周知
It was told that …	有人曾说
It is generally considered that …	大家认为
It is evident that …	显然
It can be shown that …	这表明
It has been proved that …	已经证明
It seems that …	看来

3. 祈使语气

科技文献的又一个特点是较多地使用祈使语气，即所谓的公式化表达方式，这主要见于理论分析和算法推导中。

eg.14　Let the forward-path transfer function be given by the linear difference equation.

译文：设前向传递函数由下列线性差分方程给出。

eg.15　Consider the case of a linear, single-input single-output discrete system regulated by a discrete feedback controller.

译文：假设线性、单输入单输出离散系统的情况由一个离散反馈控制器来调节。

eg.16　Action：Tranquilize anxiety and reinforce memory, nourish vigor and invigorate strength.

译文：功能:宁神益智、养心活血、滋补强身。

4. The more …, The more …结构的句型

eg.17　The faster the data is transmitted, the greater the bandwidth will need to be to accommodate it

译文：数据传输速率越快，所需要的传输带宽越宽。

eg.18　The resistance being higher, the current in the circuit was lower.

译文：电阻越大，电路中通过的电流就越小。

5. 否定句的翻译

英语表达否定有全部否定、部分否定、双重否定，分别以不同的否定词进行表达。

全部否定词：not, never, not…nor 等。

部分否定词：not many, not much, not all, not every, not both, not some 等。

双重否定词：not, no, never, neither, nobody, nothing 等与其他具有否定意义的词搭配。

还有一些词本身并非not, un-, dis-等，但也同样具有较强的否定意义，如few, too…to, but for, instead of, rather than 等。

eg.19　Without electricity, a computer can not work.

译文：没有电，计算机就不能工作。

eg.20　Not all of these results are right.

译文：不是所有的结果都是正确的。

eg.21　Teletype, telex and facsimile transmission are all methods for transmitting text rather than sounds.

译文：电传打字机、电报、传真都是用来传送文字而不是声音的技术。

eg.22　We cannot estimate the value of modern science enough.

译文：我们对现代科学的评价，无论如何估计，都是不过分的。

eg.23　Both instruments are not precision ones.

译文：这两台仪器并不都是精密仪器。

eg.24　All these various losses, great as they are, do not in any way contradict the law of conservation of energy.

译文：所有这些各种各样的损耗，尽管它们的数量很大，但都没有违反能量守恒定律。

eg.25　The increase in mass is not appreciable until the velocity approaches that of light and therefore it ordinarily escapes detection.

译文：直到速度接近光速时，才能觉察到质量的增加，因此，通常很难检测出质量的变化。

eg.26　Aside from the fact that electrons are too small to be seen, we would find it impossible to count them as they flowed by.

译文：且不谈电子小得看不见这一事实，当电子从旁边流过，也不可能数一数它们。

6. 倍数增减(包括比较)的汉译

科技英语中倍数增减句型究竟应当如何汉译，在我国翻译界中一直存在着争论，国内出版的一些语法书和工具书中所持的看法也不尽一致，因此影响了对这种句型的正确翻译。这个问题比较重要，数据上的一倍之差往往会造成不可估量的损失。

1) 倍数增加的译法

英语中说"增加了多少倍"，都是连基数也包括在内的，是表示增加后的结果；而在汉语里所谓"增加了多少倍"，则只表示纯粹增加的数量。所以英语里凡表示倍数增加的句型，汉译时都可译成"是……的几倍"，或"比……增加(n-1)倍"。

eg.27　The production of various stereo recorders has been increased four times as against 1977.

译文：各种立体声录音机的产量比 1977 年增加了 3 倍。

eg.28　The output of color television receivers increased by a factor of 3 last year.

译文：去年彩色电视接收机的产量增加了两倍。

2) 倍数比较的译法

(1) "n times + larger than + 被比较对象"，表示其大小"为……的 n 倍"，或"比……大 n-1 倍"。

eg.29　This thermal power plant is four times larger than that one.

译文：这个热电站比那个热电站大 3 倍。

(2) "n times + as + 原级 + as + 被比较对象"，表示"是……的 n 倍"。

eg.30　Iron is almost three times as heavy as aluminium.

译文：铁的重量几乎是铝的 3 倍。

3) 倍数减少的译法

英语中一切表示倍数减少的句型，汉译时都要把它换成分数，而不能按照字面意义将其译成减少了多少倍。因为汉语是不用这种表达方式的，所以应当把它译成减少了几分之几，或减少到几分之几。人们所说的增减多少，指的都是差额，差额应当是以原来的数量为标准，而不能以减少后的数量作标准。英语表示倍数减少时第一种表达方式为："…… + 减少意义的谓语 + by a factor of n 或 by n times"。这种表达法的意思是"成 n 倍地减少"，即减少前的数量为减少后数量的 n 倍。

eg.31　The automatic assembly line can shorten the assembling period(by)ten times.

译文：自动装配线能够将装配时间缩短为原来的十分之一。

eg.32　This metal is three times as light as that one.

译文：这种金属比那种金属轻三分之二。

eg.33　The dosage for a child is sometimes twice less than that for an adult.

译文：小孩的剂量有时为成年人剂量的 1/3，或小孩的剂量有时比成年人的剂量少 2/3。

7. 隐含因果关系句的翻译

在科技英语中，表示因果关系的词和词组很多。最常见的有从属连词 because、并列连词 for、复合连词 in that、普通介词 from、短语介词 due to 等。这些表示因果关系的词或词组的意思一目了然，非常明显。而有些因果关系句并没有也不需要明确地表达出来，而是隐含在某些句型或结构中、词语里或上下文内，间接地表现出来。如果不能很好地识别、理解这类隐含的因果关系句，译出来的句子就会层次不清、意义不明、逻辑性不强、让人费解。

1) 隐含在并列句中的因果关系

在科技英语中，人们越来越多地使用并列句来表示原因和结果。这主要是因为在这种结构中有的在逻辑上存在着因果关系。可以是前因后果，也可以是前果后因。在译这样的并列句时，要把两个简单句合译为汉语的一个复合句，必要时可加上适当的表示因果关系的关联词。如"因为，所以"等。

eg.34　Aluminium is used as the engineering material for planes and spaceship and it is both light and tough.

译文：铝用作制造飞机和宇宙飞船的工程材料，因为铝质轻而韧性好。(前果后因)

eg.35　Silicon does not occur in the free state in nature, and very few people have seen the pure substance.

译文：自然界中没有游离状态的硅，所以很少有人见过纯硅。(前因后果)

有时 and 之前用祈使句表示条件或假设，"祈使句+and"是科技英语中常见的一种特殊结构，用祈使句表示条件，而用 and 连接的陈述句表示由此得出的结果。结构的句子在语法上是并列复合句，但在意义上却是主从复合句，这里的祈使句相当于 if 引出的条件状语从句，后用陈述句表示结果或推论。汉译时可按条件从句处理，译成："只要……就……""如果……就……"等。

eg.36　Wave your hand in front of your face, and you can feel the air moving.

译文：只要在自己面前挥动手，你就会感到空气在流动。

eg.37　Heat the test tube further, and a yellow gas will be seen to escape into the air.

译文：将试管进一步加热，就可以看到有一种黄色的气体逸到空气中。

2）隐含在某些从句中的因果关系

（1）在定语从句中。在科技英语中，有些定语从句跟主句之间的关系很复杂。有的定语从句(包括限制性和非限制性)对先行词限制修饰作用很弱，而起着状语的作用。这类定语从句中隐含着原因、结果等意义，如按其定语性质来对待，往往对原句的意思理解不清，引起费解。要仔细分析主句与从句之间的逻辑关系，把具有原因及结果职能的定语从句转换成适当的表示因果关系的状语从句译出，往往译成"由于……，所以……"、"因为"、"之所以……，是因为……"等。

eg.38　Electric wires are made of copper or some other metals. The reason they are is that electric currents flow readily through metals.

译文：电线由铜或某种其他金属制成。之所以采用这些金属，是因为它们导电性能较好。

eg.39　Aluminium, which possesses high conductivity of heat and electricity, finds wide application in industry.

译文：由于铝具有高度的导热性和导电性，所以在工业上得到广泛应用。

（2）在状语从句中。在科技英语中，从字面上看是时间、条件、比较、地点状语从句，但在逻辑意义上这些从句有时隐含着因果关系。因此，对这些状语从句的翻译需转换成一个表示因果关系的偏正结构。

eg.40　The more intense the ionization of a region is, the more the energy will be refracted.

译文：电离越强烈的空域，对射频能量的折射也越严重。（比较状语从句表因果关系）

eg.41　Why use copper when you can use aluminium ?

译文：既然能用铝，为什么要用铜呢？(时间状语从句表示因果关系)

3）隐含在某些结构或者句型中的因果关系

（1）"there being + 名词"。这是由 there be 句型构成的分词复合结构。名词是逻辑主语，位于逻辑谓语 being 之后，保留原来 there be 句型的倒装语序。这种复合结构隐含因果关系，译成汉语时常译成"因为"、"由于"等。

eg.42　There being no iron, people had to use stone for making tools.

译文：因为那时没有铁，人们只得用石头制造工具。

eg.43　There being a lot of problems to deal with, the scientists worked till midnight.

译文：由于有许多问题要研究，科学家们一直工作到午夜。

（2）"what with…and what with"。what 在这里是副词，相当于副词 partly(部分地)。副词 what 与表示原因意义的介词 with 组成习惯用语，用来引出两个并列的原因状语。译成汉语时常译成"一方面由于……，一方面由于……"或"因为……和……的缘故"。

eg.44　What with lack of raw materials and what with shortage of labour, they just managed to fulfil the production quota.

译文：一方面由于原料缺乏，一方面由于劳力不足，他们好不容易才完成了生产定额。

eg.45 What with the weather and what with the heavy load board, this ship was late in getting to port .

译文：因为天气不好和负载过重的缘故，船抵港迟了。

(3) "in that"。in 与 that 构成短语连词隐含着因果关系，在意义上相当于 because 或 since，连接状语从句。in that 所说的原因范围比较窄，着重指某一方面的原因，属于庄重的文体，多用于正式的论述中。译成汉语时常译成"因为"、"既然"。

eg.46 All of above changes are alike, in that they do not produce new substances.

译文：上述所有的反应都相同，因为它们都没有产生新的物质。

eg.47 In that silver is expensive, it cannot be widely used as a conductor.

译文：由于银的成本很高，所以不可能广泛地用作导体。

(4) "inasmuch as"。这是一个短语连词，用来引导状语从句，其中就隐含有因果关系。其意义与 because 和 since 相同。但比较正式，现只用于书面语，所以在科技英语中能见到。译成汉语时常译成"因为"、"由于"、"既然"。

eg.48 Machining is not an economical method of producing a shape, inasmuch as good raw material is converted into scrap chips.

译文：机械加工不是一种经济的成形方法，因为它把宝贵的原材料变成了废屑。

eg.49 Inasmuch as the pressure increases with depth, there is a great pressure at the lower surface of the submerged body than at the upper surface.

译文：由于压力随深度的增加而增加，所以浸入水中的物体的底面所受到的压力比顶面大。

1.6 科技文体的翻译

1.6.1 文体浅说

科技英语的文体与普通英语和文学英语相比，既有共性也有差异。根据英国兰开斯特大学著名语言学家杰弗里·李切教授下的定义，文体是某个人在某种环境中为了某种目的而使用某种语言的方式。所以影响文体的因素是多方面的，或是地理环境的，或是社会背景的，或是讲话内容的，或是个人特点的，或是时间场合的。根据语言运用的范围，通常将其分为两大类：口语文体和书面文体。根据语言的基本功能可分为信息文体(包括科学专著、技术论文、商业文摘等)、寄情文体(包括诗歌、小说、戏剧、电影等)和鼓动文体(包括广告、标语口号等)。在理论和实践上，还有人提出了日常会话文体、广告文体、新闻报道文体、圣经文体、法律文体、科技文体；等等。语言学家埃弗林·海切在《话语与语言教育》一书中指出，从修辞结构来看，文体可分为叙事体、描述体、程序体和议论体；从语言使用场合来看，文体可分为正式书面体和信息交流体。

因此要确定和划分一篇话语的文体往往是很艰难的。这不仅是门户之见的障碍，而且更重要的是因为这些文体都是互相渗透的。然而从大量的科技英语文献资料分析来看，科技英语作者运用语言的目的和风格主要体现在正式书面文体和信息交流文体。

1.6.2 科技文体的特点及翻译要求

1. 科技英语的特点

科技英语(English for Science and Technology, EST)是从事科学技术活动时所使用的英语，是英语的一种变体。科技英语自 20 世纪 70 年代以来引起了人们的广泛关注，目前已发展成为一种重要的英语语体。本节所讨论的科技英语主要指描述、探讨自然科学各专业的著作、论文、实验报告、科技实用手段(包括仪器、仪表、机械、工具等)的结构描述和操作说明等。

科技英语由于其内容、使用域和语篇功能的特殊性，加之科技工作者长期以来的语言使用习惯，形成了自身的一些特点，使其在许多方面有别于日常英语、文学英语等语体。这些特点主要表现在词汇和句法两个层面上。

1) 大量使用名词化结构

《当代英语语法》(A Grammar of Contemporary)在论述科技英语时提出，大量使用名词化结构(nominalization)是科技英语的特点之一。因为科技文体要求行文简洁、表达客观、内容确切、信息量大、强调存在的事实，而非某一行为。举例如下。

(1) Turing's other contributions to the world of AI came in the area of defining what constitutes intelligence.

译文： 图灵的另一个在人工智能领域方面的贡献是定义智能的组成成分。

句中, of defining what constitutes intelligence 系名词化结构，一方面简化了同位语从句，另一方面强调了 area 这一事实。

(2) A modern method of producing complete, miniature circuits in quantity is to use paper-thin sheets of semiconductor material.

译文：大批量生产整体微型电路的一项新方法，就是采用薄如纸片的半导体材料。

名词化结构 A modern method of producing complete, miniature circuits in quantity 使复合句简化成简单句，而且使表达的概念更加确切严密。

(3) Television is the transmission and reception of images of moving objects by radio waves.

译文：电视通过无线电波发射和接收活动物体的图像。

名词化结构 the transmission and reception of images of moving objects by radio waves 强调客观事实，而谓语动词则着重其发射和接收的能力。

2) 广泛使用被动语句

根据英国利兹大学 John Swales 的统计，科技英语中的谓语至少三分之一是被动语态。这是因为科技文章侧重叙事推理，强调客观准确。第一、二人称使用过多，会造成主观臆断的印象。因此尽量使用第三人称叙述，采用被动语态。例如：Fibers can be used throughout the video distribution network, including the final link into the subscriber's home. 用光纤穿过视频分布网络，包括最终连到用户的家中。而很少说：We can use fibers throughout the video distribution network, including the final link into the subscriber's home. 我们能用光纤穿过视频分布网络，包括最终连到用户的家中。

此外，科技文章将主要信息前置，放在主语部分，这也是广泛使用被动语态的主要原因。试观察并比较下列短文的主语。

Electrical energy can be stored in two metal plates separated by an insulating medium. Such a device is called a capacitor, and its ability to store electrical energy capacitance is called condenser .It is measured in farads.

译文：电能可储存在由某绝缘介质隔开的两块金属极板内。这样的装置称为电容器，其储存电能的能力称为电容。电容的测量单位是法拉。

这一段短文中各句的主语分别为：Electrical energy，Such a device，Its ability to store electrical energy，It (Capacitance)。它们都包含了较多的信息，并且处于句首的位置，非常醒目。4 个主语完全不同，避免了单调重复，前后连贯，自然流畅。足见被动结构可达到简洁客观之效。

3) 非限定动词

如前所述，科技文章要求行文简练，结构紧凑，为此，往往使用分词短语代替定语从句或状语从句；使用分词独立结构代替状语从句或并列分句；使用不定式短语代替各种从句；介词加动名词短语代替定语从句或状语从句。这样可缩短句子，又比较醒目。举例如下。

(1) A capacitor is a device consisting of two conductors separated by a non-conductor.
译文：电容器是由非导体隔开的两个导体组成的一种装置。

(2) Expressed in a formula, the relationship between voltage, current and resistance can be written as V=IR.
译文：若用公式表示的话，电压、电流、电阻之间的关系可写成 V=IR。

(3) This reduction of Boolean expressions eliminates unnecessary gates, thereby saving cost、space and weight.
译文：布尔表达式经过这样的简化之后，去掉了不必要的门电路，从而节省了成本，缩小了体积，减轻了重量。

(4) Almost all metals are good conductors, silver being the best.
译文：几乎所有的金属都是良导体，而银为最好。

(5) For a transistor to function normally, it is necessary to apply proper voltages to its electrodes.
译文：为了使晶体管正常工作，必须给其电极加上合适的电压。
(一般不写成"To make a transistor function normally…")

4) with 结构
所谓"with 结构"一般是指以下形式。

With + 名词(或代词)+ 分词(短语)或介词短语或形容词(短语)或副词或不定式短语或名词(短语)等。举例如下。

Both practical design techniques and theoretical problems are covered with emphasis on general concepts.
译文：(本节)既讲了实际的设计方法，同时也讲了理论问题，而重点则放在一般概念上。

The discovery of quarks with a charge smaller than an electron charge will shake the foundation of modern physics.

译文：夸克带有的电荷小于一个电子的电荷的(这一)发现将动摇现代物理学的基础。

科技文体崇尚严谨周密，概念准确，逻辑性强，行文简练，重点突出，句式严整，少有变化，常用前置性陈述，即在句中将主要信息尽量前置，通过主语传递主要信息。详细来讲，如果科技英语是作为一种正式书面文体出现的话，在使用词汇方面，多数用的是科技专门术语，而且在普通词汇和半技术词汇方面都属于正式书面语体的范畴。科技英语的语法结构主要为一般现在时、被动句、非谓语动词、逻辑性定语、名词化结构、静态结构和各种类型的复合句(表示时间、原因、条件、让步等)。一般来说，科技英语句子较长而句型变化较少，关系代词"that"和"which"以及非人称代词"it"的使用频率较高，这是因为在严谨的科技主体中，作者为了表达缜密的思想和客观的事实，必须增加限制性和扩展性的成分，所以需要借助于它们，从而使句子的平均长度增加，结构更复杂，客观性大大增强。科技英语的著述来不得半点虚假，一定不能带有丝毫的作者个人的感情色彩。它主要应集中论述科学事实、解释科学现象、归纳科学概念和进行严密的逻辑推理。所以在科技英语中很少采用夸张、比喻、拟人、反语、幽默等文学修饰手法。

科技英语作为一种信息交流文体，以准确、简明、客观、新颖为主要特征。而这些特征的实现主要依靠科技英语中使用的普通词汇、半技术词汇和专业词汇。虽然普通词汇在科技英语中占绝大部分，半技术词汇也属于普通词汇，专业词汇在科技英语中仅占很小一部分，但决定了科技英语具有很高的正式程度和很强的信息功能。大多数专业词汇来自拉丁语和希腊语，其意义单一，用法稳定，一般只在特定的学科中出现。

总而言之，科技文体的特点是：清晰、准确、精练、严密。那么，科技文章的语言结构特色在翻译过程中如何处理，是进行英汉科技翻译时需要探讨的问题。

2. 科技英语的翻译

要做好科技英语的翻译工作，译者必须注意以下几点。

(1) 了解相关专业知识。由于科技英语涉及自然科学的各个领域，因此译者应有较宽的知识面，尤其要具备翻译材料所属学科的一些基本的专业知识，为此，一般翻译工作者都应努力学习各科知识。要勤于向书本和专家求教，不可不懂装懂或是想当然地乱译一通。

(2) 准确理解词义。要注意那些常用词在特定学科中的特定含义，不可以常义代特定义，但同时也不应将所有的常用词全部作为专业或准专业词理解，这一点很重要，因为科技英语只是英语的一种文体，并非完全不同的另一种语言，其中的词汇大部分仍是共核词汇。科技翻译中不仅要勤查词典，而且更要结合一个词的上下文及所在的专业领域来确定其真实含义。其次，科学技术发展迅速，相应的新词不断出现，而翻译最新科技成果与信息又往往是我们翻译实践的主要内容，所以译者应随时关注相关领域的最新动态与发展，同时要勤于动手动脑，这样才能准确理解并再现那些新词的意义。

(3) 仔细分析长句。科技英语中有大量长句，这些长句中往往又含有若干分句和许多短语及其他修饰限定成分，这给理解带来了一定的困难。翻译时首先必须对长句进行深入细致的分析，先理清主干，再层层明确各成分之间的语法关系和语义逻辑关系，然后根据情况，选择采用顺译、逆译或综合译法。表达时一定要将意义的准确性和明晰性放在首位，该断句就断句，该增译就增译，不可死抠原文形式。

(4) 用词要得体。总的来讲，科技英语语体较为正式，因此翻译时要尽可能选择与该文体相当的较为正式的词语，行文要向严谨规范的书面语靠拢。此外，原文因语篇内容与功能的不同(如科普文章与学术论文)而在语气的正式程度上也会有所不同，阅读对象的接受能力和文化层次也各异。因此，翻译时应先对原文的正式程度和译文的潜在读者进行一番分析，以求得译文和原文在文体和功能上最大程度的对等。对于学术性和专业性较强的语篇中正式程度高的语汇，译者一般也应将之译成正式程度相当的语汇，如原文正式程度偏低，则译文的语体也应相应降低。如 pink eye 译为"红眼病"，the runs 译为"拉肚子"。如果一些专业性较强的词语出现在通俗性的语篇中，翻译时出于为读者着想也可适当降低其译文的正式程度。

(5) 熟悉构词法。熟悉构词法，特别是科技词汇的常见构词法，对于准确理解词义，特别是新词词义，有着非常重要的意义。

要注意的是，一种缩略形式可能是好几个不同词或词组的共同的缩略形成，翻译时必须依据上下文加以分析。

例如：APC，它可以是 American Power Conference (美国动力会议) 的缩写，也可是 adjustable pressure conveyor (调压输送机) 的缩写，还可以代表 automatic phase control (自动相位调整)或是 automatic program control (自动程序控制)。

而 AC 在不同的语境中，则可有多达 28 个不同的意义，如：①absorption coefficient (吸收系数)，②adapter cable (适配电缆)，③adjustment calibration (调整—校准)，④air condenser (空气冷凝器，空气电容器)，⑤air conditioner(空调器)，⑥analog computer(模拟计算机) 等。所以，翻译缩略词一定要搞清它是哪些词或词组的缩写，手头有一本英汉科技词典和缩略语大词典是很有必要的。

(6) 熟悉数量增减表达法。科技英语中表述数量增减的方式多种多样，译者稍不留神就会出错，所以不仅要小心谨慎，还要熟悉它们常用的表达方式。

(7) 注意术语的准确表达与翻译。术语翻译常被视为科技英语翻译的难中之难，这主要和译者的专业知识欠缺以及原文中新词多有关。因此译者一定要拓宽自己的知识面，增加自己对所译材料涉及的专业知识的了解，准确理解原文的含义，并用妥帖的术语将其意义表达出来。

第 2 章　Application and Appreciation

Lesson One　Modern Digital Design & Digital Signal Processing

Text A　Introduction to Digital Signal Processing

1. What is Digital Signal Processing

Digital Signal Processing, or DSP, as the term suggests, is the processing of signals by digital means. A signal in this context can represent a number of different things. Historically the origins of signal processing are in electrical engineering, and a signal here means an electrical signal carried by a wire or telephone line, or perhaps by a radio wave. More generally, however, a signal is a stream of information representing anything from stock prices to data from a remote-sensing satellite. The term "digital" comes from "digit", meaning a number (you count with your fingers - your digits), so "digital" literally means numerical; the French word for digital is numerique. A digital signal consists of a stream of numbers, usually (but not necessarily) in binary form. The processing of a digital signal is done by performing numerical calculations.

Digital Signal Processing is one of the most powerful technologies that will shape science and engineering in the twenty-first century. Revolutionary changes have already been made in a broad range of fields: communications, medical imaging, radar & sonar, high fidelity music reproduction, and oil prospecting, to name just a few. Each of these areas has developed a deep DSP technology, with its own algorithms, mathematics, and specialized techniques. This combination of breath and depth makes it impossible for any individual to master all of the DSP technology that has been developed.[1] DSP education involves two tasks: learning general concepts that apply to the field as a whole, and learning specialized techniques for your particulararea of interest.

2. Analog and Digital Signals

In many cases, the signal of interest is initially in the form of an analog electrical voltage or current, produced for example by a microphone or some other type of transducer. In some situations, such as the output from the readout system of a CD (compact disc) player, the data is already in digital form. An analog signal must be converted into digital form before DSP techniques can be applied. An analog electrical voltage signal, for example, can be digitized using an electronic circuit called an analog-to-digital converter or ADC. This device generates a digital output as a stream of binary numbers whose values represent the input electrical voltages at each sampling instant.

3. Signal Processing

Signals commonly need to be processed in a variety of ways. For example, the output signal from a transducer may well be contaminated with unwanted electrical "noise". The electrodes attached to a patient's chest when an ECG is taken measure tiny electrical voltage changes due to the activity of the heart and other muscles. The signal is often strongly affected by "mains pickup" due to electrical interference from the mains supply. Processing the signal using a filter circuit can remove or at least reduce the unwanted part of the signal. Increasingly nowadays, the filtering of signals to improve signal quality or to extract important information is done by DSP techniques rather than by analog electronics.

4. Development and Applications of DSP

The development of digital signal processing dates from the 1960's with the use of mainframe digital computers for number-crunching applications such as the Fast Fourier Transform (FFT), which allows the frequency spectrum of a signal to be computed rapidly.[2] These techniques were not widely used at that time, because suitable computing equipment was generally available only in universities and other scientific research institutions.

Because computers were expensive during this time, DSP was limited to only a few critical applications. Pioneering efforts were made in four key areas: radar & sonar, where national security was at risk; oil exploration, where large amounts of money could be made; space exploration, where data are irreplaceable; and medical imaging, where lives could be saved.

The personal computer revolution of the 1980s and 1990s caused DSP to explode with new applications. Rather than being motivated by military and government needs, DSP was suddenly driven by the commercial marketplace. Anyone who thought they could make money in the rapidly expanding field was suddenly a DSP vendor. DSP reached the public in such products as: mobile telephones, compact disc players, and electronic voice mail.

This technological revolution occurred from the top-down. In the early 1980s, DSP was taught as a graduate level course in electrical engineering. A decade later, DSP had become a standard part of the undergraduate curriculum. Today, DSP is a basic skill needed by scientists and engineers in many fields. As an analogy, DSP can be compared to a previous technological revolution: electronics. While still the realm of electrical engineering, nearly every scientist and engineer has some background in basic circuit design. Without it, they would be lost in the technological world.[3] DSP has the same future. DSP has revolutionized many areas in science and engineering. A few of these diverse applications are shown in Figure 1.

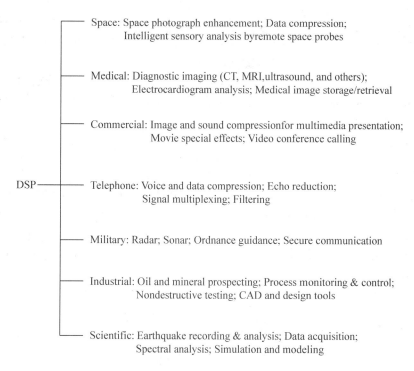

Space: Space photograph enhancement; Data compression;
Intelligent sensory analysis byremote space probes

Medical: Diagnostic imaging (CT, MRI,ultrasound, and others);
Electrocardiogram analysis; Medical image storage/retrieval

Commercial: Image and sound compressionfor multimedia presentation;
Movie special effects; Video conference calling

DSP

Telephone: Voice and data compression; Echo reduction;
Signal multiplexing; Filtering

Military: Radar; Sonar; Ordnance guidance; Secure communication

Industrial: Oil and mineral prospecting; Process monitoring & control;
Nondestructive testing; CAD and design tools

Scientific: Earthquake recording & analysis; Data acquisition;
Spectral analysis; Simulation and modeling

Fig.1　The application area of DSP

5. Digital Signal Processors (DSPs)

The introduction of the microprocessor in the late 1970's and early 1980's made it possible for DSP techniques to be used in a much wider range of applications. However, general-purpose microprocessors such as the Intel x86 family are not ideally suited to the numerically-intensive requirements of DSP, and during the 1980's the increasing importance of DSP led several major electronics manufacturers (such as Texas Instruments, Analog Devices and Motorola) to develop Digital Signal Processor chips—specialized microprocessors with architectures designed specifically for the types of operations required in digital signal processing. (Note that the acronym DSP can variously mean Digital Signal Processing, the term used for a wide range of techniques for processing signals digitally, or Digital Signal Processor, a specialized type of microprocessor chip).[4] Like a general-purpose microprocessor, a DSP is a programmable device, with its own native instruction code. DSP chips are capable of carrying out millions of floating point operations per second, and like their better-known general-purpose cousins, faster and more powerful versions are continually being introduced. DSPs can also be embedded within complex "system-on-chip" devices, often containing both analog and digital circuitry.

Although some of the mathematical theory underlying DSP techniques, such as Fourier and Hilbert Transforms, digital filter design and signal compression, can be fairly complex, the numerical operations required actually to implement these techniques are very simple, consisting mainly of operations that could be done on a cheap four-function calculator. The architecture of a DSP chip is designed to carry out such operations incredibly fast, processing hundreds of millions of samples every second, to provide real-time performance: that is, the ability to process a signal "live" as it is sampled and then output the processed signal, for example to a loudspeaker or video display. All of the practical examples of DSP applications mentioned earlier, such as hard disc drives and mobile phones, demand real-time operation.

The major electronics manufacturers have invested heavily in DSP technology. Because they now find application in mass-market products, DSP chips account for a substantial proportion of the world market for electronic devices. Sales amount to billions of dollars annually, and seem likely to continue to increase rapidly.

6. The Depth of DSP

As you go through each application, note that DSP is very interdisciplinary, relying on the technical work in many adjacent fields. As Fig.2 suggests, the borders between DSP and other technical disciplines are not sharp and well defined, but rather fuzzy and overlapping. If you want to specialize in DSP, these are the allied areas you will also need to studys areas of science, engineering and mathematics.

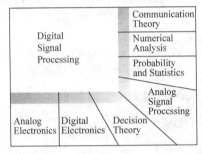

Fig.2   Digital Signal Processing has fuzzy and overlapping borders with many other

7. Some Area of DSP Affected

1) Telecommunications

DSP has revolutionized the telecommunications industry in many areas: signaling tone generation and detection, frequency band shifting, filtering to remove power line hum, etc. Three specific examples from the telephone network will be discussed here: multiplexing, compression, and echo control.

(1) Multiplexing

There are approximately one billion telephones in the world. At the press of a few buttons, switching networks allow any one of these to be connected to any other in only a few seconds. The immensity of this task is mind boggling! Until the 1960s, a connection between two telephones required passing the analog voice signals through mechanical switches and amplifiers. One connection required one pair of wires. In comparison, DSP converts audio signals into a stream of serial digital data. Since bits can be easily intertwined and later separated, many telephone conversations can be transmitted on a single channel. This technology is called multiplexing.[5]

(2) Compression

When a voice signal is digitized at 8000 samples/sec, most of the digital information is redundant. That is, the information carried by any one sample is largely duplicated by the neighboring samples.[6] Dozens of DSP algorithms have been developed to convert digitized voice signals into data streams that require fewer bits/sec. These are called data compression algorithms. Matching uncompression algorithms are used to restore the signal to its original form. These algorithms vary in the amount of compression achieved and the resulting sound quality. In general, reducing the data rate from 64 kilobits/sec to 32 kilobits/sec results in no loss of sound quality.

(3) Echo control

Echoes are a serious problem in long distance telephone connections. When you speak into a telephone, a signal representing your voice travels to the connecting receiver, where a portion of it returns as an echo. If the connection is within a few hundred miles, the elapsed time for receiving the echo is only a few milliseconds. The human ear is accustomed to hearing echoes with these small time delays, and the connection sounds quite normal. As the distance becomes larger, the echo becomes increasingly noticeable and irritating. The delay can be several hundred milliseconds for intercontinental communications, and is particularly objectionable. Digital Signal Processing attacks this type of problem by measuring the returned signal and generating an appropriate antisignal to cancel the offending echo. The same technique allows speakerphone users to hear and speak at the same time without fighting audio feedback (squealing).It can also be used to reduce environmental noise by canceling it with digitally generated antinoise.

2) Audio Processing

The two principal human senses are vision and hearing. Correspondingly, much of DSP is related to image and audio processing. People listen to both music and speech. DSP has made evolutionary changes in both these areas.

(1) Music

The path leading from the musician's microphone to the audiophile's speaker is remarkably long. Digital data representation is important to prevent the degradation commonly associated with analog storage and manipulation. This is very familiar to anyone who has compared the musical quality of cassette tapes with compact disks. In a typical scenario, a musical piece is recorded in a sound studio on multiple channels or tracks. In some cases, this even involves recording individual instruments and singers separately. This is done to give the sound engineer greater flexibility in creating the final product. The complex process of combining the individual tracks into a final product is called mix down. DSP can provide several important functions during mix down, including: filtering, signal addition and subtraction, signal editing, etc.

One of the most interesting DSP applications in music preparation is artificial reverberation. If the individual channels are simply added together, the resulting piece sounds frail and diluted, much as if the musicians were playing outdoors. This is because listeners are greatly influenced by the echo or reverberation content of the music, which is usually minimized in the sound studio. DSP allows artificial echoes and reverberation to be added during mix down to simulate various ideal listening environments. Echoes with delays of a few hundred milliseconds give the impression of cathedral like locations. Adding echoes with delays of 10~20 milliseconds provide the perception of more modest size listening rooms.

(2) Speech generation

Speech generation and recognition are used to communicate between humans and machines. Rather than using your hands and eyes, you use your mouth and ears. This is very convenient when your hands and eyes should be doing something else, such as: driving a car, performing surgery, or (unfortunately) firing your weapons at the enemy. Two approaches are used for computer generated speech: digital recording and vocal tract simulation.

(3) Speech recognition

The automated recognition of human speech is immensely more difficult than speech generation. Digital Signal Processing generally approaches the problem of voice recognition in two steps: feature extraction followed by feature matching. Each word in the incoming audio signal is isolated and then analyzed to identify the type of excitation and resonate frequencies. These parameters are then compared with previous examples of spoken words to identify the closest match. Often, these systems are limited to only a few hundred words; can only accept speech with distinct pauses between words; and must be retrained for each individual speaker.

8. Image Processing

Images are signals with special characteristics. First, they are a measure of a parameter over space (distance), while most signals are a measure of a parameter over time. Second, they contain a great deal of information. For example, more than 10 megabytes can be required to store one second of television video. This is more than a thousand times greater than for a similar length voice signal. Third, the final judge of quality is often a subjective human evaluation, rather than an objective criterion. These special characteristics have made image processing a distinct subgroup within DSP.

New Words and Expressions

historically	adv.	历史上，从历史的观点看
algorithm	n.	算法
sonar	n.	声呐，声波定位仪
analog	adj.	模拟的
transducer	n.	传感器，变频器，变换器
contaminate	vt.	污染
ECG=Electrocardiograph	abbr.	心电图
irreplaceable	adj.	不能代替的
acronym	n.	只取首字母的缩写词
Fourier Transform		傅里叶变换
incredibly	adv.	不能相信地
programmable	adj.	可编程的
interdisciplinary	adj.	各学科间的
multiplexing		多路技术

amplifier	*n.*	放大器
uncompression		解压缩
digital recording		数字式录音
speech recognition		语音识别
feature extraction		特征抽取
reproduction	*n.*	再现，再生
prospecting	*n.*	采矿
digitize	*vt.*	数字化
electrode	*n.*	电极
noise	*n.*	噪声
mains supply		交流电源
electronic voice mail		语音邮件
Microprocessor	*n.*	微处理器
Hilbert Transform		希尔伯特变换
embed	*vt.*	使插入，使嵌入，深留，嵌入
redundant	*adj.*	多余的，冗余的
filtering	*n.*	滤波
data compression		数据压缩
artificial reverberation		人工混响
vocal tract simulation		声音模拟器
speech generation		语音产生
feature matching		特征匹配

Notes

1. Each of these areas has developed a deep DSP technology, with its own algorithms, mathematics, and specialized techniques. This combination of breath and depth makes it impossible for any one individual to master all of the DSP technology that has been developed.

译文：每个研究领域都在它自身特有的算法、数学和技术的基础上更深入地开发 DSP 技术，从而使 DSP 技术在广度和深度两个方面都得到拓展，因此，任何人都不可能掌握所有现存的 DSP 技术。

2. The development of digital signal processing dates from the 1960's with the use of mainframe digital computers for number-crunching applications such as the Fast Fourier Transform (FFT), which allows the frequency spectrum of a signal to be computed rapidly.

译文：数字信号处理技术源于 20 世纪 60 年代，彼时，大型计算机开始用于处理计算量较大的运算，例如，可以快速获得信号的频谱的快速傅里叶变换(FFT)等。

在本句中，The development of digital signal processing 是主语，dates from 是谓语，意思是起源于历史上的某一个年代。后面以 which 引导的定语从句用于修饰 FFT。

3. Without it, they would be lost in the technological world.

译文：没有基本的电路设计的背景(经验)，他们将会被技术界淘汰。

it 是指前一句中的 some background in basic circuit design.

lost 的原意是丢失，这里意译为"淘汰"。

4. Note that the acronym DSP can variously mean Digital Signal Processing, the term used for a wide range of techniques for processing signals digitally, or Digital Signal Processor, a specialized type of microprocessor chip.

译文：需要注意的是，缩写 DSP 有多种含义，它既可以解释为"数字信号处理"，也可以解释为"数字信号处理器"，前者表示一种目前被广泛采用的数字信号处理技术，后者则表示一种专用的微处理器芯片。

5. In comparison, DSP converts audio signals into a stream of serial digital data. Since bits can be easily intertwined and later separated, many telephone conversations can be transmitted on a single channel. This technology is called multiplexing.

译文：比较而言，DSP 可以将音频信号转变为数据流。由于数字比特易于组合与分离，因此，多路电话信号可以通过一条信道实现传输，这种技术称为复用。

6. When a voice signal is digitized at 8000 samples/sec, most of the digital information is redundant. That is, the information carried by any one sample is largely duplicated by the neighboring samples.

译文：当对话音信号在 8000 次/秒的采样率基础上进行编码时，获得的数字信号存在冗余，也就是说，某一采样点的信息在很大程度上与其他采样点的信息重复。

Exercises

Ⅰ. Comprehension questions.

1. What is DSP? Please explain in a sentence.

2. Please explain the application area of DSP.

3. What areas you need to study if you want to specialize in DSP?

4. How has DSP revolutionized the telecommunications industry?

5. How does DSP solve the problem of voice recognition?

6. Why image processing is a distinct subgroup within DSP?

Ⅱ. Translate the following paragraph into Chinese.

Digital Signal Processing is one of the most powerful technologies that will shape science and engineering in the twenty-first century. Revolutionary changes have already been made in a broad range of fields: communications, medical imaging, radar & sonar, high fidelity music reproduction, and oil prospecting, to name just a few. Each of these areas has developed a deep DSP technology, with its own algorithms, mathematics, and specialized techniques. This combination of breath and depth makes it impossible for any one individual to master all of the

DSP technology that has been developed. DSP education involves two tasks: learning general concepts that apply to the field as a whole, and learning specialized techniques for your particular area of interest.

Text B   Modern Digital Design

1. Overview

The speed of light is just too slow. Commonplace, modern, volume-manufactured digital designs require control of timings down to the picosecond range. The amount of time it takes light from your nose to reach your eye is about 100 picoseconds (in 100 ps, light travels about 1.2 in.). This level of timing must not only be maintained at the silicon level, but also at the physically much larger level of the system board, such as a computer motherboard. These systems operate at high frequencies at which conductors no longer behave as simple wires, but instead exhibit high-frequency effects and behave as transmission lines that are used to transmit or receive electrical signals to or from neighboring components.[1] If these transmission lines are not handled properly, they can unintentionally ruin system timing. Digital design has acquired the complexity of the analog world and more. However, it has not always been this way. Digital technology is a remarkable story of technological evolution. It is a continuing story of paradigm shifts, industrial revolution, and rapid change that is unparalleled. Indeed, it is a common creed in marketing departments of technology companies that "by the time a market survey tells you the public wants something, it is already too late."

This rapid progress has created a roadblock to technological progress that this book will help solve. The problem is that modern digital designs require knowledge that has formerly not been needed. Because of this, many currently employed digital system designers do not have the knowledge required for modern high-speed designs. This fact leads to a surprisingly large amount of misinformation to propagate through engineering circles. Often, the concepts of high-speed design are perceived with a sort of mysticism. However, this problem has not come about because the required knowledge is unapproachable. In fact, many of the same concepts have been used for several decades in other disciplines of electrical engineering, such as radio-frequency design and microwave design. The problem is that most references on the necessary subjects are either too abstract to be immediately applicable to the digital designer, or they are too practical in nature to contain enough theory to fully understand the subject. This book will focus directly on the area of digital design and will explain the necessary concepts to understand and solve contemporary and future problems in a manner directly applicable by practicing engineers and/or students. It is worth noting that everything in this book has been applied to a successful modern design.

2. The basics

As the reader undoubtedly knows, the basic idea in digital design is to communicate information with signals representing 1s or 0s. Typically this involves sending and receiving a series of trapezoidal shaped voltage signals such as shown in Figure 3 in which a high voltage is a 1 and a low voltage is a 0. The conductive paths carrying the digital signals are known as interconnects. The interconnect includes the entire electrical pathway from the chip sending a signal to the chip receiving the signal. This includes the chip packages, connectors, sockets, as well as a myriad of additional structures. A group of interconnects is referred to as a bus. The region of voltage where a digital receiver distinguishes between a high and a low voltage is known as the threshold region. Within this region, the receiver will either switch high or switch low. On the silicon, the actual switching voltages vary with temperature, supply voltage, silicon process, and other variables. From the system designers point of view, there are usually high-and low-voltage thresholds, known as Vih and Vil, associated with the receiving silicon, above which and below which a high or low value can be guaranteed to be received under all conditions.[2] Thus the designer must guarantee that the system can, under all conditions, deliver high voltages that do not, even briefly, fall below Vih, and low voltages that remain below Vil, in order to ensure the integrity of the data.

Fig.3　Digital waveform

In order to maximize the speed of operation of a digital system, the timing uncertainty of a transition through the threshold region must be minimized. This means that the rise or fall time of the digital signal must be as fast as possible. Ideally, an infinitely fast edge rate would be used, although there are many practical problems that prevent this. Realistically, edge rates of a few hundred picoseconds can be encountered. The reader can verify with Fourier analysis that the quicker the edge rate, the higher the frequencies that will be found in the spectrum of the signal. Herein lies a clue to the difficulty. Every conductor has a capacitance, inductance, and frequency-dependent resistance. At a high enough frequency, none of these things is negligible. Thus a wire is no longer a wire but a distributed parasitic element that will have delay and a transient impedance profile that can cause distortions and glitches to manifest themselves on the waveform propagating from the driving chip to the receiving chip.[3] The wire is now an element that is coupled to everything around it, including power and ground structures and other traces. The signal is not contained entirely in the conductor itself but is a combination of all the local electric and magnetic fields around the conductor.[4] The signals on one interconnect will affect and be affected by the signals on another. Furthermore, at high frequencies, complex interactions occur between the different parts of the same interconnect, such as the packages、connectors、and bends. All these high-speed effects tend to produce strange, distorted waveforms that will indeed give the designer a completely different view of high-speed logic signals. The physical and electrical attributes of every structure in the vicinity of the interconnect has a vital role in the simple task of guaranteeing proper signaling transitions through Vih and Vil with the appropriate timings. These things also determine how much energy the system will radiate into space, which will lead to determining whether the system complies with governmental emission requirements.

We will see in later chapters how to account for all these things. When a conductor must be considered as a distributed series of inductors and capacitors, it is known as a transmission line. In general, this must be done when the physical size of the circuit under consideration approaches the wavelength of the highest frequency of interest in the signal. In the digital realm, since edge rate pretty much determines the maximum frequency content, one can compare rise and fall times to the size of the circuit instead, as shown in Figure 4 On a typical circuit board, a signal travels about half the speed of light (exact formulas will be in later chapters). Thus a 500 ps edge rate occupies about 3 in. in length on a circuit trace. Generally, any circuit length at least 1/10th of the edge rate must be considered as a transmission line.

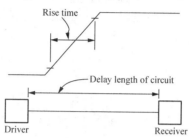

Fig.4   Rise time and circuit length

One of the most difficult aspects of high-speed design is the fact that there are a large number of codependent variables that affect the outcome of a digital design. Some of the variables are controllable and some force the designer to live with the random variation. One of the difficulties in high-speed design is how to handle the many variables, whether they are controllable or uncontrollable. Often simplifications can be made by neglecting or assuming values for variables, but this can lead to unknown failures down the road that will be impossible to "root cause" after the fact. As timing becomes more constrained, the simplifications of the past are rapidly dwindling in utility to the modern designer. This book will also show how to incorporate a large number of variables that would otherwise make the problem intractable. Without a methodology for handling the large amount of variables, a design ultimately resorts to guesswork no matter how much the designer physically understands the system. The final step of handling all the variables is often the most difficult part and the one most readily ignored by a designer. A designer crippled by an inability to handle large amounts of variables will ultimately resort to proving a few "point solutions" instead and hope that they plausibly represent all known conditions. While sometimes such methods are unavoidable, this can be a dangerous guessing game. Of course, a certain amount of guesswork is always present in a design, but the goal of the system designer should be to minimize uncertainty.

3. The Past and the Future

Gordon Moore, co-founder of Intel Corporation, predicted that the performance of computers will double every 18 months. History confirmed this insightful prediction. Remarkably, computer performance has doubled approximately every 1.5 years, along with substantial decreases in their price. One measure of relative processor performance is internal clock rates.

Figure 5 shows several processors through history and their associated internal clock rates. By the time this is in print, even the fastest processors on this chart will likely be considered unimpressive. The point is that computer speeds are increasing exponentially. As core frequency increases, faster data rates will be demanded from the buses that feed information to the processor, as shown in Figure 6, leading to an interconnect timing budget that is decreasing exponentially. Decreased timing budgets mean that it is evermore important to properly account for any phenomenon that may increase the timing uncertainty of the digital waveform as it arrives at the receiver. This is the root cause of two inescapable obstacles that will continue to make digital system design difficult. The first obstacle is simply that the sheer amount of variables that must be accounted for in a digital design is increasing. As frequencies increase, new effects, which may have been negligible at slower speeds, start to become significant. Generally speaking, the complexity of a design increases exponentially with increasing variable count. The second obstacle is that the new effects, which could be ignored in designs of the past, must be modeled to a very high precision. Often these new models are required to be three-dimensional in nature, or require specialized analog techniques that fall outside the realms of the digital designer's discipline. The obstacles are perhaps more profound on the subsystems surrounding the processor since they evolve at a much slower rate, but still must support the increasing demands of the processor system increases.

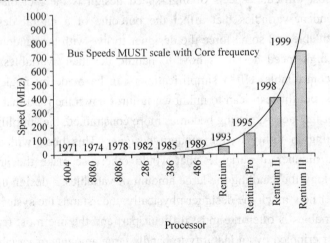

Fig.5　Moore's law in action

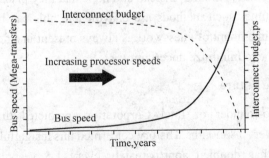

Fig.6　The interconnect budget shrinks as the performance and the frequency

All of this leads to the present situation: There are new problems to solve. Engineers who can solve these problems will define the future. This book will equip the reader with the necessary practical understanding to contend with modern high-speed digital design and with enough theory to see beyond this book and solve problems that the authors have not yet encountered.

New Words and Expressions

commonplace	*adj.*	平常的，一般的
picosecond	*n.*	皮(可)秒，百亿分之一秒(时间单位，符号为 psec 或 ps)
conductor	*n.*	导线，导体
transmission	*n.*	发射，发送，传输
unintentionally	*adv.*	无意地
roadblock	*n.*	障碍，障碍物
discipline	*n.*	纪律，学科
trapezoidal	*adj.*	梯形的
interconnect	*vt.*	互连(横向连接)
	n.	内连
socket	*n.*	插座(承窝，管套)
bus	*n.*	母线，总线
silicon process		硅过程，硅加工
realistically	*adv.*	实际地
herein	*adv.*	在这里
distributed	*adj.*	分布式的
transient	*n.*	瞬变现象，瞬态，暂态
delay	*n.*	延迟
glitch	*n.*	(俚)短时脉冲波形干扰，失灵，小故障
via	*prep.*	经过，经由；凭借，通过
transmission line		传输线，波导线
codependent	*adj.*	相互依赖的
controllable	*adj.*	可控制的
dwindle	*v.*	缩小
methodology	*n.*	方法学，方法论
resort	*vi.*	求助，诉诸，采取(某种手段等)
	n.	凭借，手段；常去之地，胜地
exponentially	*adv.*	指数地，幂数地
obstacle	*n.*	障碍，妨害物
precision	*n.*	精确，精密度，精度
volume-manufactured		大量制造的

motherboard	*n.*	母板
high-frequency effects		高频效应
ruin	*n.*	损坏(毁灭)
	vt.	破坏(毁灭)
mysticism	*n.*	神秘，神秘主义，谬论
contemporary	*adj.*	当代的，同时代的
conductive	*adj.*	传导的(导电的)
connector	*n.*	连接物(接线器，插头)
myriad	*n.*	无数，无数的人或物，<诗>一万
	adj.	无数的，一万的，各种的
threshold region		临界域
integrity	*n.*	完整性
encounter	*v.*	遇到(碰撞，遭遇)
negligible	*adj.*	可以忽略的，不予重视的
parasitic	*adj.*	寄生的
impedance	*n.*	阻抗
distortion	*n.*	失真
ground	*n.*	地，接地
vicinity	*n.*	邻近，附近，接近
realm	*n.*	领域
outcome	*n.*	结果
intractable	*adj.*	难处理的
guesswork	*n.*	臆测，猜测，凭猜测所作之工作
insightful	*adj.*	富有洞察力的，有深刻见解的
phenomenon	*n.*	现象
complexity	*n.*	复杂(性)，复杂的事物，复杂性

Notes

1. These systems operate at high frequencies at which conductors no longer behave as simple wires, but instead exhibit high-frequency effects and behave as transmission lines that are used to transmit or receive electrical signals to or from neighboring components.

译文：当系统工作于高频段时，导体不再是简单的导线，此时，导体将表现出高频特性，即具有传输线的功能和特性，该特性使得导体能与相邻器件之间实现信号的发送和接收。

transmit to 和 receive from 是固定搭配。

2. From the system designer's point of view, there are usually high-and low-voltage thresholds, known as Vih and Vil, associated with the receiving silicon, above which and below which a high or low value can be guaranteed to be received under all conditions.

译文：从系统设计者的角度来说，高电压门限(Vih)和低电压门限(Vil)的取值与硅的品质有关，在任何条件下，高于 Vih 的值或低于 Vil 的值都可以保证被正确接收。

from one's point of view: 从某人的角度来看，从某人的观点来看。

3. Every conductor has a capacitance, inductance, and frequency-dependent resistance. At a high enough frequency, none of these things is negligible. Thus a wire is no longer a wire but a distributed parasitic element that will have delay and a transient impedance profile that can cause distortions and glitches to manifest themselves on the waveform propagating from the driving chip to the receiving chip.

译文：每个导体都有电容和电感，它们的阻抗因频谱而变，当频率足够高时，必须要考虑这些因素的影响，此时，导线不再仅仅是简单的导线，而是分布参数元件，这样的元件会带来延时和瞬变阻抗，从而导致驱动芯片和接收芯片之间传输的波形发生畸变。

4. The signal is not contained entirely in the conductor itself but is a combination of all the local electric and magnetic fields around the conductor.

译文：信号不再仅仅存在于导体内，也在导体外产生磁场。

Exercises

Ⅰ. Comprehension questions.

1. Why are the concepts of high-speed design often perceived with a sort of mysticism?

2. How to communicate information with signal 1s or 0s in digital design?

3. What does the interconnect include?

4. What does the designer must do in order to ensure the integrity of the data?

5. What will you do to maximize the speed of operation of a digital system?

6. Please tell the difference of a conductor between high frequency and low frequency.

7. What is the most difficult thing in high-speed designing?

8. What is the two inescapable obstacles that will make digital system design difficult?

9. According to the author, what will happen in the future?

Ⅱ. Translate the following paragraph into Chinese.

One of the most difficult aspects of high-speed design is the fact that there are a large number codependent variables that affect the outcome of a digital design. Some of the variables are controllable and some force the designer to live with the random variation. One of the difficulties in high-speed design is how to handle the many variables, whether they are controllable or uncontrollable. Often simplifications can be made by neglecting or assuming values for variables, but this can lead to unknown failures down the road that will be impossible to "root cause" after the fact. As timing becomes more constrained, the simplifications of the past are rapidly dwindling in utility to the modern designer.

Lesson Two　Embedded Systems and Applications

Text A　Characteristics of Embedded Systems

What are embedded systems?

A completely new branch of computer engineering is that of embedded systems. It is the development of specialized computer equipment that is not programmable by the user, but is dedicated to drive or control a piece of equipment, such as medical equipment or machinery. The skill of embedded systems is marrying the computer technology with the mechanical engineering design.

An embedded system is a special purpose computer that is used inside of a device. For example, a microwave contains an embedded system that accepts input from the panel, controls the LCD display, and turns on and off the heating elements that cook the food. Embedded systems generally use micro-controllers that contain many functions of a computer on a single device. Motorola and Intel make some of the most popular micro-controllers.

The embedded systems market is getting wider all the time as engineers think of other engineering projects that can benefit from the embedded systems technology. We now have embedded systems in everything from food processors to cars and beyond. Living in the computer age means that in all likelihood, before this decade is out, we will be hard put to find a mechanical device that has not been subjected to embedded systems of some sort.

There are different grades of embedded systems. Computerized toys and kitchen implements are a very simple form of embedded systems. Many of the more complicated medical machines actually benefit from the use of more than one embedded system. Although this means that the machines we use as a matter of course in daily life are a lot more effective in general, it does also mean that the repair process of embedded systems machinery can be difficult and costly. But it does also mean that our time is freed up by embedded systems machinery so that we can spend more time doing what we love. We all use washing machines with embedded systems, for example. More and more, the cars we buy have embedded system.

Even the tools we use for manufacturing are the result of embedded systems. It stands to reason that there are companies that specialize in the development of embedded systems, either independently, or in tandem with the machinery with which they're to be used. More and more, engineering firms are calling on this kind of expertise to upgrade their products in every way imaginable.[1]

1. Without embedded systems

You get into your car and turn the key on. You take a 3.5' floppy disk from the glove compartment, insert it into a slot on the dashboard, and drum your fingers on the steering wheel until the operating system prompt appears on the dashboard LCD. Using the cursor keys on the center console you select the program for electronic ignition, then turn the key to start the engine.

On the way to work you want to listen to some music, so you insert the program CD into the player, wait for the green light to flash indicating that the digital signal processor in the player is ready, then put in your music CD.

2. With embedded systems

(1) You don't need a traditional user interface to decide which programs should be running—the car's electronic ignition program will respond to the car key.

(2) You don't need to load programs into your devices—the ones needed to make it work should already be loaded (although in some new mobile phones you can download extra programs).

(3) You don't need to waste time waiting for the O/S to load—if one is needed, then it doesn't have baggage that make it slow to load .

(4) You don't need to load programs or data from a slow disk drive—most information needed will be in fast ROM.

Embedded systems can be roughly defined as "a system that is not primarily a computer but contains a processor". But rather than focusing on a definition, it is useful to consider aspects that most embedded systems share, at least to some degree.

1) Embedded systems are frequently price and size sensitive

Many embedded systems such as PDAs or cell-phones are high-volume, low-cost and low-margin. This requires use of the cheapest components possible, which typically means simple processors and small memory (RAM and NVRAM/flash). This causes embedded systems software to trade off maintainability aspects such as portability, clarity, or modularity for performance optimization aspects such as a small boot image footprint, a small RAM footprint, and small cycle requirements. The increased up-front software development costs and periodic maintenance costs are amortized by the high-volume sales, and outweighed by the continuous hardware cost savings of cheaper components.

Many other embedded systems, though not so price-sensitive, have physical constraints on form factor or weight to use the smallest components possible. Again, this favors performance optimization at the cost of maintainability.[2]

In addition to trading off portability, clarity, or modularity, embedded systems may also require optimization by using a low-level language, e.g. assembly rather than C, or C rather than code automatically generated from a UML model. However, this hand tuning is typically only applied to small portions of the software identified by the "90/10" guideline as being the major performance bottlenecks.

2) Embedded systems often have power limitations

Many embedded systems run from a battery, either continually or during emergencies. Therefore, power consumption performance is favored in many embedded systems at the cost of complexity and maintainability.

3) Embedded systems are frequently real-time

By nature, most embedded systems are built to react in real-time to data flowing to and through the system. The real-time constraints again favor performance aspects (particularly cycles usage) over maintainability aspects. There are generally both hard real-time constraints, which require an event to be handled by a fixed time, and soft real-time constraints, which set limits on the average event response time.[3] Real-time operating systems use preemptive prioritized scheduling to help ensure that real-time deadlines are met, but careful thought is required to divide processing into execution contexts (threads), set the relative priorities of the execution contexts, and manage control/data flow between the contexts.

4) Embedded systems frequently use custom hardware

Embedded systems are frequently comprised of off-the-shelf processors combined with off-the-shelf peripherals. Even though the components may be standard, the custom mixing and matching requires a high degree of cohesion between the hardware and the software—a significant portion of the software for an embedded system is operating system and device driver software. Though this low-level software is often available for purchase, license, or free use, frequently a large portion of the operating system for an embedded system is custom-developed in-house, either to precisely match the hardware system at hand, or to glue together off-the-shelf software in a custom configuration.

Often the functionality of an embedded system is distributed between multiple peer processors and/or a hierarchy of master/slave processors. Careful thought is required regarding the distribution of processing tasks across processors, and the extent, method, and timing of communication between processors.

Furthermore, many embedded systems make use of specialized FPGAs or ASICs, and thus require low-level software to interact with the custom hardware.

5) Embedded systems are predominantly hidden from view

By nature, embedded systems typically have a limited interface with their "user"(real user or another component of the super-system). Thus, much of the system is developed to meet the software functional specifications developed during architecture and high-level design, rather than the user requirements.

6) Embedded systems frequently have monolithic functionality

Most embedded systems are built for a single primary purpose. They can be decomposed into components, and potentially the components could have low cross-cohesion and cross-coupling. That is, each component could serve a distinct purpose, and the interactions between components could be restricted to a few well-defined points. Nevertheless, the system as a whole will not function unless most or all of the components are operational. A system that requires all components to function before the system as a whole achieves useful functionality is a "monolithic system". This non-linear jump in system functionality as a function of component functionality is in contrast to some other types of software, where the system may be 50% functional (or more) when the software is 50% complete.

For example, a space probe is built to travel by or to other planets and send back information about them. Though there are many lower-level responsibilities of the space probe components, such as targeting, landing, deploying sensors, deploying solar panels, and communications. Each of these lower-level responsibilities is an indispensable component of the over-arching functionality. The space probe will fail if any of these vital components is missing, even if all other components are completely functional.

Another example is a cell phone, in which all the sub-features such as the user interface, the cellular base station selection, the vocoder, and the communications protocols are all vital aspects of the over-arching goal to transfer bi-directional audio information between the user and specific remote nodes.

These are in contrast to other software regimes, such as web services or desktop tools, in which lower-level responsibilities are more likely to contribute independently to the aggregate system functionality rather than serving as indispensable parts of a monolithic whole.

Though the software components of an embedded system are combined into a monolithic functionality, the components themselves are often very distinct. Embedded systems will frequently combine software components that perform signal processing, low-level device driver I/O, communications protocols, guidance and control, and user interfaces. Each of these specialized components requires a distinct developer skill set.

7) Embedded systems frequently have limited development tools

Though some software regimes have a whole host of tools to assist with software development, embedded systems software development are more limited, and frequently use only basic compiler tools. This is in part because embedded systems often use custom hardware, which may not have tool support, and because embedded systems are often real-time and performance constrained, making it difficult to freeze the entire execution context under the control of a debugger or transfer control and data between the embedded target and a host-based tool, or capture extensive execution-tracing logs.

Because of the limited choices of commercial tools for embedded systems software development, many embedded system projects create their own tools to use for debugging and testing, or at least augment commercial tools with in-house tools.

8) Embedded systems frequently have stringent robustness requirements

Embedded systems are often used in harsh environments and for mission-critical or medical purposes. Therefore, requirements for reliability, correct exception handling, and mean time between failures are typically more stringent for embedded systems than for many other types of software. This translates into rigorous development processes and testing requirements. In turn, this increases the overhead needed to make a release of software.

Some types of embedded systems are subject to regulatory requirements that purport to reduce fault rates by mandating the software development process, or at least specifying what documentation must accompany the embedded systems product.

Furthermore, for several types of embedded systems, it is difficult or even impossible to upgrade firmware, which emphasizes the need to "get it right" in the system's initial commercial release.[4]

9) Embedded systems are frequently very long-lived

Embedded systems often stay in use for many years. Frequently the duration of support for an embedded system is far greater than the turnover rate of the original software developers. This makes it paramount to have good documentation to explain the embedded systems software, particularly since the source code itself may have its self-documentation quality compromised due to performance trade-offs.

New Words and Expressions

embedded systems		嵌入式系统
microwave	*n.*	微波炉
micro-controller	*n.*	微控制器
console	*n.*	控制台
a matter of course		理所当然的事，必然的结果
in tandem with		同……串联，同……合作
roughly	*adv.*	概略地，粗糙地
form factor		外形因素
real-time		实时
off-the-shelf		从商店可以直接购买的，非顾客订制的
PDA	*abbr.*	Personal Digital Assistant 个人数字助理(即掌上型计算机)
trade off		交替换位，交替使用，卖掉
portability	*n.*	可携带，轻便
clarity	*n.*	清楚，透明
modularity	*n.*	[计]模块性
up-front	*adv*	在前面，在最前面
amortize	*v.*	分期清偿
peripheral	*adj.*	外围的
harsh	*adj.*	粗糙的，荒芜的，苛刻的，刺耳的，刺目的
emergency	*n.*	紧急情况，突然事件，非常时刻，紧急事件
stringent	*adj.*	严厉的，迫切的
robustness	*n.*	健壮性
preemptive	*adj.*	有先买权的，有强制收购权的，抢先的
execution context		[计]执行文本
FPGA	*abbr.*	可编程器件
ASIC	*abbr.*	[电]特定用途集成电路
predominantly	*adv.*	支配性地，主要地，有影响地
monolithic	*n.*	单片电路，单块集成电路
architecture	*n.*	建筑，建筑学；体系机构
cohesion	*n.*	结合，凝聚，[物理]内聚力

cross-coupling		交叉耦合
non-linear	*adj.*	非线性的
solar panels		太阳电池板
vital	*adj.*	生死攸关的，重大的，生命的，生机的， 至关重要的，所必需的
communications protocols		通信协议
bi-directional		双向的
compiler	*n.*	编辑者，[计]编译器
rigorous	*adj.*	严格的，严厉的，严酷的，严峻的
be subject to		受支配
paramount	*adj.*	极为重要的
compromise	*n.*	妥协，折中
	v.	妥协，折中，危及……的安全
stand to reason		显而易见

Notes

1. It stands to reason that there are companies that specialize in the development of embedded systems, either independently, or in tandem with the machinery with which they're to be used. More and more, engineering firms are calling on this kind of expertise to upgrade their products in every way imaginable.

译文：这就很容易理解为什么越来越多的公司致力于嵌入式系统的开发，他们或独立开发操作系统，或连带开发相关芯片，与此同时，越来越多的工程公司也在不断研究这种技术，运用它从而实现其产品的全面升级。

2. Many other embedded systems, though not so price-sensitive, have physical constraints on form factor or weight to use the smallest components possible. Again, this favors performance optimization at the cost of maintainability.

译文：还有一种可能，即用户并不在乎嵌入式系统的价格，而对外形尺寸、重量等物理条件有较高的要求，要求使用体积最小的器件，针对尺寸的优化过程是以牺牲系统的稳定性为代价的。

3. Embedded systems are generally both hard real-time constraints, which require an event to be handled by a fixed time, and soft real-time constraints, which set limits on the average event response time.

译文：嵌入式系统既要受到硬实时限制，也要受到软实时限制，前者要求某个进程必须在固定时间内完成，后者则确定了平均响应时间。

4. Furthermore, for several types of embedded systems, it is difficult or even impossible to upgrade firmware, which emphasizes the need to "get it right" in the system's initial commercial release.

译文：另外，有的嵌入式系统固化软件升级困难，甚至不能实现升级，这就要求系统在投入市场时必须做到"起步正确"。

Exercises

I. Comprehension questions.

1. What are embedded systems?

2. Explain the reasons why embedded systems are frequently price and size sensitive.

3. Explain the reasons why embedded systems often have power limitations.

4. Explain the reasons why embedded systems are frequently real-time.

5. Explain the reasons why embedded systems frequently use custom hardware.

6. Explain the reasons why embedded systems frequently have monolithic functionality.

7. Explain the reasons why embedded systems frequently have stringent robustness requirements.

8. Explain the reasons why embedded systems are frequently very long-lived.

9. Explain the reasons why embedded systems frequently have limited development tools.

10. What can we learn from the article?

II. Translate the following paragraph into Chinese.

Embedded systems are frequently comprised of off-the-shelf processors combined with off-the-shelf peripherals. Even though the components may be standard, the custom mixing and matching requires a high degree of cohesion between the hardware and the software—a significant portion of the software for an embedded system is operating system and device driver software. Though this low-level software is often available for purchase, license, or free use, frequently a large portion of the operating system for an embedded system is custom-developed in-house, either to precisely match the hardware system at hand, or to glue together off-the-shelf software in a custom configuration.

Often the functionality of an embedded system is distributed between multiple peer processors and/or a hierarchy of master/slave processors. Careful thought is required regarding the distribution of processing tasks across processors, and the extent, method, and timing of communication between processors.

Furthermore, many embedded systems make use of specialized FPGAs or ASICs, and thus require low-level software to interact with the custom hardware.

Text B Design Languages for Embedded Systems

An embedded system is a computer masquerading as a non-computer that must perform a small set of tasks cheaply and efficiently. A typical system might have communication, signal processing, and user interface tasks to perform.

Because the tasks must solve diverse problems, a language general-purpose enough to solve them all would be difficult to write, analyze, and compile. Instead, a variety of languages have evolved, each best suited to a particular problem domain.[1] For example, a language for signal processing is often more convenient for a particular problem than, say, assembly, but might be poor for control-dominated behavior.[2]

This article describes popular hardware, software, dataflow, and hybrid languages, each of which excels a certain problems. Dataflow languages are good for signal processing, and hybrid languages combine ideas from the other three classes.

Due to space limit, this article only describes the main features of each language.

1. Hardware Languages

Verilog and VHDL are the most popular languages for hardware description and modeling. Both model systems with discrete-event semantics that ignore idle portions of the design for efficient simulation. Both describe systems with structural hierarchy: a system consists of blocks that contain instances of primitives, other blocks, or concurrent processes. Connections are listed explicitly.

Verilog provides more primitives geared specifically toward hardware simulation. VHDL's primitive are assignments such as $a = b + c$ or procedural code. Verilog adds transistor and logic gate primitives, and allows new ones to be defined with truth tables. Both languages allow concurrent processes to be described procedurally. Such processes sleep until awakened by an event that causes them to run, read and write variables, and suspend. Processes may wait for a period of time, a value change.

VHDL communication is more disciplined and flexible. Verilog communicates through wires or regions: shared memory locations that can cause race conditions. VHDL's signals behave like wires but the resolution function may be user-defined. VHDL's variables are local to a single process unless declared as shared.

Verilog's type system models hardware with four-valued bit vectors and arrays for modeling memory. VHDL does not include four-valued vectors, but its type system allows them to be added. Furthermore, composite types such as C structures can be defined.

Overall, Verilog is the leaner language more directly geared toward simulating digital integrated circuits. VHDL is a much larger, more verbose language capable of handing a wider class of simulation and modeling tasks.

2. Software Languages

Software languages describe sequences of instructions for a processor to execute. As such, most consist of sequences of imperative instructions that communicate through memory: an array of numbers that hold their values until changed.

Each machine instruction typically does little more than, say, add two numbers, so high-level languages aim to specify many instructions concisely and intuitively. Arithmetic expressions are typical: coding an expression such as $ax^2 + bx + c$ in machine code is straightforward, tedious, and best done by a compiler. The C language provides such expressions, control-flow constructs such as loops and conditionals, and recursive functions. The C++ language adds classes as a way to build new data types, templates for polymorphic code, exceptions for error handling, and a standard library of common data structures. Java is a still higher-level language that provides automatic garbage collection, threads and monitors to synchronize them.

1) Assembly Language

An assembly language program is a list of processor instructions written in a symbolic, human-readable form. Each instruction consists of an operation such as addition along with some operands. E.g. add r5, r2, r4 might add the contents of registers r2 and r4 and write the result to r5. Such arithmetic instructions are executed in order, but branch instructions can perform conditionals and loops by changing the processor's program counter the address of the instruction being executed.

A processor's assembly language is defined by its op-codes addressing modes, registers, and memories. The op-code distinguishes, say, addition from conditional branch and an addressing mode defines how and where data is gathered and stored. Registers can be thought of as small fast easy-to-access pieces of memory.

2) The C Language

A C program contains functions built from arithmetic expressions structured with loops and conditionals. Instructions in a C program run sequentially, but control-flow constructs such as loops of conditionals can affect the order in which instructions execute. When control reaches a function call in an expression control is passed to the called function, which runs until it produces a result, and control returns to continue evaluating the expression that called the function.[3]

C derives its types from those a processor manipulates directly: signed and unsigned integers ranging from bytes to words, floating point numbers, and pointers. These can be further aggregated into arrays and structures—groups of named fields.

C programs use three types of memory. Space for global data is allocated when the program is compiled, the stack stores automatic variables allocated and released when their function is called and returns, and the heap supplies arbitrarily-sized regions of memory that can be deal-Located in any order.

3) C++

C++ extends C with structuring mechanisms for big programs: user-defined data types, a way to reuse code with different types, name spaces for group objects to and avoid accidental name collisions when program pieces are assembled, and exceptions to handle errors. The C++ standard library provides a collection of important and powerful common classes and interfaces, including containers, iterators and algorithms. A class defines a new data type by specifying its representation and the operations that may access and modify it. Classes may be defined though inheritance, which extends and modifies existing classes. For example, a rectangle class might add length and width fields and an area method to a shape class.

A template is a special function or class that can work with multiple types. The compiler generates custom code for each different use of the template. For example, the same min template could be used for both integers and floating-point numbers.

4) Java

Java language resembles C++ but is incompatible. Like C++, Java is object-oriented, providing classes and inheritance. It is a higher-level language than C++ since it uses object references, arrays, and strings instead of pointers. Java's automatic garbage collection frees the programmer from memory management.

Java provides concurrent threads. Creating a thread involves extending the thread class, creating instances of these objects, and calling their start methods to start a new thread of control that executes the objects' run methods.

Synchronizing a method or block uses a per-object lock to resolve contention when two or more threads attempt to access the same object simultaneously. A thread that attempts to gain a lock owned by another thread will block until the lock is released which can be used to grant a thread exclusive access to a particular object.

5) RTOS

Many embedded systems use a real-time operating system (RTOS) to simulate concurrency on a single processor. An RTOS manages multiple running processes, each written in sequential language such as C. The processes perform the system's computation and the RTOS schedules them—attempts to meet deadlines by deciding which process runs when.

Most RTOS uses fixed-priority preemptive scheduling in which each process is given a particular priority (a small integer) when the system is designed. At any time, the RTOS runs the highest-priority running process, which is expected to run for a short period of time before suspending itself to wait for more data. Priorities are usually assigned using rate-monotonic analysis, which assigns higher priorities to processes that must meet more frequent dead lines.

3. Data flow Languages

Dataflow languages describe systems of procedural processes that run concurrently and communicate through queues. Although clumsy for general applications data flow languages area perfect fit for signal-processing algorithms, which use vast quantities of arithmetic derived from linear system theory to decode, compress, or filter data streams that represent periodic samples of continuously-changing values such as sound or video. Dataflow semantics are natural for expressing the block diagrams typically used to describe signal-processing algorithms, and their regularity makes dataflow implementations very efficient because otherwise costly run-time scheduling decisions can be made at compile time even in systems containing multiple sampling rates.[4]

1) Kahn Process Networks

Kahn Process Networks form a formal basis for dataflow computation. Kahn's systems consist of processes that communicate exclusively through unbounded point-to-point first-in, first-out queues. Reading from a port makes a process wait until data is available, so the behavior of Kahn's networks does not depend on execution speeds.

Balancing processes' relative execution rates to avoid an unbounded accumulation of tokens is the challenge in scheduling a Kahn network. Any process that writes to a full buffer blocks until space is available, but if the system deadlocks because all buffers are full, the scheduler increases the capacity of the smallest buffer.

2) Synchronous Data Flow

Synchronous data flow fixes the communication patterns of the blocks in a Kahn network. Each time a block runs, it consumes and produces a fixed number of data tokens on each of its ports. This predictability allows SDF to be scheduled completely at compile-time, producing very efficient code.

Scheduling operates in two steps. First, the rate at which each block fires is established by considering the production and consumption rates of each block at the source and sink of each queue. Once the rates are established, any algorithm that simulates the execution of the network without buffer underflow will produce a correct schedule if one exists. However, more sophisticated techniques reduce generated code and buffer sizes by better ordering the execution of the blocks.

4. Hybrid Languages

Hybrid languages combine ideas from others to solve different types of problems. Esterel excels at discrete control by blending software-like control flow with the synchrony and concurrency of hardware. Communication protocols are SDL's forte; it uses extended finite-state machines with single input queues. System C provides a flexible discrete event simulation environment built on C++. CoCentric[TM] System Studio combines dataflow with Esterel-like finite-state machine semantics to simulate and synthesize dataflow applications that also require control.

1) Esterel

Intended for specifying control-dominated reactive systems, Esterel combines the control constructs of an imperative software language with concurrency, preemption, and a synchronous model of time like that used in synchronous digital circuits. In each clock cycle, the program awakens, reads its inputs, produces outputs, and suspends.

An Esterel program communicates through signals that are either present or absent each cycle. In each cycle, each signal is absent unless an emit statement for the signal runs and makes the signal present for that cycle only. Esterel guarantees determinism by requiring each emitter of a signal to run before any statement that tests the signal.

2) SDL

SDL is a graphical specification language developed for describing telecommunication protocols defined by the ITU.[5] A system consists of concurrently-running FSMs, each with a single input queue, connected by channels that define which messages they carry. Each FSM consumes the most recent message in its queue, reacts to it by changing internal state or sending messages to other FSMs, changes to its next state, and repeats the process. Each FSM is deterministic, but because messages from other FSMs may arrive in any order because of varying execution speed and communication delays, an SDL system may behave nondeterministically.

3) System C

The System C language is a C++ subset for system modeling. A System C specification is simulated by compilng it with a standard C++ compiler and linking in freely distributed class libraries from www.systemc.org.

The System C language builds systems from Verilog and VHDL-like modules. Each has a collection of I/O ports and may contain instances of other modules or processes defined by a block of C++ code.

System C uses a discrete-event simulation model. The System C scheduler executes the code in a process in response to an event such as a clock signal, or a delay. This model resembles that used in Verilog and VHDL, but has the flexibility of operating with a general-purpose programming language.

4) Co-Centric System Studio

Co-Centric System Studio^{TM} uses a hierarchical formalism that combines Kahn-like dataflow and hierarchical, concurrent FSMs.

A CCSS model is built hierarchically from Dataflow, AND, OR, and Gated models. Dataflow models are Kahn Process networks. The blocks may be dataflow primitives written in a C++ subset or other hierarchical models. AND models run concurrently and communicate with Esterel-like synchronous semantics. OR models are finite-state machines that may manipulate data and whose states may contain other models. Gated models contain sub-models whose execution can be temporarily suspended under external control.

New Words and Expressions

masquerade	*n.*	化妆舞会
	v.	化装
general-purpose	*adj.*	多方面的，多种用途的
evolve	*v.*	(使)发展(使)进展，(使)进化
due to		由于，应归于
discrete	*adj.*	不连续的，离散的
semantics	*n.*	[语]语义学
hierarchy	*n.*	层次，层级
memory locations		存储单元
race conditions		[电]紊乱情况；竞态条件
iterator	*n.*	[计]迭代器，迭代程序
verbose	*adj.*	详细的，冗长的

imperative	*n.*	命令，诫命，需要，规则
	adj.	命令的，强制的，紧急的，势在必行的，[语法]祈使的
concisely	*adv.*	简明地
intuitively	*adv.*	直觉地，直观地
arithmetic expressions		算术表达式
tedious	*adj.*	单调乏味的，冗长乏味的
function call		函数引用[调用]
manipulate	*vt.*	(熟练地)操作，使用(机器等)，操纵(人或市价、市场)，应付，假造
	vt.	(熟练地)操作，巧妙地处理
group objects		[计](程序)组对象
representation	*n.*	表示法，表现，陈述，请求，扮演，画像，继承，代表
providing	*conj.*	倘若
synchronize	*v.*	同步，使……同步化
simultaneously	*adv.*	同时地
single processor		单一处理机
sequential	*adj.*	连续的，相续的，有继的，有顺序的，结果的
preemptive	*adj.*	有先买权的，有强制收购权的，抢先的
clumsy	*adj.*	笨拙的
algorithms		[计]算法库
block diagrams		结构图，方块图，简图
implementation	*n.*	执行
exclusively	*adv.*	排外地，专有地
unbounded	*adj.*	极大的
point-to-point	*adj.*	点对点的，一一对应的
suspend	*vt.*	吊，悬挂
	v.	延缓
deterministic	*adj.*	确定性的
nondeterministic	*adj.*	非定常的，非确定的
formalism	*n.*	拘泥形式，(艺术或宗教上的)形式主义，虚礼

Notes

1. Because the tasks must solve diverse problems, a language general-purpose enough to solve them all would be difficult to write, analyze, and compile. Instead, a variety of languages have evolved, each best suited to a particular problem domain.

译文：由于这些任务需要解决很多问题，若采用通用语言，无论是程序的编写，还是程序的分析和编译都会十分困难，因此需要采用多种语言，在解决不同的特定问题时采用不同的语言。

2．A language for signal processing is often more convenient for a particular problem than, say, assembly, but might be poor for control-dominated behavior.

译文：信号处理中采用的语言，如汇编语言，比其他语言更适合解决特定问题，但是，它却不适合于控制领域的应用。

3．When control reaches a function call in an expression, control is passed to the called function, which runs until it produces a result, and control returns to continue evaluating the expression that called the function.

译文：当程序计算包涵某个功能函数的表达式时，将会调用这个功能函数，功能函数返回运行结果后，程序代入该结果，并继续计算表达式。

4．Dataflow semantics are natural for expressing the block diagrams typically used to describe signal-processing algorithms, and their regularity makes dataflow implementations very efficient because otherwise costly run-time scheduling decisions can be made at compile time even in systems containing multiple sampling rates.

译文：数据流语言适合于表示方块图，常用于描述信号处理算法。数据流语言能提高数据流的运行效率，因为即使在多种抽样速率下，它也能在编译时完成耗费系统资源较多的进程，如运行模式选择进程。

5．SDL is a graphical specification language developed for describing telecommunication protocols defined by the ITU.

译文：SDL 是用于描述国际电信联盟(ITU)定义的电信协议的一种图形说明语言。

Exercises

Ⅰ. Comprehension questions.

1. What are the most popular languages for hardware description and modeling in the embedded systems?

2. What's the difference between Verilog and VHDL?

3. Explain the relations between C and C++.

4. Which Software Languages are mentioned in this article?

5. What's the characteristics of data flow Languages?

6. What's the SDL?

7. What can we learn from the article?

Ⅱ. Translate the following into Chinese.

Many embedded systems use a real-time operating system (RTOS) to simulate concurrency on a single processor. An RTOS manages multiple running processes, each written in sequential language such as C. The processes perform the system's computation and the RTOS schedules them—attempts to meet deadlines by deciding which process runs when.

Most RTOS uses fixed-priority preemptive scheduling in which each process is given a particular priority (a small integer) when the system is designed. At any time, the RTOS runs the highest-priority running process, which is expected to run for a short period of time before suspending itself to wait for more data. Priorities are usually assigned using rate-monotonic analysis, which assigns higher priorities to processes that must meet more frequent dead lines.

Lesson Three　Virtual Instruments

Text A　About Virtual Instrumentation

With more than 6 million new measurement channels sold last year, National Instruments is a worldwide leader in virtual instrumentation. Engineers have used virtual instrumentation for more than 25 years to bring the power of flexible software and PC technology to test, control, and design applications making accurate analog and digital measurements from DC to 2.7 GHz. This document provides an excellent introduction to virtual instrumentation as well as additional resources for continued research.

1. What is virtual instrumentation

With virtual instrumentation, software based on user requirements defines general-purpose measurement and control hardware functionality. Virtual instrumentation combines mainstream commercial technologies, such as the PC, with flexible software and a wide variety of measurement and control hardware, so engineers and scientists can create user-defined systems that meet their exact application needs.[1] (see Figure 1) With virtual instrumentation, engineers and scientists reduce development time, design higher quality products, and lower their design costs.

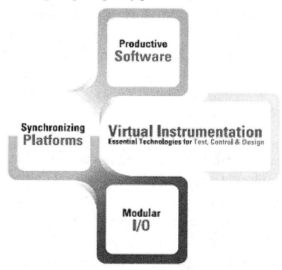

Fig.1　Virtual instrumentation system

National Instruments introduced virtual instrumentation more than 25 years ago, changing the way engineers and scientists measure and automate the world around them. In 2004, National Instruments sold more than 6 million channels of virtual instrumentation in 90 countries. Today, virtual instrumentation has reached mainstream acceptance and is used in thousands of applications around the world in industries from automobile, to consumer electronics, to oil and gas.

2. Why is virtual instrumentation necessary

Virtual instrumentation is necessary because it delivers instrumentation with the rapid adaptability required for today's concept, product, and process design, development, and delivery. Only with virtual instrumentation can engineers and scientists create the user-defined instruments required to keep up with the world's demands.[2]

To meet the ever-increasing demand to innovate and deliver ideas and products faster, scientists and engineers are turning to advanced electronics, processors, and software. Consider that most modern cell phones contain the latest features of the last generation, including audio, phone book, and text messaging capabilities. Newer versions include a camera, MP3 player, and Bluetooth networking and Internet browsing.

The increased functionality of advanced electronics is possible because software is playing a more important role in these devices. Engineers and scientists can add new functions to the device without changing the hardware, resulting in improved concepts and products without costly hardware redevelopment. This extends product life and usefulness and reduces product delivery times. Engineers and scientists can improve functionality through software instead of developing further specific electronics to do a particular job.

However, this increase in functionality comes with a price. Upgraded functionality introduces the possibility of unforeseen interaction or error. So, just as device-level software helps rapidly develop and extend functionality, design and test instrumentation also must adapt to verify the improvements.[3]

The only way to meet these demands is to use test and control architectures that are also software centric. Because virtual instrumentation uses highly productive software, modular I/O, and commercial platforms, it is uniquely positioned to keep pace with the required new idea and product development rate. National Instruments LabVIEW, a premier virtual instrumentation graphical development environment, uses symbolic or graphical representations to speed up development. The software symbolically represents functions. Consolidating functions within rapidly deployed graphical blocks further speeds development.

Another, virtual instrumentation component is modular I/O, designed to be rapidly combined in any order or quantity to ensure that virtual instrumentation can both monitor and control any development aspect. Using well-designed software drivers for modular I/O, engineers and scientists quickly can access functions during concurrent operation.

The third, virtual instrumentation element – using commercial platforms, often enhanced with accurate synchronization – ensures that virtual instrumentation takes advantage of the very latest computer capabilities and data transfer technologies. This element delivers virtual instrumentation on a long-term technology base that scales with the high investments made in processors, buses, and more.[4]

In summary, as innovation mandates software to accelerate new concept and product development, it also requires instrumentation to rapidly adapt to new functionality. Because virtual instrumentation applies software, modular I/O, and commercial platforms, it delivers instrumentation capabilities uniquely qualified to keep pace with today's concept and product development.

3. Why has virtual instrumentation been so successful

Virtual instrumentation achieved mainstream adoption by providing a new model for building measurement and automation systems. Keys to its success include rapid PC advancement; explosive low-cost, high-performance data converter (semiconductor) development; and system design software emergence. These factors make virtual instrumentation systems accessible to a very broad base of users.

PC performance, in particular, has increased more than 10,000X over the past 20 years. (see Figure 2) Virtual instruments takes advantage of this PC performance increase by analyzing measurements and solving new application challenges with each new-generation PC processor, hard drive, display, and I/O bus. These rapid advancements, combined with the general trend that technical and computer literacy starts early in school, contribute to successful computer-based virtual instrumentation adoption.

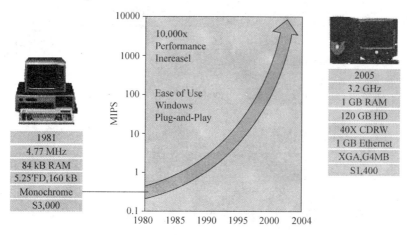

Fig.2　A 10,000X performance increase for PCs helps drive virtual instrumentation system performance

Another virtual instrumentation driver is the proliferation of high-performance, low-cost analog-to-digital (ADC) and digital-to-analog (DAC) converters. Applications such as wireless communication and high-definition video impact these technologies relentlessly. While traditional proprietary converter technology tends to move slowly, commercial semiconductor technologies tend to follow Moore's law – doubling performance every 18 months. Virtual instrumentation hardware uses these widely available semiconductors to deliver high-performance measurement front ends.

Finally, system design software that provides an intuitive interface for designing custom instrumentation systems furthers virtual instrumentation. LabVIEW is an example of such software. The LabVIEW graphical development environment offers the performance and flexibility of a programming language, as well as high-level functionality and configuration utilities designed specifically for measurement and automation applications.[5]

4. What makes National Instruments a leader in virtual instrumentation

In one word, the answer is software. Software that enables engineers and scientists to create user-defined instruments.

At the heart of any virtual instrument is flexible software, and National Instruments invented one of the world's best virtual instrumentation software platforms – LabVIEW. LabVIEW is a powerful graphical development environment for signal acquisition, measurement analysis, and data presentation, giving the flexibility of a programming language without the complexity of traditional development tools. Since 1986, when National Instruments introduced LabVIEW for the Macintosh, it has quickly and consistently attracted engineers and scientists looking for a productive, powerful programming language to use in test, control and design applications. Today, LabVIEW is the preferred graphical development environment for thousands of engineers and scientists. (see Figure 3)

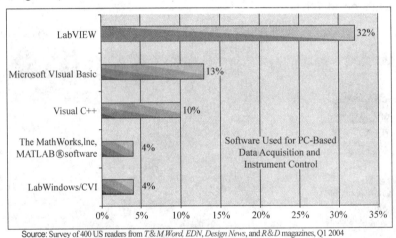

Source: Survey of 400 US readers from *T&M Word*, *EDN*, *Design News*, and *R&D* magazines, Q1 2004

Fig.3   LabVIEW is a leader in application software used in PC-based data acquisition and instrument control

For engineers who prefer text-based programming, National Instruments also offers LabWindows/CVI, an application development environment for ANSI C, as well as tools for virtual instrument development using Visual Studio .NET, Measurement Studio.

While software is the heart of every virtual instrument, almost every virtual instrument requires measurement hardware to accurately acquire the measurement. Independent of the programming environment chosen, virtual instrumentation software must provide excellent integration with system measurement hardware. National Instruments software, including LabVIEW, offers open connectivity to tens of thousands of sensors, cameras, actuators, traditional instruments and plug-in devices (USB, PCI, etc.) from thousands of third-party hardware vendors.

In 2004, National Instruments measurement hardware provided customers with more than 6,000,000 virtual instrumentation measurement channels. From low-cost USB data acquisition, to image acquisition and process control vision systems, to RF measurements at 2.7GHz, to GPIB bus communication, National Instruments has shown more than 25,000 companies that it offers the measurement hardware and scalable hardware platforms required to complete virtual instruments.

5. What makes National Instruments different from other virtual instrumentation companies

National Instruments has been a virtual instrumentation leader for more than 25 years. This leadership has grown and been sustained through constant and consistent innovation.

Because National Instruments invented and innovated the premier virtual instrumentation graphical development environment, LabVIEW, it attracts thousands of engineers and scientists building virtual instruments. By understanding customer project development needs, National Instruments has consistently delivered significant software innovations, including Express technology, the LabVIEW Real-Time Module and LabVIEW PDA Module, and SignalExpress:

1) Express technology

National Instruments created Express technology for LabVIEW, LabWindow/CVI, and Measurement Studio in 2003 to reduce code complexity while preserving power and functionality. Today, more than 50 percent of data acquisition customers use DAQ Assistant to simplify data acquisition tasks.

2) The LabVIEW Real-Time Module and LabVIEW PDA Modules

National Instruments extended LabVIEW for deterministic execution using the LabVIEW Real-Time Module and developed matching hardware platforms to make embedded application deployment a reality. The LabVIEW PDA Module extended virtual instrumentation and the LabVIEW platform to handheld devices.

3) NI Signal Express

Design and test engineers asked National Instruments for virtual instrumentation software that interactively measures and analyzes data. In response, National Instruments created SignalExpress – a drag-and-drop, no-programming-required environment ideal for exploratory measurements.

In addition to the strong software differentiator, National Instruments offers the most broad and innovative I/O selection among virtual instrumentation companies. To help engineers and scientists meet accelerating demands, National Instruments constantly releases products to further extend breadth. A few recent examples of NI hardware innovation include USB DAQ devices, M Series DAQ devices, and National Instruments CompactRIO。

(1) USB DAQ Devices

In a recent survey, 70 percent of National Instruments data acquisition (DAQ) customers said they plan to purchase multifunction USB DAQ in the near future. That month, National Instruments released the USB-6008, setting a new low price point for multifunction DAQ at $145 (US).

(2) M Series DAQ Devices

National Instruments helped establish leadership in plug-in data acquisition when it released the M Series DAQ products in late 2004. The first 18-bit PCI devices, first PCI data acquisition devices with six DMA channels for maximum throughput, and a patent-pending device calibration scheme are just a few of the features that set these products apart.

(3) CompactRIO Reconfigurable Control and I/O

One of the most innovative additions to National Instruments I/O products is CompactRIO. With an FPGA chip at the heart of this I/O platform, engineers can create custom hardware and customize it repeatedly using LabVIEW FPGA.

6. Who uses National Instruments virtual instrumentation

National Instruments customers include engineers, scientists, and technical professionals in a wide range of industries. From testing DVD recorders to researching advanced medicines, they use National Instruments software and hardware to develop user-defined instruments and deliver a diverse set of products and services, faster and at a lower cost.

Here are a few examples of how customers use National Instruments virtual instrumentation products。

1) AP Racing – Building Formula 1 Caliper and Brake Test Dynamometers

For more than 30 years, AP Racing has been a world leader in brake caliper and race clutch technology and manufacturing. AP Racing concluded that a unique new dynamometer would be a distinct advantage, and virtual instrumentation using National Instruments DAQ devices and LabVIEW provided the flexibility it needed to innovate in the marketplace.

2) Lexmark – Ink Cartridge Electrical Test

Ed Coleman, with Lexmark International, Inc., said, "As we continue to adapt our test systems to meet our latest requirements with minimal development time with the use of PC-based modular instruments and industry-standard software. Upgrading to the NI 5122, NI 6552, and LabVIEW 7 Express, we increased the quality of our products and production yields while increasing our test performance with minimal development expense."

3) Texas Instruments – RF and Wireless Component Characterization

With close to $4 billion in revenue, Texas Instruments (TI) is one of the leading wireless IC providers. To streamline its characterization process, TI created test development, management, and automation software powered by NI TestStand and LabVIEW. Using NI products, it expanded its business without sacrificing quality and resources.

4) Drivven – Motorcycle Engine Control Unit (ECU) Prototype

In past projects, Drivven spent at least two man-years and $500,000US to develop ECU prototyping systems from custom hardware. For this project, the equipment costs (including the motorcycle and CompactRIO) totaled $15,000US, and development time took approximately three man-months. FPGA-based reconfigurable hardware, CompactRIO, and the LabVIEW

Real-Time Module delivered reliability and precise timing resources, and the system was rugged enough to withstand the high-temperature and high-vibration operating environment.

New Words and Expressions

automotive	*adj.*	自动的
centric	*adj.*	中心的
keep pace with		跟上，与……同步
consolidate	*v.*	统一；巩固
concurrent operation		并发操作
mandate	*v.*	批准；委任
literacy	*n.*	读写的能力
proliferation	*n.*	增加；增多
relentlessly	*adv.*	不懈地；坚韧地
moore's law		摩尔氏定律
actuator	*n.*	[电信]激励器；调节器
vendor	*n.*	[法律]卖主
sustain	*v.*	支持；提供
deterministic	*adj.*	确定性的
drag-and-drop		拖放
exploratory	*adj.*	探险的；勘察的
breadth	*n.*	宽度；幅度
revenue	*n.*	税收
streamline	*v.*	使现代化；使效率更高
sacrifice	*v.*	牺牲
prototyping	*n.*	原型；标准
rugged	*adj.*	强健的
withstand	*v.*	抵抗；经得起
vibration	*n.*	振动

Notes

1. Virtual instrumentation combines mainstream commercial technologies, such as the PC, with flexible software and a wide variety of measurement and control hardware, so engineers and scientists can create user-defined systems that meet their exact application needs.

译文：虚拟仪器将主流商业技术，如 PC，与灵活的软件和多种测量控制硬件相结合，使得工程师和科学家得以根据用户的需要组成用户自定义系统。

2. Only with virtual instrumentation can engineers and scientists create the user-defined instruments required to keep up with the world's demands.

译文：只有采用虚拟仪器，工程师和科学家们才能适应不断变化的需求，组成由用户定义的设备，句中"Only with…"引导了一个倒装结构。

3. So, just as device-level software helps rapidly develop and extend functionality, design and test instrumentation also must adapt to verify the improvements.

译文：设备级的软件能快速开发、扩展系统功能，而设计与测试设备必须为这些功能提供验证工具。

4. This element delivers virtual instrumentation on a long-term technology base that scales with the high investments made in processors, buses, and more.

译文：这个因素使得虚拟仪器成为一种影响处理器、总线等产业技术投资力度的长线技术。

5. The LabVIEW graphical development environment offers the performance and flexibility of a programming language, as well as high-level functionality and configuration utilities designed specifically for measurement and automation applications.

译文：LabVIEW 图形开发环境提供了灵活、有效的编程语言，同时也提供了用于测量和自动化应用的高级功能模块和配置工具程序。

Exercises

I. Translate the following paragraph into Chinese.

When you run a series of experiments to test different parameters, you typically need to associate the input parameters with the resulting output. In most cases, you also need an efficient way to document this information for further analysis, future reference, and to the ensure repeatability of your experiments. Users familiar with the Mathematica Notebook know that Mathematica allows you to save your entire session in a single file. With Mathematica Link for LabVIEW, you can extend this capability into the LabVIEW domain. Simply call your test VI from Mathematica, return the LabVIEW data to the Mathematica Notebook, then process the data in the Notebook as necessary. When you save the Notebook file, all the steps of your experiment are automatically recorded—including the VIs you called, the parameters passed, the data return, the subsequent post-processing steps, and so on. Should you need to review the experiment at a later date, all of the information has been meticulously documented—automatically!

II. Translate the following paragraph into English.

软件是虚拟仪器技术中最重要的部分。使用正确的软件工具、通过设计或调用特定的程序模块，工程师和科学家们可以高效地创建自己的应用以及友好的人机交互界面。NI 公司提供的行业标准图形化编程软件——LabVIEW，不仅能轻松方便地完成与各种软硬件的连接，更能提供强大的后续数据处理能力，设置数据处理、转换、存储的方式，并将结果显示给用户。此外，NI 提供了更多交互式的测量工具和更高层的系统管理软件工具，例如，连接设计与测试的交互式软件 SignalExpress、用于传统 C 语言的 LabWindows/CVI、针对微软 Visual Studio 的 Measurement Studio 等，均可满足客户对高性能应用的需求。有了功能强大的软件，您就可以在仪器中创建智能性和决策功能，从而发挥虚拟仪器技术在测试应用中的强大优势。

Text B　What Exactly Is LabVIEW, and What Can It Do For Me

You'd probably like to know what exactly LabVIEW is before you go much further. What can you do with it and what can it do for you? LabVIEW, short for Laboratory Virtual Instrument Engineering Workbench, is a programming environment in which you create programs with graphics; in this regard it differs from traditional programming languages like C, C++, or Java, in which you program with text.[1] However, LabVIEW is much more than a language. It is a program development and execution system designed for people, such as scientists and engineers, who need to program as part of their jobs. LabVIEW works on PCs running Windows, MacOS, Linux, Solaris, and HP-UX.

Providing you with a very powerful graphical programming language, LabVIEW can increase your productivity by orders of magnitude.[2] Programs that take weeks or months to write using conventional programming languages can be completed in hours using LabVIEW, because it is specifically designed to take measurements, analyze data, and present results to the user. And because LabVIEW has such a versatile graphical user interface and is so easy to program with, it is also ideal for simulations, presentation of ideas, general programming, or even teaching basic programming concepts.

LabVIEW offers more flexibility than standard laboratory instruments because it is software-based. You, not the instrument manufacturer, define instrument functionality. Your computer, plug-in hardware, and LabVIEW comprise a completely configurable virtual instrument to accomplish your tasks. Using LabVIEW, you can create exactly the type of virtual instrument you need, when you need it, at a fraction of the cost of traditional instruments. When your needs change, you can modify your virtual instrument in moments.

LabVIEW tries to make your life as hassle-free as possible. It has extensive libraries of functions and subroutines to help you with most programming tasks, without the fuss of pointers, memory allocation, and other arcane programming problems found in conventional programming languages. LabVIEW also contains application-specific libraries of code for data acquisition (DAQ), General Purpose Interface Bus (GPIB), and serial instrument control, data analysis, data presentation, data storage, and communication over the Internet. The Analysis library contains a multitude of useful functions, including signal generation, signal processing, filters, windows, statistics, regression, linear algebra, and array arithmetic.

Because of LabVIEW's graphical nature, it is inherently a data presentation package. Output appears in any form you desire. Charts, graphs, and user-defined graphics comprise just a fraction of available output options. This book will show you how to present data in all of these forms.

LabVIEW's programs are portable across platforms, so you can write a program on a Macintosh and then load and run it on a Windows machine without changing a thing in most applications. You will find LabVIEW applications improving operations in any number of industries, from every kind of engineering and process control to biology, farming, psychology, chemistry, physics, teaching, and many others.

1. Dataflow and the Graphical Programming Language

The LabVIEW program development environment is different from commercial C or Java development systems in one important respect. Whereas other programming systems use text-based languages to create lines of code, LabVIEW uses a graphical programming language to create programs in a pictorial form called a block diagram, eliminating a lot of the syntactical details. With this method, you can concentrate on the flow of data within your application; the simpler syntax doesn't obscure what the program is doing.[3] LabVIEW user interface and the code behind it.

LabVIEW uses terminology, icons, and ideas familiar to scientists and engineers. It relies on graphical symbols rather than textual language to describe programming actions. The principle of dataflow, in which functions execute only after receiving the necessary data, governs execution in a straightforward manner.[4] You can learn LabVIEW even if you have little or no programming experience, but you will find knowledge of programming fundamentals very helpful.

2. How Does LabVIEW Work

LabVIEW programs are called *virtual instruments* (*VI*s) because their appearance and operation imitate actual instruments. However, behind the scenes they are analogous to main programs, functions, and subroutines from popular programming languages like C or Basic. Hereafter, we will refer to a LabVIEW program as a "VI" (pronounced "vee eye," not the Roman numeral six as we've heard some people say). Also, be aware that a LabVIEW program is always called a VI, whether its appearance or function relates to an actual instrument or not.

3. A VI has three main parts

(1) The *front panel* is the interactive user interface of a VI, so named because it simulates the front panel of a physical instrument. The front panel can contain knobs, push buttons, graphs, and many other controls (which are user inputs) and indicators (which are program outputs). A user will input data using a mouse and keyboard and then view the results produced by the program on the screen.

(2) The *block diagram* is the VI's source code, constructed in LabVIEW's graphical programming language, G. The block diagram is the actual executable program. The components of a block diagram are lower-level VIs, built-in functions, constants, and program execution control structures. You draw wires to connect the appropriate objects together to indicate the flow of data between them. Front panel objects have corresponding terminals on the block diagram so that data can pass from the user to the program and back to the user.

(3) In order to use a VI as a subroutine in the block diagram of another VI, it must have an icon and a connector. A VI that is used within another VI is called a subVI and is analogous to a

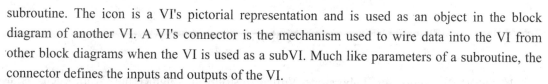

subroutine. The icon is a VI's pictorial representation and is used as an object in the block diagram of another VI. A VI's connector is the mechanism used to wire data into the VI from other block diagrams when the VI is used as a subVI. Much like parameters of a subroutine, the connector defines the inputs and outputs of the VI.

Virtual instruments are hierarchical and modular. You can use them as top-level programs or subprograms. With this architecture, LabVIEW promotes the concept of modular programming. First, you divide an application into a series of simple subtasks. Next, you build a VI to accomplish each subtask and then combine those VIs on a top-level block diagram to complete the larger task.

Modular programming is a plus because you can execute each subVI by itself, which facilitates debugging. Furthermore, many low-level subVIs often perform tasks common to several applications and can be used independently by each individual application.

Just so you can keep things straight, we've listed a few common LabVIEW terms with their conventional programming equivalents in Table 1.

Table 1   LabVIEW Terms and Their Conventional Equivalents.

LabVIEW	Conventional Language
VI	program
function	function or method
subVI	subroutine, subprogram, object
front panel	user interface
block diagram	program code
"G" or LabVIEW	C, C++, Java, Pascal, BASIC, etc.

New words and expressions

MacOS		苹果机操作系统
Solaris		诸如 SUN 这种大型工作站所用的一种操作系统
HP-UX		隶属于 Unix 的一种操作系统
versatile	*adj.*	多方面的；多用途的
plug-in hardware		插入式硬件
hassle-free		免麻烦的；免困扰的
subroutine	*n.*	子程序
fuss	*n.*	小题大做；无谓纷扰
memory allocation		内存配置
arcane	*adj.*	神秘的；难懂的
multitude	*n.*	多数；许多
regression	*n.*	回归
array arithmetic		队列算术
syntactical	*adj.*	句法的

Notes

1. LabVIEW, short for Laboratory Virtual Instrument Engineering Workbench, is a programming environment in which you create programs with graphics; in this regard it differs from traditional programming languages like C, C++, or Java, in which you program with text.

译文：实验室虚拟仪器工程平台，简称"LabVIEW"，提供一种图形化编程环境，它与传统的，用文本编程的编程语言(如 C，C++，Java)是不同的。

2. Providing you with a very powerful graphical programming language, LabVIEW can increase your productivity by orders of magnitude.

译文：LabVIEW 提供一种功能强大的图形化编程语言，可以大大地提高工作效率。

3. With this method, you can concentrate on the flow of data within your application; the simpler syntax doesn't obscure what the program is doing.

译文：出于这种思路，你可以将注意力集中在应用的数据流上，编程所采用的简单句法使得程序的功能目的一目了然。

4. The principle of *dataflow*, in which functions execute only after receiving the necessary data, governs execution in a straight forward manner.

译文："数据流"原理：只有在获得必要数据后，才运行功能模块，它的控制执行方式采用的是直接方式。

Exercises

Translate the following paragraph into Chinese.

Countless technical users worldwide have standardized on LabVIEW. With its rapid application development capabilities, integrated GUI (graphical user interface) panels, robust I/O connectivity, and run-time productivity advantages, it is not hard to understand why. Still, imagine how flexible LabVIEW could become with the addition of Mathematica's powerful, integrated "Notebook" interface. Mathematica—complete with its advanced function libraries and symbolic mathematical capabilities, is the perfect complement to LabVIEW's graphical VI ("Virtual Instrument") metaphor.

Consider how convenient a hybrid LabVIEW/Mathematica system might be-particularly during the early stages of the design cycle, before the parameters of the design problem have been completely defined. Rather than committing to several wire-test-then-rewire cycles, you could use Mathematica's rich command-style interface from within LabVIEW, developing, testing, and verifying your mathematical models in a single, integrated workflow. Imagine the productivity advantages of a single environment that transparently accommodates both advanced mathematical notation and real-world, LabVIEW-acquired data. This is the Mathematica Link for LabVIEW advantage.

Lesson Four   Design Patterns

Text A   Intro to Design Patterns (1)

1. Someone has already solved your problems

In this chapter, you'll learn why (and how) you can exploit the wisdom and lessons learned by other developers who've been down the same design problem road and survived the trip. Before we're done, we'll look at the use and benefits of design patterns, look at some key OO design principles, and walk through an example of how one pattern works. The best way to use patterns is to load your brain with them and then recognize places in your designs and existing applications where you can apply them. Instead of code reuse, with patterns you get experience reuse.[1]

2. It started with a simple SimuDuck app

Joe works for a company that makes a highly successful duck pond simulation game, SimuDuck. The game can show a large variety of duck species swimming and making quacking sounds. The initial designers of the system used standard OO techniques and created one Duck superclass from which all other duck types inherit. The class diagram shows as Figure 1.

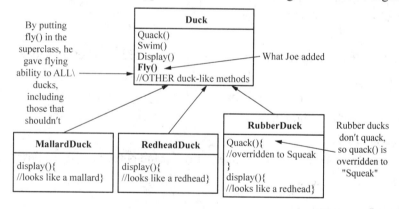

Fig.1   Class diagram of SimuDuck application

In the last year, the company has been under increasing pressure from competitors. After a week-long off-site brainstorming session over golf, the company executives think it's time for a big innovation. They need something really impressive to show at the upcoming shareholders meeting in Maui next week.[2]

3. But now we need the ducks to FLY

The executives decided that flying ducks is just what the simulator needs to blow away the other duck simulation competitors. And of course Joe's manager told them it'll be no problem for Joe to just whip something up in a week. "After all", said Joe's boss, "He's an OO programmer…, how hard can it be?"

Joe: I just need to add a fly() method in the Duck class and then all the ducks will inherit it. Now is my time to really show my true OO genius.

The new class diagram shows as Figure 2.

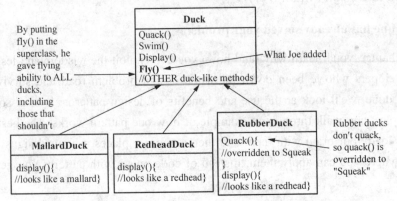

Fig.2 The new class diagram

4. But something went horribly wrong

The boss telephoned Joe: "Joe, I'm at the shareholder's meeting. They just gave a demo and there were rubber ducks flying around the screen. Was your idea of a joke? You might want to spend some time on Monster.com…"

5. What happened

Joe failed to notice that not all subclasses of duck should fly. When Joe added new behavior to the Duck superclass, he was also adding behavior that was not appropriate for some Duck subclasses. He now has flying inanimate objects in the SimuDuck program.

Joe: OK, so there's a slight flaw in my design. I don't see why they can't just call it a "feature". It's kind of cute…

What he thought was a great use of inheritance for the purpose of reuse hasn't turned out so well when it comes to maintenance.

6. Joe thinks about inheritance

Joe: I could always just override the fly() method in rubber duck, the way I am with the quack() method. But then what happens when we add wooden decoy ducks to the program? They aren't supposed to fly or quack…

Here's another class in the hierarchy; notice that like RubberDuck, it doesn't fly, but it also doesn't quack.

7. Sharpen your pencil

Which of the following are disadvantages of using inheritance to provide Duck behavior? (Choose all that apply.)

A. Code is duplicated across subclasses.

B. Runtime behavior changes are difficult.

C. We can't make ducks dance.

D. Hard to gain knowledge of all duck behaviors.

E. Ducks can't fly and quack at the same time.

F. Changes can unintentionally affect other ducks.

8. How about an interface

Joe realized that inheritance probably wasn't the answer, because he just got a memo that says that the executives now want to update the product every six months (in ways they haven't yet decided on). Joe knows the spec will keep changing and he'll be forced to look at and possibly override fly() and quack() for every new Duck subclass that's ever added to the program… forever.[3]

So, he needs a cleaner way to have only some (but not all) of the duck types fly or quack.

Joe: I could take fly() out of the Duck superclass, and make a Flyable() interface with a fly() method. That way, only the ducks that are supposed to fly will implement that interface and have a fly() method. And I might as well make a Quackable, too, since not all ducks can quack. The new design is shown in Figure 3. What do you think about this design?

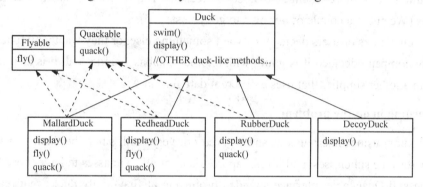

Fig.3   The new design by interface

9. What would you do if you were Joe

We know that not all of the subclasses should have flying or quacking behavior, so inheritance isn't the right answer. But while having the subclasses implement Flyable and /or Quackable solves part of the problem (no inappropriately flying rubber ducks), it completely destroys code reuse for those behaviors, so it just creates a different maintenance nightmare. And of course there might be more than one kind of flying behavior even among the ducks that do fly…

At this point you might be waiting for a Design Pattern to come riding in on a white horse and save the day. But what fun would that be? No, we're going to figure out a solution the old-fashioned way—by applying good OO software design principles.[4]

Joe: Wouldn't it be dreamy if only there were a way to build software so that when we need to change it, we could do so with the least possible impact on the existing code? We could spend less time reworking code and more making the program do cooler things…

10. The one constant in software development

Okay, what's the one thing you can always count on in software development?

No matter where you work, what you're building, or what language you are programming in, what's the one true constant that will be with you always?

(use a mirror to see the answer)

Fig.4　The constant of programming

No matter how well you design an application, over time an application must grow and change or it will die.[5] (An example of program designed see Figure 4.)

11. Sharpen your pencil

Lots things can drive change. List some reasons you've had to change code in your applications (We put in a couple of our own to get you started).

(1) My customers or users decide they want something else, or they want new functionality.

(2) My company decided it is going with another database vendor and it is also purchasing its data from another supplier that uses a different data format Argh!

12. Zeroing in on the problem

So we know using inheritance hasn't worked out very well, since the duck behavior keeps changing across the subclasses, and it's not appropriate for all subclasses to have those behaviors. The Flyable and Quackable interface sounded promising at first—only ducks that really do fly will be Flyable, etc.—except Java interfaces have no implementation code, so no code reuse. And that means that whenever you need to modify a behavior, you're forced to track down and change it in all the different subclasses where that behavior is defined, probably introducing new bugs along the way! Luckily, there's a design principle for just this situation. The first design principle is: Identify the aspects of your application that vary and separate them from what stays the same.

Take what varies and "encapsulate" it so it won't affect the rest of your code. The result? Fewer unintended consequences from code changes and more flexibility in your systems! In other words, if you've got some aspect of your code that is changing, say with every new requirement, then you know you've got a behavior that needs to be pulled out and separated from all the stuff that doesn't change. Here's another way to think about this principle: take the parts that vary and encapsulate them, so that later you can alter or extend the parts that vary without affecting those that don't. As simple as this concept is, it forms the basis for almost every design pattern. All patterns provide a way to let some part of a system vary independently of all other parts. Okay, time to pull the duck behavior out of the Duck classes!

13. Separating what changes from what stays the same

Where do we start? As far as we can tell, other than the problems with fly() and quack(), the Duck class is working well and there are no other parts of it that appear to vary or change frequently. So, other than a few slight changes, we're going to pretty much leave the Duck class alone.

Now, to separate the "parts that change from those that stay the same", we are going to create two sets of classes (totally apart from Duck), one for fly and one for quack. Each set of classes will hold all the implementations of their respective behavior. For instance, we might have one class that implements quacking, another that implements squeaking, and another that implements silence.

We know that fly() and quack() are the parts of the Duck class that vary across ducks.

To separate these behaviors from the Duck class, we'll pull both methods out of the Duck class and create a new set of classes to represent each behavior. Please look at figure 5.

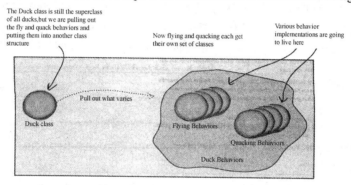

Fig.5   Separate what changes from that stays the same

14. Designing the Duck Behaviors

So how are we going to design the set of classes that implement the fly and quack behaviors? We'd like to keep things flexible; after all, it was the inflexibility in the duck behaviors that got us into trouble in the first place. And we know that we want to assign behaviors to the instances of Duck. For example, we might want to instantiate a new MallardDuck instance and initialize it with a specific type of flying behavior. And while we're there, why not make sure that we can change the behavior of a duck dynamically? In other words, we should include behavior setter methods in the Duck classes so that we can, say change the MallardDuck's flying behavior at runtime.

Given these goals, let's look at our second design principle: Program to an interface, not an implementation.

From now on, the Duck behaviors will live in a separate class—a class that implements a particular behavior interface.

That way, the Duck classes won't need to know any of the implementation details for their own behaviors.

We'll use an interface to represent each behavior—for instance, FlyBehavior (see Figure 6) and QuackBehavior—and each implementation of a behavior will implement one of those interfaces.

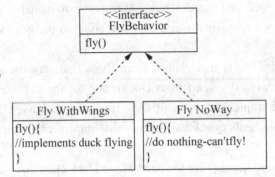

Fig.6   The FlyBehavior interface

So this time it won't be the Duck classes that will implement the flying and quacking interfaces. Instead, we'll make a set of classes whose entire reason for living is to represent a behavior (fox example, "squeaking"), and it's the behavior class, rather than the Duck class, that will implement the behavior interface.

This is in contrast to the way we were doing things before, where a behavior either came from a concrete implementation in the superclass Duck, or by providing a specialized implementation in the subclass itself. In both cases we were relying on an implementation. We were locked into using that specific implementation and there was no room for changing out the behavior (other than writing more code).

With our new design, the Duck subclasses will use a behavior represented by an interface (FlyBehavior and QuackBehavior), so that the actual implementation of the behavior (in other words, the specific concrete behavior coded in the class that implements the FlyBehavior or QuackBehavior) won't be locked into the Duck subclass.

Joe: I don't see why you have to use an interface for FlyBehavior. You can do the same thing with an abstract superclass. Isn't the whole point to use polymorphism?

15. "Program to an interface" really means "Program to a supertype"

The world interface is overloaded here. There's the concept of interface, but there's also the Java construct interface. You can program to an interface, without having to actually use a Java interface. The point is to exploit polymorphism by programming to a supertype so that the actual runtime object isn't locked into the code. And we could rephrase "program to a supertype" as "the declared type of the variables should be a supertype, usually an abstract class or interface, so that the objects assigned to those variables can be of any concrete implementation of the supertype, which means the class declaring them doesn't have to know about the actual object types!"

This is probably old news to you, but just to make sure we're all saying the same thing, here's a simple example of using a polymorphic type—imagine an abstract class Animal, with two concrete implementations, Dog and Cat.

Programming to an implementation would be

```
    Dog d=new Dog();    //Declaring the variable "d" as type Dog (a concrete
implementation
    d.bark();        // of Animal forces us to code to a concrete implementation
```

But programming to an interface/supertype would be:

```
    Animal animal=new Dog();    //We know it's a Dog, but we can now use the animal
    Animal.makeSound();        //reference polymorphically
```

Even better, rather than hard-coding the instantiation of the subtype (like new Dog()) into the code (see Figure 7).

assign the concrete implementation object at runtime:

```
    a=getAnimal();    //we don't know what the actual animal subtype is... all
we care about
    animal.makeSound(); //is that it knows how to respond to makeSound()
```

Implement the Duck Behavior see Figure 8.

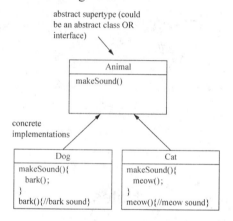

Fig.7   Program to supertype

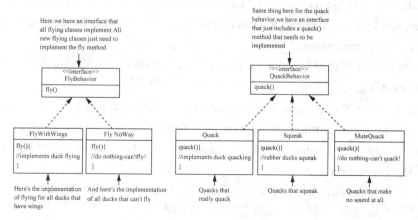

Fig.8   Implement the Duck Behavior

New Words and Expressions

design pattern	*n.*	设计模式
exploit	*v.*	充分利用
lesson	*n.*	教训
superclass	*n.*	超类；父类
inherit	*vt.*	继承
competitor	*n.*	竞争者
brainstorming	*n.*	头脑风暴
executive	*n.*	经理主管人员
innovation	*n.*	改革；创新
impressive	*adj.*	给人印象深刻的
shareholders meeting	*n.*	股东大会
blow away		吹走，驱散
OO		面向对象的
horribly	*adv.*	可怕的；非常的
monster.com		美国著名的求职网站
subclass		子类
inanimate	*adj.*	没有生命的
quack	*v.*	(指鸭)呷呷地叫
nightmare	*n.*	梦魇；噩梦；可怕的事物
encapsulate	*vt.*	封装
dynamically	*adv.*	动态地

Notes

1. The best way to use patterns is to load your brain with them and then recognize places in your designs and existing applications where you can apply them. Instead of code reuse, with patterns you get experience reuse.

译文：使用设计模式最好的办法是将它们装进你的脑袋里，然后在你设计的现有程序中找到合适的地方把它们放进去。它不是代码复用，使用模式是经验复用。

2. In the last year, the company has been under increasing pressure from competitors. After a week-long off-site brainstorming session over golf, the company executives think it's time for a big innovation. They need something really impressive to show at the upcoming shareholders meeting in Maui next week.

译文：去年，公司的竞争压力加剧。在为期一周的高尔夫假期兼头脑风暴会议之后，公司主管认为该是创新的时候了，他们需要在"下周"毛伊岛股东会议上展示一些"真正"让人印象深刻的东西来振奋人心。

3. Joe realized that inheritance probably wasn't the answer, because he just got a memo that says that the executives now want to update the product every six months (in ways they haven't yet decided on). Joe knows the spec will keep changing and he'll be forced to look at and possibly override fly() and quack() for every new Duck subclass that's ever added to the program...forever.

译文：Joe 认识到继承可能不是答案，因为他刚刚拿到来自主管的备忘录，希望以后每 6 个月更新一次产品（至于更新的方法，他们还没想到）。Joe 知道规格会常常改变，每当有新的鸭子子类出现，他就要被迫检查并可能需要覆盖 fly()和 quark()...这简直是无穷无尽的噩梦。

4. At this point you might be waiting for a Design Pattern to come riding in on a white horse and save the day. But what fun would that be? No, we're going to figure out a solution the old-fashioned way—by applying good OO software design principles.

译文：此时，你可能正期盼着设计模式能骑着白马来解救你离开苦难的一天。但是，如果直接告诉你答案，这有什么乐趣？我们会用老方法找出一个解决之道："采用良好的面向对象软件设计原则"。

5. No matter where you work, what you're building, or what language you are programming in, what's the one true constant that will be with you always?

No matter how well you design an application, over time an application must grow and change or it will die.

译文：不管你在何处工作，构建些什么，用何种编程语言，在软件开发上，一直伴随你的那个不变真理是什么？

不管当初软件设计得有多好，一段时间之后，总是需要成长与改变，否则软件会"死亡"。

Exercises

1. Why we should learn design patterns?

2. What is the best way to use patterns?

3. Think what will lead your application change in your work.

4. What is the first design principle? Please explain it in your words.

5. What is the second design principle? What is the difference between interface and implementation?

6. What does "program to a supertype" mean?

Text B   Intro to Design Patterns (2)

1. Implementing the Duck Behaviors

Here we have the two interfaces, FlyBehavior and QuackBehavior along with the corresponding classes that implement each concrete behavior. Please look at figure 8. With this design, other types of objects can reuse our fly and quack behaviors because these behaviors are no longer hidden away in our Duck classes!

And we can add new behaviors without modifying any of our existing behavior classes or touching any of the Duck classes that use flying behaviors.

So we get the benefit of REUSE without all the baggage that comes along with inheritance.

2. Dumb Questions

Q: Do I always have to implement my application first, see where things are changing, and then go back and separate & encapsulate those things?

A: Not always; often when you are designing an application, you anticipate those areas that are going to vary and then go ahead and build the flexibility to deal with it into your code. You'll find that the principles and patterns can be applied at any stage of the development lifecycle.

Q: Should we make Duck an interface too?

A: Not in case. As you'll see once we've got everything hooked together, we do benefit by having Duck be a concrete class and having specific ducks, like MallardDuck, inherit common properties and methods. Now that we've removed what varies from the Duck inheritance, we get the benefits of this structure without the problems.

Q: It feels a little weird to have a class that's just a behavior. Aren't classes supposed to represent things? Aren't classes supposed to have both state and behavior?

A: In an OO system, yes, classes represent things that generally have both state (instance variables) and methods. And in this case, the thing happens to be a behavior. But even a behavior can still have stage and methods; a flying behavior might have instance variables representing the attributes for the flying (wing beats per minute、max altitude and speed, etc.) behavior.

3. Integrating the Duck Behavior

Integrating the Duck Behavior see Figure 9. The key is that a Duck will now delegate its flying and quacking behavior, instead of using quacking and flying methods defined in the Duck class (or subclass). Here is how.

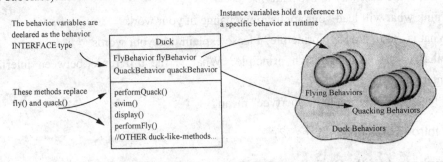

Fig.9   Integrating the Duck Behavior

(1) First we'll add two instance variables to the Duck class called FlyBehavior and QuackBehavior, those are declared as the interface type (not a concrete class implementation type). Each duck object will set these variables polymorphically to reference the specific behavior type it would like at runtime (FlyWithWings, Squeak, etc.).

We'll also remove the fly() and quack() methods from the Duck class (and any subclasses) because we've moved this behavior out into the FlyBehavior and QuackBehavior classes.

We'll replace fly() and quack() in the Duck class with two similar methods, called performFly() and performQuack(); you'll see how they work next.

(2) Now we implement performQuack().

```
Public class Duck{
    QuackBehavior quackBehavior; //Each Duck has a reference to something
that
                            //more implement the QuackBehavior
interface
    Public void performQuack(){ //Rather than handling the quack
behavior itself,
        quackBehavior.quack(); //the Duck object delegates that
behavior to the
        }                      //object referenced by quackBehavior
    }
```

Pretty simple, huh? To perform the quack, a Duck just allows the object that is referenced by quackBehavior to quack for it.

In this part of the code we don't care what kind of object it is, all we care about is that it knows how to quack()!

(3) Okay, it's time to worry about how the flyBehavior and quackBehavior instance variables are set. Let's take a look at the MallardDuck class.

```
Public class MallardDuck extends Duck{
    Public MallardDuck(){          //A Mallard Duck uses the Quack class
to handle
        quackBehavior=new Quack();    //its quack, so when performQuack is
called, the
        flyBehavior=new FlyWithWings();//responsibility for the quack is
delegated to the
        }        //Quack object and we get a real quack and it uses FlywithWings
as its
            . //FlyBehavior type Remember, MallardDuck inherits the
quackBehavior
            //and flyBehavior instance variables from class Duck.
    Public void display(){
        System.out.println("I'm a real Mallard duck");
    }
    }
```

So MallardDuck's quack is a real live duck quack, not a squeak and no a mute quack. So what happens here? When a MallardDuck is instantiated, its constructor initializes the MallardDuck's inherited quackBehavior instance variable to a new instance of type Quack (a QuackBehvior concrete implementation class).

And the same is true for the duck's flying behavior—the MallardDuck's constructor initializes the flyBehavior instance variable with an instance of type FlyWithWings (a FlyBehavior concrete implementation class).

Good catch, that's exactly what we're doing… for now.

Later in the book we'll have more patterns in our toolbox that can help us fix it.

Still, notice that while we are setting the behaviors to concrete classes (by instantiating a behavior class like Quack or FlyWithWings and assigning it to our behavior reference variable), we could easily change that at runtime.

So, we still have a lot of flexibility here, but we're doing a poor job of initializing the instance variables in a flexible way. But think about it, since the quackBehavior instance variable is an interface type, we could (through the magic of polymorphism) dynamically assign a different QuackBehavior implementation class at runtime.

Take a moment and think about how you would implement a duck so that its behavior could change at runtime. (You'll see the code that does this a few pages from now.)

4. The Big Picture on encapsulated behaviors

Okay, now that we've done the deep dive on the duck simulator design, it's time to come back up for air and take a look at the Big Picture.[1]

Figure 10 is the entire reworked class structure. We have everything you'd expect: ducks extending Duck, fly behaviors implementing FlyBehavior and quack behaviors implementing QuackBehavior.

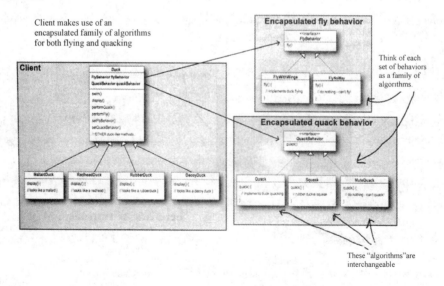

Fig.10 The Big Picture on encapsulated behaviors

Notice also that we've started to describe things a little differently. Instead of thinking of the duck behaviors as a set of behaviors, we'll start thinking of them as a family of algorithms. Think about it: in the SimuDuck design, the algorithms represent things a duck would do (different ways of quacking or flying), but we could just as easily use the same techniques for a set of classes that implement the ways to compute state sales tax by different states.

Pay careful attention to the relationships between the classes. In fact, grab your pen and write the appropriate relationship (IS-A, HAS-A and IMPLEMENTS) on each arrow in the class diagram.

5. HAS-A can be better than IS-A

The HAS-A relationship is an interesting one: each duck has a FlyBehavior and a QuackBehavior to which it delegates flying and quacking.

When you put two classes together like this you're using composition. Instead of inheriting their behavior, the ducks get their behavior by being composed with the right behavior object.

This is an important technique; in fact, we've been using our third design principle: Favor composition over inheritance.

As you've seen, creating systems using composition gives you a lot more flexibility. Not only does it let you encapsulate a family of algorithms into their own set of classes, but it also lets you change behavior at runtime as long as the object you're composing with implements the correct behavior interface.[2]

Composition is used in many design patterns and you'll see a lot more about its advantages and disadvantages throughout the book.

Brain Power: A duck call is a device that hunters use to mimic the calls (quacks) of ducks. How would you implement your own duck call that does not inherit from the Duck class?

6. Master and Student

Master: Grasshopper, tell me what you have learned of the object-Oriented ways.

Student: Master, I have learned that the promise of the object-oriented way is reuse.

Master: Grasshopper, continue…

Student: Master, through inheritance all good things may be reused and so we will come to drastically cut development time like we swiftly cut bamboo in the woods.

Master: Grasshopper, is more time spent on code before or after development is complete?

Student: The answer is after, Master. We always spend more time maintaining and changing software than initial development.

Master: So Grasshopper, should effort go into reuse above maintainability and extensibility?

Student: Master, I believe that there is truth in this.

Master: I can see that you still have much to learn. I would like for you to go and meditate on inheritance further. As you've seen, inheritance has its problems, and there are other ways of achieving reuse.

7. Speaking of design patterns

You just applied your first design pattern—the Strategy Pattern. That's right, you used the Strategy Pattern to rework the SimuDuck app. Thanks to this pattern, the simulator is ready for any changes those execs might cook up on their next business trip to Vegas.

Now that we've made you take the long road to apply it, here's the formal definition of this pattern.

The strategy pattern defines a family of algorithms, encapsulates each one, and makes them interchangeable. Strategy lets the algorithm vary independently from clients that use it.[3]

Use this definition when you need to impress friends and influence key executives.

8. Overheard at the local diner

Alice: I need a Cream cheese with jelly on white bread, a chocolate soda with vanilla ice cream, a grilled cheese sandwich with bacon, a tuna fish salad on toast, a banana split with ice cream & sliced bananas and a coffee with a cream and two sugars,…oh, and put a hamburger on the grill.

Flo: Give me a C.J. White, a black & white, a Jack Benny, a radio, a house boat, a coffee regular and burn one!

What's the difference between these two orders? Not a thing! They're both the same order, except Alice is using twice the number of words and trying the patience of a grumpy short order cook.

What's Flo got that Alice doesn't? A shared vocabulary with the short order cook. Not only is it easier to communicate with the cook, but it gives the cook less to remember because he's got all the diner patterns in his head.

Design Patterns give you a shared vocabulary with other developers. Once you've got the vocabulary you can more easily communicate with other developers and inspire those who don't know patterns to start learning them. It also elevates your thinking about architectures by letting you think at the pattern level, not the nitty gritty object level.[4]

9. Overheard in the next cubicle

Rick: So I created this broadcast class. It keeps track of all the objects listening to it and anytime a new piece of data comes along it sends a message to each listener. What's cool is that the listeners can join the broadcast at any time or they can even remove themselves. It is really dynamic and loosely-coupled!

Joe: Rick, why didn't you just say you were using the Observer pattern?

Jack: Exactly. If you communicate in patterns, then other developers know immediately and precisely the design you've describing. Just don't get Pattern Fever…You'll know you have it when you start using patterns for Hello World…

Brain Power: Can you think of other shared vocabularies that are used beyond OO design and diner talk?(Hint: how about auto mechanics、carpenters、gourmet chefs、air traffic control). What qualities are communicated along with lingo? Can you think of aspects of OO design that get communicated along with pattern names? What qualities get communicated along with the name "Strategy Pattern"?

10. The power of a shared pattern vocabulary

When you communicate using patterns you are doing more than just sharing lingo.

Shared pattern vocabularies are powerful. When you communicate with another developer or your team using patterns, you are communicating not just a pattern name but a whole set of qualities, characteristics and constraints that the pattern represents.

Patterns allow you to say more with less. When you use a pattern in a description, other developers quickly know precisely the design you have in mind.

"We've using the strategy pattern to implement the various behaviors of our ducks." This tells you the duck behavior has been encapsulated into its own set of classes that can be easily expanded and changed, even at runtime if needed.

Talking at the pattern level allows you to stay "in the design" longer. Talking about software systems using patterns allows you to keep the discussion at the design level, without having to dive down to the nitty gritty details of implementing objects and classes.[5]

How many design meetings have you been in that quickly degrade into implementation details?

Shared vocabularies can turbo charge your development team. A team well versed in design patterns can move quickly with less room for misunderstanding.

As your team begins to share design ideas and experience in terms of patterns, you will build a community of patterns users.

Shared vocabularies encourage more junior developers to get up to speed. Junior developers look up to experienced developers. When senior developers make use of design patterns, junior developers also become motivated to learn them. Build a community of pattern users at your organization.

Think about starting a patterns study group at your organization, maybe you can even get paid while you're learning...

11. How do I use design patterns

We've all used off-the-shelf libraries and frameworks. We take them, write some code against their APIs, compile them into our programs, and benefit from a lot of code someone else has written. Think about the Java APIs and all the functionality they give you: network, GUI, IO, etc. Libraries and frameworks go a long way towards a development model where we can just pick and choose components and plug them right in. But... they don't help us structure our own applications in ways that are easier to understand, more maintainable and flexible. That's where Design Patterns come in.

Design patterns don't go directly into your code, they first go into your brain. Once you've loaded your brain with a good working knowledge of patterns, you can then start to apply them to your new designs, and rework your old code when you find it's degrading into an inflexible mess of jungle spaghetti code. Figure11 shows how design patterns work.

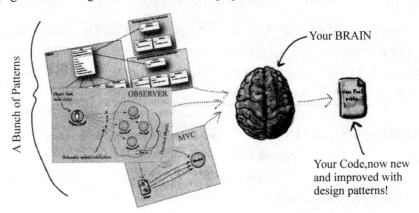

Fig.11　How design patterns work

New Words and Expressions

composition	*n.*	合成
overhear	*vt.*	无意中听到；偷听
jelly	*n.*	果子冻；一种果冻甜品
vanilla	*n.*	[植]香草；香子兰
bacon	*n.*	咸肉；熏肉
grill	*n.*	烤架；铁格子；烤肉
grumpy	*adj.*	脾气坏的；性情乖戾的；脾气暴躁的
inspire	*vt.*	鼓舞；感动；激发
elevate	*vt.*	举起；提拔；提升
cubicle	*n.*	小隔档
constraint	*n.*	约束
dive down	*v.*	压低
nitty	*adj.*	多虱卵的；多小虫卵的
gritty	*adj.*	多砂的；粗砂质的
spaghetti	*n.*	意大利式细面条

Notes

1. Okay, now that we've done the deep dive on the duck simulator design, it's time to come back up for air and take a look at the big picture.

译文：好，我们已经深入研究了鸭子模拟器的设计，该是将头探出水面，呼吸空气的时候了。现在就来看看整体的格局。

2. As you've seen, creating systems using composition gives you a lot more flexibility. Not only does it let you encapsulate a family of algorithms into their own set of classes, but it also lets you change behavior at runtime as long as the object you're composing with implements the correct behavior interface.

译文：如你所见，使用组合建立系统具有很大的弹性，不仅可将算法封装成类，更可以"在运行时动态地改变行为"，只要组合的行为对象符合正确的接口标准即可。

3. The strategy pattern defines a family of algorithms, encapsulates each one, and makes them interchangeable. Strategy lets the algorithm vary independently from clients that use it.

译文：策略模式定义了一组算法，将每个算法封装起来，并使其可以互换。策略模式使得算法可以独立于使用它们的客户变化。

4. Design patterns gives you a shared vocabulary with other developers. Once you've got the vocabulary you can more easily communicate with other developers and inspire those who don't know patterns to start learning them. It also elevates your thinking about architectures by letting you think at the pattern level, not the nitty gritty object level.

译文：设计模式让你和其他开发人员之间有共享的词汇，一旦懂得这些词汇，和其他开发人员之间沟通就很容易，也会促使那些不懂的程序员想开始学习设计模式。设计模式也可以把你的思考架构的层次提高到模式层面，而不是仅反停留在琐碎的对象上。

5. Talking at the pattern level allows you to stay "in the design" longer. Talking about software systems using patterns allows you to keep the discussion at the design level, without having to dive down to the nitty gritty details of implementing objects and classes.

译文：将说话的方式保持在模式层次，可让你待在"设计圈子"久一点。使用模式谈论软件系统，可以让你保持在设计层次，不会被压低到对象与类这种琐碎的事情上面。想想看，有多少次的设计会议中，你们一不小心就进入了琐碎的实现细节的讨论上。

Exercises

1. What is the difference between interface and implementation?

2. What is the principle "Favor composition over inheritance" means?

3. What is the strategy pattern?

4. Why should we learn design patterns?

5. How does a shared pattern vocabulary work?

6. How do you use design patterns?

Lesson Five　Digital Image Processing & Video Compression

Text A　An Introduction to Digital Image Processing

1. Introduction

Digital image processing remains a challenging domain of programming for several reasons. First the issue of digital image processing appeared relatively late in computer history. It had to wait for the arrival of the first graphical operating systems to become a true matter. Secondly, digital image processing requires the most careful optimizations especially for real time applications. Comparing image processing and audio processing is a good way to fix ideas. Let us consider the necessary memory bandwidth for examining the pixels of a 320x240, 32 bits bitmap, 30 times a second: 10 Mo/sec. Now with the same quality standard, an audio stereo wave real time processing needs 44100 (samples per second) x 2 (bytes per sample per channel) x 2 (channels) = 176Ko/sec, which is 50 times less. Obviously we will not be able to use the same techniques for both audio and image signal processing. Finally, digital image processing is by definition a two dimensions domain; this somehow complicates things when elaborating digital filters. We will explore some of the existing methods used to deal with digital images starting by a very basic approach of color interpretation. As a more advanced level of interpretation comes the matrix convolution and digital filters. Finally, we will have an overview of some applications of image processing. The aim of this document is to give the reader a little overview of the existing techniques in digital image processing. We will neither penetrate deep into theory, nor will we in the coding itself; we will more concentrate on the algorithms themselves, the methods.[1] Anyway, this document should be used as a source of ideas only, and not as a source of code.

2. A simple approach to image processing

1) The color data: Vector representation

(1) Bitmaps

The original and basic way of representing a digital colored image in a computer's memory is obviously a bitmap. A bitmap is constituted of rows of pixels, contraction of the words "Picture Element". Each pixel has a particular value which determines its appearing color. This value is qualified by three numbers giving the decomposition of the color in the three primary colors Red, Green and Blue. Any color visible to human eye can be represented this way. The decomposition of a color in the three primary colors is quantified by a number between 0 and 255. For example, white will be coded as R = 255, G = 255, B = 255; black will be known as (R,G,B) = (0,0,0); and say, bright pink will be : (255,0,255). In other words, an image is an enormous two-dimensional array of color values, pixels, each of them coded on 3 bytes, representing the three primary colors. This allows the image to contain a total of 256×256×256 = 16.8 million different colors. This technique is also known as RGB encoding, and is specifically adapted to human vision. With cameras or other measure instruments we are capable of "seeing" thousands of other "colors", in which cases the RGB encoding is inappropriate.

The range of 0~255 was agreed for two good reasons: The first is that the human eye is not sensible enough to make the difference between more than 256 levels of intensity (1/256 = 0.39%) for a color. That is to say, an image presented to a human observer will not be improved by using more than 256 levels of gray (256 shades of gray between black and white). Therefore 256 seems enough quality. The second reason for the value of 255 is obviously that it is convenient for computer storage. Indeed on a byte, which is the computer's memory unit, can be coded up to 256 values.

As opposed to the audio signal which is coded in the time domain, the image signal is coded in a two dimensional spatial domain. The raw image data is much more straightforward and easy to analyze than the temporal domain data of the audio signal. This is why we will be able to do lots of stuff and filters for images without transforming the source data, while this would have been totally impossible for audio signal. This first part deals with the simple effects and filters you can compute without transforming the source data, just by analyzing the raw image signal as it is.

The standard dimensions, also called resolution, for a bitmap are about 500 rows by 500 columns. This is the resolution encountered in standard analogical television and standard computer applications. You can easily calculate the memory space a bitmap of this size will require. We have 500×500 pixels, each coded on three bytes, this makes 750 Ko. It might not seem enormous compared to the size of hard drives, but if you must deal with an image in real time then processing things get tougher. Indeed rendering images fluidly demands a minimum of 30 images per second, the required bandwidth of 10 Mo/sec is enormous. We will see later that the limitation of data access and transfer in RAM has a crucial importance in image processing, and sometimes it happens to be much more important than limitation of CPU computing, which may seem quite different from what one can be used to in optimization issues.[2] Notice that, with modern compression techniques such as JPEG 2000, the total size of the image can be easily reduced by 50 times without losing a lot of quality, but this is another topic.

(2) Vector representation of colors

As we have seen, in a bitmap, colors are coded on three bytes representing their decomposition on the three primary colors. It sounds obvious to a mathematician to immediately interpret colors as vectors in a three-dimension space where each axis stands for one of the primary colors.[3] Therefore we will benefit of most of the geometric mathematical concepts to deal with our colors, such as norms, scalar product, projection, rotation or distance. This will be really interesting for some kind of filters we will see soon. Figure 1 illustrates this new interpretation:

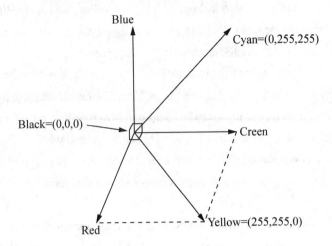

Vector representation of colors in a three dimensions space

Fig.1　Vector representation of colors

2) Immediate application to filters

(1) Edge Detection

From what we have said before we can quantify the 'difference' between two colors by computing the geometric distance between the vectors representing those two colors. Lets consider two colors $C1 = (R1,G1,B1)$ and $C2 = (R2,B2,G2)$, the distance between the two colors is given by the formula :

$$D(C1,C2) = \sqrt{(R1 - R2)^2 + (G1 - G2)^2 + (B1 - B2)^2}$$

This leads us to our first filter: edge detection. The aim of edge detection is to determine the edge of shapes in a picture and to be able to draw a result bitmap where edges are in white on black background (for example).[4] The idea is very simple; we go through the image pixel by pixel and compare the color of each pixel to its right neighbor, and to its bottom neighbor. If one of these comparison results in a too big difference the pixel studied is part of an edge and should be turned to white, otherwise it is kept in black. The fact that we compare each pixel with its bottom and right neighbor comes from the fact that images are in two dimensions. Indeed if you imagine an image with only alternative horizontal stripes of red and blue, the algorithms wouldn't see the edges of those stripes if it only compared a pixel to its right neighbor. Thus the two comparisons for each pixel are necessary.

This algorithm was tested on several source images of different types and it gives fairly good results. It is mainly limited in speed because of frequent memory access. The two square roots can be removed easily by squaring the comparison; however, the color extractions cannot be improved very easily. If we consider that the longest operations are the get pixel function and put pixel functions, we obtain a polynomial complexity of 4*N*M, where N is the number of rows and M the number of columns. This is not reasonably fast enough to be computed in real time. For a 300×300×32 image I get about 26 transforms per second on an Athlon XP 1600+. Quite slow indeed.

Figure 2 shows the results of the algorithm on an example image:

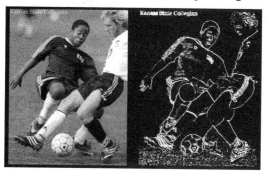

Fig.2　Edge detection Results

A few words about the results of this algorithm: Notice that the quality of the results depends on the sharpness of the source image. If the source image is very sharp edged, the result will reach perfection. However if you have a very blurry source you might want to make it pass through a sharpness filter first, which we will study later. Another remark, you can also compare each pixel with its second or third nearest neighbors on the right and on the bottom instead of the nearest neighbors. The edges will be thicker but also more exact depending on the source image's sharpness. Finally we will see later on that there is another way to make edge detection with matrix convolution.

(2) Color extraction

The other immediate application of pixel comparison is color extraction. Instead of comparing each pixel with its neighbors, we are going to compare it with a given color C1. This algorithm will try to detect all the objects in the image that are colored with C1. This was quite useful for robotics for example. It enables you to search on streaming images for a particular color. You can then make you robot go get a red ball for example. We will call the reference color, the one we are looking for in the image $C0 = (R0,G0,B0)$.

Once again, even if the square root can be easily removed it doesn't really improve the speed of the algorithm. What really slows down the whole loop is the NxM get pixel accesses to memory and put pixel. This determines the complexity of this algorithm: 2xNxM, where N and M are respectively the numbers of rows and columns in the bitmap. The effective speed measured on my computer is about 40 transforms per second on a 300×300×32 source bitmap.

(3) Color to grayscale conversion

Regarding the 3D color space, grayscale is symbolized by the straight generated by the (1,1,1) vector. Indeed, the shades of grays have equal components in red, green and blue, thus their decomposition must be (n,n,n), where n is an integer between 0 and 255 (example : (0,0,0) black, (32,32,32) dark gray, (128,128,128) intermediate gray, (192,192,192) bright gray, (255,255,255) white etc. Now the idea of the algorithm is to find the importance a color has in the direction of the (1,1,1) vector. We will use scalar projection to achieve this. The projection of a color vector C = (R,G,B) on the vector (1,1,1) is computed this way :

$$agb = PaPgPb\,Pg\cos(\alpha)$$

$$\operatorname{Pr}oj(C/(1,1,1)) = Pb\,Pg\cos(\alpha) = \frac{1\times R + 1\times G + 1\times B}{\sqrt{3}}$$

However the projection value can reach up to 441.67, which is the norm of the white color (255,255,255). To avoid having numbers above 255 limit we will multiply our projection value by a factor 255/441,67=1/sqrt(3). Thus the formula simplifies a little giving:

$$Grayscale(C) = \frac{255}{\sqrt{255^2 + 255^2 + 255^2}} \cdot \operatorname{Pr}oj(C/(1,1,1)) = \frac{1}{\sqrt{3}}\frac{1\times R + 1\times G + 1\times B}{\sqrt{3}} = \frac{R+G+B}{3}$$

So in fact converting a color to a grayscale value is just like taking the average of its red, green and blue components. You can also adapt the (R3) formula to other color-scales. For example you can choose to have a red-scale image, Redscale(C)=R, or a yellow-scale image, Yellowscale(C)=(G+B)/sqrt(6) etc.

It's impossible to optimize this algorithm regarding its simplicity but we can still give its computing complexity which is given by the number of pixel studied: NxM, (N,M) is the resolution of the bitmap.[5] The execution time on my computer is the same as in the previous algorithm, still about 35 transforms per second.

3. Conclusions

Digital image processing is far from being a simple transpose of audio signal principles to a two dimensions space. Image signal has its particular properties, and therefore we have to deal with it in a specific way. The Fast Fourier Transform, for example, which was such a practical tool in audio processing, becomes useless in image processing. Oppositely, digital filters are easier to create directly, without any signal transforms, in image processing.

Digital image processing has become a vast domain of modern signal technologies. Its applications pass far beyond simple aesthetical considerations, and they include medical imagery, television and multimedia signals, security, portable digital devices, video compression, and even digital movies. We have been flying over some elementary notions in image processing but there is yet a lot more to explore. If you are beginning in this topic, I hope this paper will have given you the taste and the motivation to carry on.

New Words and Expressions

digital image processing		数字图像处理
optimization	*n.*	最佳化，最优化
elaborate	*v.*	精心制作
	adj.	精心制作的
penetrate	*v.*	穿透，渗透，看穿，洞察
decomposition	*n.*	分解

RGB encoding RGB		编码
temporal	*adj.*	暂时的，短暂的
vector	*n.*	矢量
formula	*n.*	公式
color extraction		彩色提取
grayscale	*n.*	灰度级
transpose	*v.*	变换
graphical operating systems		图形操作系统
bitmap	*n.*	[计]位图
digital filter		数字滤波器
pixel	*n.*	像素
the three primary colors		三原色
two dimensional spatial domain		二维空域
resolution	*n.*	分辨率
Edge detection		边缘检测
square root		平方根
robotics	*n.*	机器人技术
scalar projection		标量投影
aesthetical	*adj.*	美学的

Notes

1. We will neither penetrate deep into theory, nor will we in the coding itself; we will more concentrate on the algorithms themselves, the methods.

译文：我们既不需要深入研究理论，也不会研究编码，我们更关注的是算法，也就是方法。

该句是由分号";"连接起来的两个句子。前一个是"neither...nor"句型，表示"不会……也不会……"。后一句中，"the methods"作"algorithms"的同位语。

2. We will see later that the limitation of data access and transfer in RAM has a crucial importance in image processing, and sometimes it happens to be much more important than limitation of CPU computing, which may seem quite different from what one can be used to in optimization issues.

译文：我们将注意到，RAM 中的数据访问与传输能力的限制对图像处理影响巨大，有时候，它的影响甚至超过由于 CPU 的处理能力限制而带来的影响，这与我们习惯的优化思路大不相同。

该句是由"and"连接起来的简单句，最后一句是由"which"引导的非限定性定语从句，which 在这里指代前面所讨论的内容。

3. It sounds obvious to a mathematician to immediately interpret colors as vectors in a three dimension space where each axis stands for one of the primary colors.

译文：很明显，一个数学家会立刻将颜色定义为三维空间矢量，三维空间的每条坐标轴代表一种基色。

这是一个由"it"引导的主语从句。主句其实是"to immediately interpret colors as vectors in a three dimension space."。由"where"引导的定语从句，用来修饰"a three dimension space"。

4. The aim of edge detection is to determine the edge of shapes in a picture and to be able to draw a result bitmap where edges are in white on black background (for example).

译文：边缘检测的目的是确定图片中不同形状的边缘位置，并将结果绘制成位图，例如，可以在黑色背景上用白色表示边缘。

5. It's impossible to optimize this algorithm regarding its simplicity but we can still give its computing complexity which is given by the number of pixel studied: N×M, (N, M) is the resolution of the bitmap.

译文：我们不可能通过优化该算法降低算法的复杂度，但是我们可以从研究的像素数目 N×M 来获得计算复杂度，其中(N, M)表示位图的分辨率。

"resolution of the bitmap"指位图的分辨率，表明该位图有 N 行 M 列。

Exercises

Ⅰ. Comprehension Questions.

1. Why does digital image processing remain a challenging domain of programming?

2. How is a digital colored image represented in a computer's memory?

3. What is the aim of edge detection?

4. Please give a simple introduction to edge detection algorithm.

5. Is digital image processing a transpose of audio signal principles to a two dimensions space? why?

6. Could you tell me the application area of digital image processing?

Ⅱ. Translate the following paragraph into Chinese.

Digital image processing is far from being a simple transpose of audio signal principles to a two dimensions space. Image signal has its particular properties, and therefore we have to deal with it in a specific way. The Fast Fourier Transform, for example, which was such a practical tool in audio processing, becomes useless in image processing. Oppositely, digital filters are easier to create directly, without any signal transforms, in image processing.

Digital image processing has become a vast domain of modern signal technologies. Its applications pass far beyond simple aesthetical considerations, and they include medical imagery, television and multimedia signals, security, portable digital devices, video compression, and even digital movies. We have been flying over some elementary notions in image processing but there is yet a lot more to explore. If you are beginning in this topic, I hope this paper will have given you the taste and the motivation to carry on.

Text B   What is Video Compression

The increasing demand to incorporate video data into telecommunications services, the corporate environment, the entertainment industry, and even at home has made digital video technology a necessity.[1] A problem, however, is that still image and digital video data rates are very large, typically in the range of 150Mbits/sec. Data rates of this magnitude would consume a lot of the bandwidth, storage and computing resources in a typical personal computer. For this reason, Video Compression standards have been developed to eliminate picture redundancy, allowing video information to be transmitted and stored in a compact and efficient manner.

1. Video Compression Standards

During the 80s and 90s, Discrete Cosine Transform (DCT) based compression algorithms and international standards were developed to alleviate storage and bandwidth limitations imposed by digital still image and motion video applications.

Today there are three DCT-based standards that are widely used and accepted worldwide:

- JPEG (Joint Photographic Experts Group)
- H.261 (Video codec for audiovisual services)
- MPEG (Motion Picture Experts Group)

Each of these standards is well suited for particular applications: JPEG for still image compression, H.261 for video conferencing, and MPEG for high-quality, multimedia systems.[2]

2. Video Compression Processing Functions

As mentioned earlier, the JPEG, H.261, and MPEG video compression standards are all based on the DCT. In addition to being DCT-based, many processing functions and compression principles are common to these standards.

The basic compression scheme for all three standards can be summarized as follows: divide the picture into 8x8 blocks, determine relevant picture information, discard redundant or insignificant information, and encode relevant picture information with the least number of bits.[3] Common functions to all three standards are:

- DCT
- Zig-Zag Scanning
- Quantization
- Entropy Coding
- Motion Estimation

1) DCT & Zig-Zag Scanning

The Discrete Cosine Transform is closely related to the Discrete Fourier Transform (FFT) and, as such, allows data to be represented in terms of its frequency components. Similarly, in image processing applications the two-dimensional (2D) DCT maps a picture or a picture segment into its 2D frequency components.

For video compression applications, since the variations in the block tend to be low, the great majority of these transformations result in a more compact representation of the block. The block energy is packed into the corresponding lower frequency bins.

The DCT component at coordinates (0,0) is referred to as the DC bin. All other components are referred to as AC bins.

Since the mapping is from lower to higher frequencies in the horizontal and vertical directions, zig-zag scanning of the resulting 2D frequency bins clusters packets of picture information from low to high frequencies into a 1D stream of bins.[4]

(a) Original picture   (b) Corresponding DCT mapping of (a)

Fig.3   The DCT operation

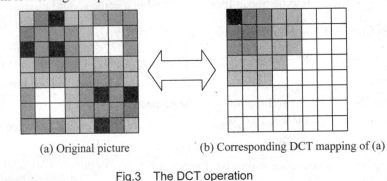

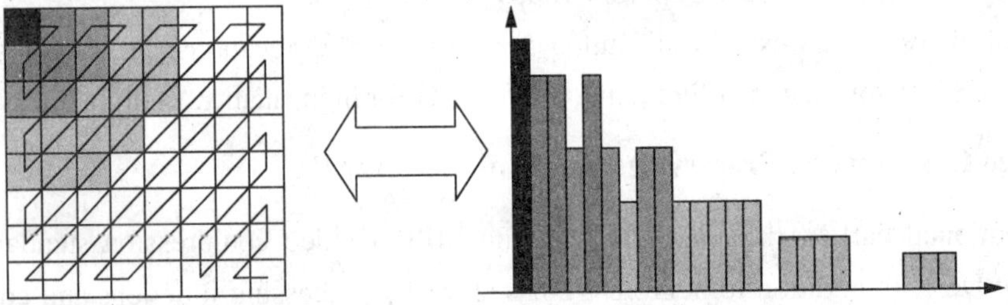

(a) 2D frequency bins of picture   (b) 1D stream of bins

Fig.4   Zig-zag scanning

2) Quantization

Quantization is the primary source of data loss in DCT-based image compression algorithms. Quantization reduces the amount of information required to represent the frequency bins by converting amplitudes that fall in certain ranges to one in a set of quantization levels. For simplicity, all standard image compression algorithms use linear quantization where the step size quantization levels are constant.

Quantization in the frequency domain has many advantages over directly quantizing the pixel values. Quantization of the pixel values results in a visual artifact called "contour" distortion where small changes in amplitude in a gradient area cause step-sized changes in the reconstructed amplitude. Except for the DC bin, quantization error for each of the frequency bins average out to zero over the 8 x 8 block.

3) Entropy Coding

Entropy coding is a loss-less compression scheme based on statistical properties of the picture or the stream of information to be compressed. Although entropy coding is implemented slightly different in each of the standards, the basic "entropy coding" scheme consists of encoding the most frequently occurring patterns with the least number of bits. In, this manner, data can be compressed by an additional factor of 3 or 4.

Entropy coding for video compression applications is a two-step process: Zero Run-Length Coding (RLC) and Huffman coding. RLC data is an intermediate symbolic representation of the quantized bins which utilizes a pair of numbers. The first number represents the number of consecutive zeros while the second number represents the value between zero-run lengths. For instance the RLC code (5,8) represents the sequence (0,0,0,0,0,8) of numbers.

Huffman coding assigns a variable length code to the RLC data, producing variable length bit stream data. This requires Huffman tables which can be pre-computed based on statistical properties of the image (as it is in JPEG) or can be pre-determined if a default table is to be used (as it is in H.261 and MPEG). In either case, the same table is used to decode the bit stream data.

As mentioned above, frequently occurring RLC patterns are coded with the least number of bits. At this point the digital stream, which is a representation of the picture, has no specific boundaries or fixed length. This information can now be stored or appropriately prepared for transmission.

4) Motion Estimation

In general, successive pictures in a motion video sequence tend to be highly correlated, that is, the pictures change slightly over a small period of time. This implies that the arithmetic difference between these pictures is small. For this reason, compression ratios for motion video sequences may be increased by encoding the arithmetic difference between two or more successive frames.

In contrast, objects that are in motion increase the arithmetic difference between frames which in turn implies that more bits are required to encode the sequence. To address this issue, motion estimation is utilized to determine the displacement of an object.

Motion estimation is the process by which elements in a picture are best correlated to elements in other pictures (ahead or behind) by the estimated amount of motion. The amount of motion is encapsulated in the motion vector. Forward motion vectors refer to correlation with previous pictures. Backward motion vectors refer to correlation with future pictures.

An efficient motion estimation algorithm increases frame correlation, which in turn minimizes pixel arithmetic difference. Resulting in not only higher compression ratios but also in higher quality decoded video sequences. Motion estimation is an extremely computationally intensive operation difficult to implement in real-time. For this reason, a variety of motion estimation algorithms have been implemented by the industry.

3. The JPEG Compression Algorithm

The JPEG algorithm was designed to efficiently compress continuous-tone still images. In addition to its use in still image compression, JPEG has also been adapted for use with motion video sequences. This adaptation (commonly called motion-JPEG) uses the JPEG algorithm to individually compress each frame in a motion video sequence.

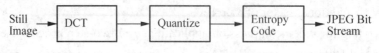

Fig.5　JPEG Encoding

Each color component of a still image is treated as a separate gray-scale picture by JPEG. Although JPEG allows any color component separation, images are usually separated into Red, Green, Blue (RGB) or Luminance (Y), with Blue and Red color differences (U=B−Y, V=R−Y). Separation into YUV color components allows the algorithm to take advantage of the human eye's lower sensitivity to color information. The U and V color components are commonly recorded at a lower bandwidth and sub-sampled to one-half in the horizontal dimension (called 4:2:2), or one-half in both the horizontal and vertical (called 4:2:0).

JPEG partitions each color component picture into 8x8 pixel blocks of image samples. An 8x8 DCT is applied to each block. For quantization, JPEG uses quantization matrices. JPEG allows a different quantization matrix to be specified for each color component.

Using quantization matrices allow each frequency bin to be quantized to a different step size. Generally the lower frequency components are quantized to a small step size and the high frequency components to a large step size. This takes advantage of the fact that the human eye is less sensitive to high frequency visual noise, but is more sensitive to lower frequency noise, manifesting itself in blocking artifacts.[5]

Modification of the quantization matrices is the primary method for controlling the quality and compression ratio in JPEG. Although the quantization step size for any one of the frequency components can be modified individually, a more common technique is to scale all the elements of the matrices together.

The final stage of compression is the zig-zag scanning and entropy coding. Although JPEG allows for two different types of entropy coders, nearly all JPEG implementations use the Huffman coding option. The JPEG standard allows for the use of user-definable Huffman coding tables. To decompress a JPEG image each operation is performed in reverse order.

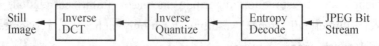

Fig.6　JPEG Decoding

4. The H.261 Compression Algorithm

Video conferencing and video telephony are the intended applications for the H.261 compression algorithm. For these applications, representation of limited motion video (talking heads) is a key component. To allow for low-cost implementations, H.261 fixes many of the system parameters. Only the YUV color component separation with the 4:2:0 sampling ratio is allowed by the standard. In addition, H.261 allows for only two frame sizes, CIF (352×288) and QCIF (176×144).

As with the JPEG standard, each color component picture is partitioned into 8x8 pixel blocks of picture samples. Instead of coding each block separately, H.261 groups 4 Y blocks, 1 U block, and 1 V block together into a unit called a macro block. The macro block is the basic unit for compression.

To compress each macro block, the H.261 standard allows the compressor to select from several compression options. The H.261 standard only specifies the decoding of each of the compression options. The method used to select the options is not standardized. This allows vendors to differentiate their products by providing methods with different cost-quality tradeoffs. A typical method used to compress H.261 is described below.

First, motion estimation is performed on each macro block. Since objects in the frame may be moving in different directions, each macro block is allowed to have a different motion vector. The motion vector is used as a displacement vector to fetch a macro block from the preceding frame to be used as a prediction. Motion estimation in H.261 is only performed relative to the preceding frame, and on full-pixel offsets up to a maximum of +/−15 in the horizontal and vertical directions. To improve the prediction, H.261 allows for an optional loop-filter to be applied to the prediction on a macro block basis.

Next, a decision must be made to code either the arithmetic difference between the offset prediction macro block and the current macro block or to code the current macro block from scratch. Since the arithmetic difference is usually small, coding the arithmetic difference results in higher compression.

An 8x8 DCT is applied to each block in either the arithmetic difference macro block or the current macro block. Instead of quantization matrices, H.261 uses one quantization scale for all frequency bins. Since the DC bin is the most important, it is separately quantized to a fixed 8-bit scale. Adjustment of the quantization scale on a per macro block basis is the primary method for controlling the quality and compression ratio in H.261.

The final stage of compression is the zig-zag scanning, run-length encoding and entropy coding. Unlike JPEG, H.261 specifies fixed Huffman coding tables for entropy coding. To decompress an H.261 frame inverse operations are performed in reverse order. Motion estimation is not necessary since the motion vectors are embedded in the compressed bit stream. The H.261 de-compressor simply applies the motion vector offset to retrieve the prediction, if necessary.

5. The MPEG Compression Algorithm

MPEG compression algorithms were developed to address the need for higher quality pictures and increased system flexibility, which are required by multi-media systems. Since it was developed later, MPEG was able to leverage the efforts behind the development of both the JPEG and H.261 algorithms.

As with H.261, only the YUV color component separation with the 4:2:0 sampling ratio is allowed by the MPEG standard. Unlike H.261, the frame size is not fixed although a 352×240 frame size is typically used. MPEG adopted the macro block of H.261 (4 Y blocks, 1 U block, and 1 V block) as the basic unit for compression. To compress each macro block, the MPEG standard allows the compressor to select from several compression options.

There are many more options available under the MPEG standard than under H.261. As with H.261, the MPEG standard only specifies the decoding of each of the compression options. The method used to select the options is not standardized, allowing vendors to differentiate their products by providing methods with different cost-quality trade-offs. A typical method used to compress MPEG is described below.

First, motion estimation is performed on each macro block. In addition to motion estimation from just the preceding frame, MPEG allows for prediction from frames in the past or future or a combination of a past and future frame (with restrictions).

Since objects in the frame may not be moving steadily from frame to frame, each macro block is allowed to have up to two motion vectors (one relative to a past frame and another relative to a future frame). Note that to allow for predictions from future frames, the extra frames must be buffered and the sequence coded out-of-order.

Motion estimation is also allowed over a greater range (up to +/−1023) and with half-pixel resolution. The loop-filter of H.261 is not included in MPEG because the half-pixel resolution motion vectors serve the same purpose.

Next, a four-way decision must be made. MPEG allows the prediction formed from the arithmetic difference between the current macro block and an offset macro block from a past frame, future frame, an average between past and future frame, to be coded; or to code the current macro block from scratch. A different decision can be made for each macro block subject to the restrictions that follow. Key frames (called Intra or I frames) which do not allow any predicted macro blocks are coded periodically to allow for random access into the video stream. Forward predicted frames (called P frames) allow macro blocks predicted from past P frames or I frames or macro blocks coded from scratch. I frames and P frames are used as past and future frames for Bi-directional predicted frames (called B frames). B frames allow for all four types of macro blocks.

An 8×8 DCT is applied to each block in either the arithmetic difference or current macro block. MPEG uses both matrices (like JPEG) and a scale factor (like H.261) for quantization. Since the DC bin is the most important, it is quantized to a fixed 8-bit scale.

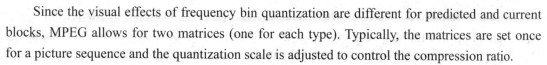
Since the visual effects of frequency bin quantization are different for predicted and current blocks, MPEG allows for two matrices (one for each type). Typically, the matrices are set once for a picture sequence and the quantization scale is adjusted to control the compression ratio.

The final stage of compression is the zig-zag scanning, run-length encoding and entropy coding. Like H.261, MPEG specifies fixed Huffman coding tables for entropy coding.

To decompress an MPEG frame each operation is performed in reverse except for motion estimation. Since the motion vectors and the decision are embedded in the compressed bit-stream, the MPEG de-compressor just needs to apply the motion vector offsets to retrieve the prediction from the past and/or future frames if necessary.

New Words and Expressions

necessity	*n.*	必要性，需要，必需品
video compression standards		视频压缩标准
Joint Photographic Experts Group (JPEG)		联合图像专家组
Motion Picture Experts Group (MPEG)		运动图像专家组
video conferencing		视频会议
motion estimation		运动估值
amplitude	*n.*	幅度
frame	*n.*	帧
luminance	*n.*	亮度
still	*adj.*	静止的
discrete cosine transform		离散余弦变换
entropy coding		熵编码
quantization	*n.*	量化
successive	*adj.*	连续的
encapsulate	*v.*	封装
matrices (pl. of matrix)	*n.*	矩阵

Notes

1. The increasing demand to incorporate video data into telecommunications services, the corporate environment, the entertainment industry, and even at home has made digital video technology a necessity.

译文：越来越多的市场需求导致视频数据与电信业务的结合，无论在办公室、娱乐场所，还是家庭中，数字视频技术都变得越来越必不可少。

本句中，"telecommunications services, the corporate environment, the entertainment industry"等都是"incorporate… into"的介词宾语。"necessity"的原意是"必需品"，在这里根据上下文译为"必需的技术"。

2. Each of these standards is well suited for particular applications: JPEG for still image compression, H.261 for video conferencing, and MPEG for high-quality, multimedia systems.

译文：每一种标准都有其特定的用途：JPEG 适用于静止图像压缩，H.261 适用于视频会议，而 MPEG 则适用于高质量的多媒体系统。

3. The basic compression scheme for all three standards can be summarized as follows: divide the picture into 8x8 blocks, determine relevant picture information, discard redundant or insignificant information, and encode relevant picture information with the least number of bits.

译文：这 3 种标准的基本压缩方案总结如下：先将图像分为 8×8 的块，然后找出相关的图像信息，去除冗余以及不重要的信息，并用最少的比特数对相关图像信息进行编码。

4. Since the mapping is from lower to higher frequencies in the horizontal and vertical directions, zig-zag scanning of the resulting 2D frequency bins clusters packets of picture information from low to high frequencies into a 1D stream of bins.

译文：由于映射在水平方向和垂直方向都是从低频到高频排列的，因此，"之"字形的扫描将从低频向高频排列的图像二维频率信息簇转换为一维数据流。

5. This takes advantage of the fact that the human eye is less sensitive to high frequency visual noise, but is more sensitive to lower frequency noise, manifesting itself in blocking artifacts.

译文：这是利用了人眼的特点，方块效应证实，人眼对高频视觉噪声不敏感，而对低频噪声比较敏感。

Exercises

Ⅰ. Comprehension questions.

1. What is the motivation of developing Video Compression standards?

2. What is the three DCT-based Video Compression standards?

3. Please introduce the common functions to all three standards.

4. Why is Zig-Zag scanning used?

5. What is the advantage of motion estimation?

6. Is JPEG compression algorithm used only in still images?

7. What is the primary method for controlling the quality and compression ratio in JPEG?

Ⅱ. Translate the following paragraph into Chinese.

Quantization is the primary source of data loss in DCT based image compression algorithms. Quantization reduces the amount of information required to represent the frequency bins by converting amplitudes that fall in certain ranges to one in a set of quantization levels. For simplicity, all the standard image compression algorithms use linear quantization where the step size quantization levels are constant.

Quantization in the frequency domain has many advantages over directly quantizing the pixel values. Quantization of the pixel values results in a visual artifact called "contour" distortion where small changes in amplitude in a gradient area cause step-sized changes in the reconstructed amplitude. Except for the DC bin, quantization error for each of the frequency bins average out to zero over the 8×8 block.

Lesson Six   Technology of Modern Communication

Text A   Bluetooth

Bluetooth wireless technology is a short-range communications technology intended to replace the cables connecting portable and fixed devices while maintaining high levels of security.[1] The key features of Bluetooth technology are robustness, low power, and low cost. The Bluetooth specification defines a uniform structure for a wide range of devices to connect and communicate with each other.

Bluetooth technology has achieved global acceptance such that any Bluetooth enabled device, almost everywhere in the world, can connect to other Bluetooth enabled devices in proximity. Bluetooth enabled electronic devices connect and communicate wirelessly through short-range, ad hoc networks known as piconets. Each device can simultaneously communicate with up to seven other devices within a single piconet.[2] Each device can also belong to several piconets simultaneously. Piconets are established dynamically and automatically as Bluetooth enabled devices enter and leave radio proximity.

A fundamental Bluetooth wireless technology strength is the ability to simultaneously handle both data and voice transmissions. This enables users to enjoy variety of innovative solutions such as a hands-free headset for voice calls, printing and fax capabilities, and synchronizing PDA, laptop, and mobile phone applications to name a few.

1. Core System

The Bluetooth core system, defined by Bluetooth specification, is a common service layer protocol which covers four lower layers in seven layer protocol. Service Discovery Protocol (SDP) and the overall profile requirements are defined by Generic Access Profile (GAP).[3] A complete Bluetooth application requires a number of additional services and higher layer protocols that are defined in the Bluetooth specification.

The lowest three layers are sometimes grouped into a subsystem known as the Bluetooth controller. This is a common implementation involving a standard physical communications interface between the Bluetooth controller and remainder of the Bluetooth system including the L2CAP, service layers and higher layers (known as the Bluetooth host). Although this interface is optional, the architecture is designed to allow for its existence and characteristics. The Bluetooth specification enables interoperability between independent Bluetooth enabled systems by defining the protocol messages exchanged between equivalent layers, and also interoperability between independent Bluetooth sub-systems by defining a common interface between Bluetooth controllers and Bluetooth hosts.

A number of functional blocks are shown and the path of services and data between these. The functional blocks shown in the diagram are informative; in general the Bluetooth specification does not define the details of implementations except where this is required for interoperability.

Standard interactions are defined for all inter-device operation, where Bluetooth devices exchange protocol signaling according to the Bluetooth specification. The Bluetooth core system protocols are the radio (RF) protocol, link control (LC) protocol, link manager (LM) protocol and logical link control and adaptation protocol (L2CAP), all of which are fully defined in subsequent parts of the Bluetooth specification.[4] In addition, the service discovery protocol (SDP) is a service layer protocol required by all Bluetooth applications.

The Bluetooth core system offers services through a number of service access points that are shown in the diagram as ellipses. These services consist of the basic primitives that control the Bluetooth core system. The services can be split into three types. There are device control services that modify the behavior and modes of a Bluetooth device, transport control services that create, modify and release traffic bearers (channels and links), and data services that are used to submit data for transmission over traffic bearers.[5] It is common to consider the first two as belonging to the C-plane and the last as belonging to the U-plane.

A service interface to the Bluetooth controller sub-system is defined such that the Bluetooth controller may be considered a standard part. In this configuration the Bluetooth controller operates the lowest three layers and the L2CAP layer is contained with the rest of the Bluetooth application in a host system. The standard interface is called the host to controller interface (HCI). Implementation of this standard service interface is optional.

As the Bluetooth architecture is defined with the possibility of a separate host and controller communicating through an HCI, a number of general assumptions are made. The Bluetooth controller is assumed to have limited data buffering capabilities in comparison with the host. Therefore the L2CAP layer is expected to carry out some simple resource management when submitting L2CAP PDUs to the controller for transport to a peer device. This includes segmentation of L2CAP SDUs into more manageable PDUs and then the fragmentation of PDUs into start and continuation packets of a size suitable for the controller buffers, and management of the use of controller buffers to ensure availability for channels with quality of service (QoS) commitments.

The baseband layer provides the basic ARQ protocol in Bluetooth technology. The L2CAP layer can optionally provide a further error detection and retransmission to the L2CAP PDUs. This feature is recommended for applications with requirements for a low probability of undetected errors in the user data. A further optional feature of L2CAP is a window-based flow control that can be used to manage buffer allocation in the receiving device. Both of these optional features augment the QoS performance in certain scenarios.

Although these assumptions may not be required for embedded Bluetooth technology implementations that combine all layers in a single system, the general architectural and QoS models are defined with these assumptions in mind, in effect a lowest common denominator.[6]

Automated conformance testing of implementations of the Bluetooth core system is required. This is achieved by allowing the tester to control the implementation through the RF interface, which is common to all Bluetooth systems, and through the test control interface (TCI), which is only required for conformance testing.

The tester uses exchanges with the implementation under test (IUT) through the RF interface to ensure the correct responses to requests from remote devices. The tester controls the IUT through the TCI to cause the IUT to originate exchanges through the RF interface so that these can also be verified as conformant.

The TCI uses a different command-set (service interface) for the testing of each architectural layer and protocol. A subset of the HCI command-set issued as the TCI service interface for each of the layers and protocols within the Bluetooth controller subsystem. A separate service interface is used for testing the L2CAP layer and protocol. As an L2CAP service interface is not defined in the Bluetooth core specification it is defined separately in the TCI specification. Implementation of the L2CAP service interface is only required for conformance testing.

2. Why Choose Bluetooth Wireless Technology

Bluetooth wireless technology is the simple choice for convenient, wire-free, and short-range communication between devices. It is a globally available standard that wirelessly connects mobile phones, portable computers, cars, stereo headsets, MP3 players, and more. Thanks to the unique concept of "profiles", Bluetooth enabled products do not need to install driver software. The technology is now available in its fourth version of the specification and continues to develop, building on its inherent strengths — small-form factor radio, low power, low cost, built-in security, robustness, ease-of-use, and ad hoc networking abilities.[7] Bluetooth wireless technology is the leading and only proven short-range wireless technology on the market today shipping over five million units every week with an installed base of over 500 million units at the end of 2005.

3. Globally Available

The Bluetooth wireless technology specification is available free-of-charge to our member companies around the globe. Manufacturers from many industries are busy implementing the technology in their products to reduce the clutter of wires, make seamless connections, stream stereo audio, transfer data or carry voice communications. Bluetooth technology operates in the 2.4 GHz, one of the unlicensed industrial, scientific, medical (ISM) radio bands. As such, there is no cost for the use of Bluetooth technology. While you must subscribe to a cellular provider to use GSM or CDMA, with Bluetooth technology there is no cost associated with the use beyond the cost of your device.

4. Range of Devices

Bluetooth technology is available in an unprecedented range of applications from mobile phones to automobiles to medical devices for use by consumers, industrial markets, enterprises, and more. The low power consumption, small size and low cost of the chipset solution enables Bluetooth technology to be used in the tiniest of devices. Have a look at the wide range products made available by our members in the Bluetooth product directory and the component product listing.

5. Ease of Use

Bluetooth technology is an ad hoc technology that requires no fixed infrastructure and is simple to install and set up. You don't need wires to get connected. The process for a new user is easy – you get a Bluetooth branded product, check the profiles available and connect it to another Bluetooth device with the same profiles. The subsequent PIN[8] code process is as easy as when you identify yourself at the ATM machine. When out-and-about, you carry your personal area network (PAN) with you and can even connect to others.

6. Globally Accepted Specification

Bluetooth wireless technology is the most widely supported, versatile, and secure wireless standard on the market today. The globally available qualification program tests member products as to their accordance with the standard. Since the first release of the Bluetooth specification in 1999, over 4000 companies have become members in the Bluetooth Special Interest Group (SIG). Meanwhile, the number of Bluetooth products on the market is multiplying rapidly. Volumes have doubled for the fourth consecutive year and are likely to reach an installed base of 500 million units by the close of 2005.

7. Secure Connections

From the start, Bluetooth technology was designed with security needs in mind. Since it is globally available in the open 2.4 GHz ISM band, robustness was built in from the beginning. With adaptive frequency hopping (AFH), the signal "hops" and thus limits interference from other signals. Further, Bluetooth technology has built-in security such as 128bit encryption and PIN code authentication. When Bluetooth products identify themselves, they use the PIN code the first time they connect. Once connected, always securely connected.

New Words and Expressions

proximity	*n.*	接近的，邻近
ad hoc		(拉丁语)特别的；变通的；特殊的自组织 对等式多跳移动通信网络
laptop		膝上型轻便计算机
ellipse	*n.*	椭圆
RF Radio Frequency		射频
PDU Protocol Data Unit		协议数据单元
peer	*adj.*	对等的
fragmentation	*n.*	分区输入程序；碎片
commitment	*n.*	行为；委托；义务
baseband	*n.*	基带
stereo headsets		立体声耳机
scenario	*n.*	剧情说明书，电影剧本

denominator	n.	[数]分母；共同的要素，共同的性质
conformance	n.	相似；相符；一致
clutter	n.	混乱
seamless	adj.	无缝的
chipset	n.	[计]芯片集
encryption	n.	加密
authentication	n.	认证

Notes

1. Bluetooth wireless technology is a short-range communications technology intended to replace the cables connecting portable and fixed devices while maintaining high levels of security.

译文：蓝牙无线技术是一种小范围无线通信技术，旨在保持高安全级的基础上，在便携式设备与固定设备之间实现无线连接。

2. Piconet：微微网，是由采用蓝牙技术的设备以特定方式组成的网络。微微网的建立以两台设备(如便携式计算机和蜂窝电话)的连接开始，最多由 8 台设备构成。所有的蓝牙设备都是对等的，以同样的方式工作。然而，当一个微微网建立时，只有一台为主设备，其他均为从设备，而且在一个微微网存在期间将一直维持此状况。所有设备都具有由主设备参数(clock 和 BD_ADDR)定义的同样的物理信道。

3. The Bluetooth core system, defined by Bluetooth specification, is a common service layer protocol which covers four lower layers in seven layer protocol. Service Discovery Protocol (SDP) and the overall profile requirements are defined by Generic Access Profile (GAP).

译文：蓝牙规范将蓝牙核心系统定义为一个普通的服务层协议，这个服务层覆盖了七层协议的下四层，通用访问应用(GAP)定义了服务发现层协议(SDP)和所需要的通用协议子集。

(1) SDP: Service Discovery Protocol 服务发现协议，蓝牙中定义的一个协议，主要用来提供一个方式，通过它能够让应用程序发现和使用有关服务，并且能够知晓这些服务的特点。

(2) GAP: Generic Access Profile 通用访问应用，该应用描述了一种设备发现和访问另外一种设备的机制，而此时，这两种设备不共享普通的应用程序。

4. The Bluetooth core system protocols are the radio (RF) protocol, link control (LC) protocol, link manager (LM) protocol and logical link control and adaptation protocol (L2CAP), all of which are fully defined in subsequent parts of the Bluetooth specification.

译文：蓝牙核心系统协议包括射频协议、链路控制协议、连接管理协议、逻辑链路控制应用协议，所有这些协议都是由蓝牙规范定义的。

(1) LC: Link Control 链路控制，链接控制器管理对其他蓝牙设备的链接。它是个低层的基带协议管理者。

(2) LM: Link Manager 链路管理，链路管理软件实体负责管理建立链接、鉴定、链路配置，以及实现其他协议等事务。

(3) L2CAP: Logical Link Control and Adaptation Protocol 逻辑信道控制和适配协议。该协议支持高层协议多路复用技术，包括分割和重组装技术，以及保证传达服务信息的质量。

5. There are device control services that modify the behavior and modes of a Bluetooth device, transport control services that create, modify and release traffic bearers (channels and links), and data services that are used to submit data for transmission over traffic bearers.

译文：设备控制服务用于改善蓝牙设备的性能和模式，传输控制服务用于创建、修改、释放(信道和链路上的)承载业务，数据服务则为基于承载业务的传输提供数据。

6. Although these assumptions may not be required for embedded Bluetooth technology implementations that combine all layers in a single system, the general architectural and **QoS** models are defined with these assumptions in mind, in effect a lowest common denominator.

译文：对于将所有层都组合成一个单一系统的嵌入式蓝牙设备来说，这样的假设是不需要的，但是，简单结构的系统以及 **QoS** 模型的定义都是在考虑这些假设的前提下确定的，而且这样的系统更具有普遍性。

QoS: Quality of Service 服务质量。

7. The technology is now available in its fourth version of the specification and continues to develop, building on its inherent strengths — small-form factor radio, low power, low cost, built-in security, robustness, ease-of-use, and ad hoc networking abilities.

译文：第 4 版的蓝牙规范已经定义了该技术，鉴于其与生俱来的优点，如小尺寸、低功耗、低价格、高安全、强生命力、操作简单、具备 ad hoc 网络能力等，该技术发展前景广阔。

8. PIN: Personal Identification Number 个人识别码。蓝牙中的 PIN 用来鉴定以前没有交换过链接关键字(link key)的两个设备。通过交换 PIN，设备之间就创建了相互信任的关系。在配对(pairing)过程中使用的 PIN 用来生成初始链接，以便进一步的鉴定。

Exercises

Ⅰ. **Translate the following English sentences into Chinese.**

1. Bluetooth SIG members are busy developing headsets, mobile phones, cars, and computers with the technology integrated, and many more are also bringing new ideas to life by implementing Bluetooth technology in new use cases and astounding the world with their new designs.

2. Bluetooth enabled hands-free systems in automobiles allow drivers to make calls directly

through the speaker systems while keeping their Bluetooth mobile phone anywhere in the vehicle, both hands on the wheel, and both eyes on the road.

3. Symantec said the latest worm attempts to use Bluetooth connections to spread by searching for other Bluetooth-using devices that will accept requests for a connection when the computer is restarted.

4. The link controller is responsible for the encoding and decoding of Bluetooth packets from the data payload and parameters related to the physical channel, logical transport and logical link.

5. These QoS settings may be used to indicate, for example, that the data is isochronous and therefore has a limited lifetime after which it becomes invalid, that the data should be delivered within a given time period, or that the data is reliable and should be delivered without error, however long this takes.

II. Translate the following sentences into English.

1. 有了蓝牙技术，存储于手机中的信息可以在电视机上显示出来，也可以将其中的声音信息数据进行转换，以便在个人计算机上聆听。

2. 蓝牙技术的传输速率设计为 1MHz，以时分方式进行全双工通信，其基带协议是电路交换和分组交换的组合。

3. 透过芯片上的无线接收器，配有蓝牙技术的电子产品能够在十公尺的距离内彼此相通，传输速度可以达到每秒钟 1 兆字节。

4. 蓝牙，是 1998 年推出的一种新的无线传输方式，实际上就是取代数据电缆的短距离无线通信技术，通过低带宽电波实现点对点，或点对多点连接之间的信息交流。

5. 红外传输是一种点对点的传输方式，无线，不能离得太远，要对准方向，且中间不能有障碍物，也就是不能穿墙而过，几乎无法控制信息传输的进度。

Text B   "Chinese standard" aims at international market

In 2004, the TD-SCDMA standards for the 3-generation (3G) mobile communications network initiated by China and ratified by the International Telecommunication Union, has become a focus of the global telecom industry, reported People Daily.[1] Both telecom operators and telecom equipment manufacturers have paid growing attentions to the "Chinese standard" for 3G. Almost all-mobile communication equipment suppliers in the world are putting more investment and efforts in R&D for the "Chinese standard".

The Chinese government has been making efforts to push forward the "Chinese standard" since the beginning of the year with the pace of R&D and industrialization becoming apparently quickened.[2] The signing of supply contract for the field test of 3G and emergence of TD-SCDMA cellular phone are proof of such progresses.

1. Technical advantages of the Chinese standard gradually come to show

In response to the questions for the so-called level problems of the "Chinese standard", Zhang Xinsheng, Vice Director of Science and Technology Department, Ministry of Information

Industry is of opinion that the underlying reason for having drawn the world's attention so far lies in the technological advantages of the TD-SCDMA.

The world mobile communication industry unanimously agrees that TD-SCDMA can serve as one of the standards for 3G after intensive researches and discussions on it. The TD-SCDMA is more extensively recognized following the auction of 3G frequencies in Europe.

At present, the "Chinese standard" for 3G has become a highlight of the world. Japan, Europe and US are all paying attention to it. Each and every major telecom corporation in the world is doing research related to the "Chinese standard". The TD-SCDMA has been recognized by the industry even though some problems still need further research. TD-SCDMA can be connected with the current telecom system, and with its features of intelligent antenna, high application rate of frequency, the TD-SCDMA's technical advantages are coming to show gradually.[3]

2. TD-SCDMA changes world's orientation of research for 3G

Zhang holds that the TD-SCDMA standard has changed the world's orientation of research for 3G in the following aspects.

1. The "Chinese Standard" for 3G is the only 3G standard based on intelligent antenna.[4] China is leading the world in this field.

2. Development of TD-SCDMA pushes the world telecom industry to make further research and discussion for the software wireless.[5] The 3G will take on a new look if software wireless is enabled.

3. The development of TD-SCDMA makes people pay more attention to the development trend of IP.

The "Chinese standard" makes the 3G research concentrate on the above three aspects, the biggest contribution of TD-SCDMA. If a breakthrough can be made in the above three aspects, the world wireless communication will take on a new look.

3. China is capable of doing fundamental researches

According to Zhang, China's economic growth as well as development of information industry have created conditions for the development of an innovative telecom system. Chinese enterprises have seen great improvements in terms of economic strength, personnel quality and ability of industrialization. Especially, the overall strength-improvement of the Chinese enterprises in the industrial chain has created conditions for the growth of TD-SCDMA. Aside from the development of core network, terminals and the most important cell site system, the development of a new telecom system still involves design of chip and components production. China has now acquired basic abilities for doing fundamental researches and development even though it is still backward in some areas as compared with foreign advanced level. This ability is a key factor that enables continuous advancement of TD-SCDMA. Chinese enterprises are competent in committing large-scale investment because they have strong R&D strength. Chinese government has been offering strong support to the "Chinese standard", but the major investment is put in by enterprises. Chinese enterprises, especially the Datang group, has put large amount of money into the development of the "Chinese standard". Without such a long-term investment, rapid growth of the TD-SCDMA standard is unimaginable.

4. The "Chinese standard" targets at the world market

Chinese government will develop the "Chinese standard" as a strategic industry. It will actively call for the domestic enterprises' participation in the industrialization of the TD-SCDMA standard. On the other hand it welcomes foreign enterprises to take part in the development of the TD-SCDMA standard, said Zhang.

Our target is not limited to the domestic market. We shall go overseas into the world market. By fully exploiting the synergy advantage in the manufacturing and operation fields, we will bend on pushing the commercialization process of the 3G "Chinese standard ahead."[6]

New Words and Expressions

ratify	*v.*	正式生效，批准
cellular phone		移动电话
IP=Internet Protocol	*Abbr.*	互联网通信协议
auction	*n.*	拍卖；拍卖人
terminal	*n.*	终端(机)
synergy	*n.*	(两公司合并后产生的)增效作用，增加生产力作用

Notes

1. In 2004, the TD-SCDMA standard for the 3-generation (3G) mobile communications network initiated by China and ratified by the International Telecommunication Union, has become a focus of the global telecom industry, reported People Daily.

译文：《人民日报》报道，2004 年，中国率先提出第三代移动通信网络标准——TD-SCDMA 标准，并由国际电信协会批准通过，该标准也因此成为全球电信产业关注的焦点。

2. The Chinese government has been making efforts to push forward the "Chinese standard" since the beginning of the year with the pace of R&D and industrialization becoming apparently quickened.

译文：鉴于研发速度与工业化节奏的明显加快，自年初以来，中国政府开始致力于推动"中国标准"的制订和完善。

3. TD-SCDMA can be connected with the current telecom system, and with its features of intelligent antenna, high application rate of frequency, the TD-SCDMA's technical advantages are coming to show gradually.

译文：TD-SCDMA 可以与目前的电信系统相连，加上智能天线的使用和高频谱利用率，

TD-SCDMA 的技术优势逐渐显露。

4. intelligent antenna：智能天线，是一种安装在基站现场的双向天线，通过一组带有可编程电子相位关系的固定天线单元获取方向特性，并可以同时获取基站和移动台之间各个链路的方向特性。智能天线的原理是将无线电的信号导向具体方向，产生空间定向波束，使天线主波束对准用户信号到达方向 DOA(Direction of Arrival)，旁瓣或零陷对准干扰信号到达方向，达到充分高效利用移动用户信号并删除或抑制干扰信号的目的。同时，智能天线技术利用各个移动用户间信号空间特征的差异，通过阵列天线技术在同一信道上接收和发射多个移动用户信号而不发生相互干扰，使无线电频谱的利用和信号的传输更为有效。在不增加系统复杂度的情况下，使用智能天线可满足服务质量和网络扩容的需要。

5. software wireless：软件无线电，是指采用通用的硬件平台，通过软件编程来实现各种功能。"通用硬件平台"实际上是一台功能强大的袖珍型电子计算机，过去它靠硬件实现的任务，现在利用软件都可完成。例如，灌进一组电视软件，它就成了电视机；灌进收音软件，它就成了收音机；灌进无线电通信软件，它就成了无线电台。将各种各样的无线电软件灌进去，就成了一种多模式终端。

6. By fully exploiting the synergy advantage in the manufacturing and operation fields, we will bend on pushing the commercialization process of the 3G "Chinese standard" ahead.

译文：在全面发掘生产与销售领域的综合优势后，我们将致力于推动 3G "中国标准"的商业化进程。

Exercises

Ⅰ. Translate the following sentences into Chinese.

1. The most likely scenario for TD-SCDMA is it may serve as an add-on technology to some operators' WCDMA networks, or as a stand-alone technology for minor operators to deploy networks.

2. It is believed that TD-SCDMA is much further behind in its development than publicly claimed by its proponents, and that many of its Western-based backers are only supporting the technology to gain favour with the Chinese Government.

3. TD-SCDMA may ultimately be deployed by an operator in China, but it will be due to necessity, not choice, and its performance will likely pale in comparison with its claimed performance.

4. TD-SCDMA-based systems satisfy all these requirements and let operators benefit from a smooth and low risk migration from 2G to 3G, rapid time to market for 3G services and an increase of their systems' capacity.

5. Time Division Multiple Access (TDMA) in combination with Time Division Duplex (TDD) significantly improves network performance by allowing radio resources to process network traffic in both directions, per uplink and downlink.

II. Translate the following sentences into English.

1. 中兴通信(ZTE)已经成为中国短消息市场中最大的供应商之一，占有将近一半的新建短消息市场，并基于该短消息平台开展了信息点播、移动银行、移动证券、Web 订制等丰富的业务。

2. 由于窄带通信采用的带宽只有几十千赫，只需要使用一个具有相同发射频率及足够大功率的发射机就可以非常容易地干扰对方的通信。

3. 如果码序列在传输中有传输时延，在接收端便不能解调恢复出原始数据，需要在接收端通过人工的时延来补偿传输及数字信号处理造成的时延。

4. GPS 是一个由 24 颗绕地球运转的卫星组成的天线导航系统，它的优势在于全球覆盖，系统时钟精度高，不易受电磁暴、低频干扰源的影响。

5. 1995 年，第一个 CDMA 商用系统运行之后，CDMA 技术理论上的诸多优势在实践中得到了检验，从而在北美、南美和亚洲等地得到了迅速推广和应用。

Lesson Seven　Wireless Sensor Networks

Text A　Sensor Networks: Evolution, Opportunities, and Challenges (I)

1. Introduction

Networked microsensors technology is a key technology for the future. In September 1999, *Business Week* heralded it as one of the 21 most important technologies for the 21st century. Cheap, smart devices with multiple onboard sensors, networked through wireless links and the Internet and deployed in large numbers, provide unprecedented opportunities for instrumenting and controlling homes, cities, and the environment. In addition, networked microsensors provide the technology for a broad spectrum of systems in the defense arena, generating new capabilities for reconnaissance and surveillance as well as other tactical applications.

Smart disposable microsensors can be deployed on the ground, in the air, under water, on bodies, in vehicles, and inside buildings. A system of networked sensors can detect and track threats (e.g., winged and wheeled vehicles, personnel, chemical and biological agents) and be used for weapon targeting and area denial. Each sensor node will have embedded processing capability, and will potentially have multiple onboard sensors, operating in the acoustic, seismic, infrared (IR), and magnetic modes, as well as imagers and microradars. Also onboard will be storage, wireless links to neighboring nodes, and location and positioning knowledge through the global positioning system (GPS) or local positioning algorithms.

Networked microsensors belong to the general family of sensor networks that use multiple distributed sensors to collect information on entities of interest. Table 1 summarizes the range of possible attributes in general sensor networks.

Table 1　Attributes of Sensor Networks

Sensors	*Size*: small (e.g., micro-electro mechanical systems (MEMS)), large (e.g., radars, satellites) *Number*: small, large *Type*: passive (e.g., acoustic, seismic, video, IR, magnetic), active (e.g., radar, ladar) *Composition or mix*: homogeneous (same types of sensors), heterogeneous (different types of sensors) *Spatial coverage*: dense, sparse *Deployment*: fixed and planned (e.g., factory networks), ad hoc (e.g., air-dropped) *Dynamics*: stationary (e.g., seismic sensors), mobile (e.g., on robot vehicles)
Sensing entities of interest	*Extent*: distributed (e.g., environmental monitoring), localized (e.g., target tracking) *Mobility*: static, dynamic *Nature*: cooperative (e.g., air traffic control), non-cooperative (e.g., military targets)
Operating environment	Benign (factory floor), adverse (battlefield)
Communication	*Networking*: wired, wireless *Bandwidth*: high, low
Processing architecture	Centralized (all data sent to central site), distributed (located at sensor or other sites), hybrid
Energy availability	Constrained (e.g., in small sensors), unconstrained (e.g., in large sensors)

Current and potential applications of sensor networks include: military sensing, physical security, air traffic control, traffic surveillance, video surveillance, industrial and manufacturing automation, distributed robotics, environment monitoring, and building and structures monitoring. The sensors in these applications may be small or large, and the networks may be wired or wireless. However, ubiquitous wireless networks of microsensors probably offer the most potential in changing the world of sensing.

While sensor networks for various applications may be quite different, they share common technical issues. This paper will present a history of research in sensor networks (Section II), technology trends (Section III), new applications (Section IV), research issues and hard problems (Section V), and some examples of research results (Section VI).

2. History of Research in Sensor Networks

The development of sensor networks requires technologies from three different research areas: sensing, communication, and computing (including hardware, software, and algorithms). Thus, combined and separate advancements in each of these areas have driven research in sensor networks. Examples of early sensor networks include the radar networks used in air traffic control. The national power grid, with its many sensors, can be viewed as one large sensor network. These systems were developed with specialized computers and communication capabilities, and before the term "sensor networks" came into vogue.

1) Early Research on Military Sensor Networks

As with many technologies, defense applications have been a driver for research and development in sensor networks. During the Cold War, the Sound Surveillance System (SOSUS), a system of acoustic sensors (hydrophones) on the ocean bottom, was deployed at strategic locations to detect and track quiet Soviet submarines. Over the years, other more sophisticated acoustic networks have been developed for submarine surveillance. SOSUS is now used by the National Oceanographic and Atmospheric Administration (NOAA) for monitoring events in the ocean, e.g., seismic and animal activity. Also during the Cold War, networks of air defense radars were developed and deployed to defend the continental United States and Canada. This air defense system has evolved over the years to include aerostats as sensors and Airborne Warning And Control System (AWACS) planes, and is also used for drug interdiction.

These sensor networks generally adopt a hierarchical processing structure where processing occurs at consecutive levels until the information about events of interest reaches the user. In many cases, human operators play a key role in the system. Even though research was focused on satisfying mission needs, e.g., acoustic signal processing and interpretation, tracking, and fusion, it provided some key processing technologies for modern sensor networks.[1]

2) Distributed Sensor Networks Program at the Defense Advanced Research Projects Agency

Modern research on sensor networks started around 1980 with the Distributed Sensor Networks (DSN) program at the Defense Advanced Research Projects Agency (DARPA). By this time, the Arpanet (predecessor of the Internet) had been operational for a number of years, with about 200 hosts at universities and research institutes. R. Kahn, who was coinventor of the TCP/IP protocols and played a key role in developing the Internet, was director of the Information Processing Techniques Office (IPTO) at DARPA. He wanted to know whether the Arpanet approach for communication could be extended to sensor networks. The network was assumed to have many spatially distributed low-cost sensing nodes that collaborate with each other but operate autonomously, with information being routed to whichever node can best use the information.

It was an ambitious program given the state of the art. This was the time before personal computers and workstations; processing was done mostly on minicomputers such as PDP-11 and VAX machines running Unix and VMS. Modems were operating at 300 to 9600 Bd, and Ethernet was just becoming popular.

Technology components for a DSN were identified in a Distributed Sensor Nets workshop in 1978. These included sensors (acoustic), communication (high-level protocols that link processes working on a common application in a resource-sharing network), processing techniques and algorithms (including self-location algorithms for sensors), and distributed software (dynamically modifiable distributed systems and language design). Since DARPA was sponsoring much artificial intelligence (AI) research at the time, the workshop also included talks on the use of AI for understanding signals and assessing situations, as well as various distributed problem-solving techniques. Since very few technology components were available off the shelf, the resulting DSN program had to address distributed computing support, signal processing, tracking, and test beds. Distributed acoustic tracking was chosen as the target problem for demonstration.

Researchers at Carnegie Mellon University (CMU), Pittsburgh, PA, focused on providing a network operating system that allows flexible, transparent access to distributed resources needed for a fault-tolerant DSN. They developed a communication-oriented operating system called Accent, whose primitives support transparent networking, system reconfiguration, and rebinding. Accent evolved into the Mach operating system, which found considerable commercial acceptance. Other efforts at CMU included protocols for network inter-process communication to support dynamic rebinding of active communicating computations, an interface specification language for building distributed system software, and a system for dynamic load balancing and fault reconfiguration of DSN software.[2] All this was demonstrated in an indoor test bed with signal sources, acoustic sensors, and VAX computers connected by Ethernet.

Researchers at the Massachusetts Institute of Technology (MIT), Cambridge, focused on knowledge-based signal processing techniques for tracking helicopters using a distributed array of acoustic microphones by means of signal abstractions and matching techniques. Signal abstractions view signals as consisting of multiple levels, with higher levels of abstraction (e.g., peaks) obtained by suppressing detailed information in lower levels (e.g., spectrum). They provide a conceptual framework for thinking about signal processing systems that resemble what people use when interactively processing and interpreting real-world signals. By incorporating human heuristics, this approach was designed for high signal-to-noise ratio situations where models are lacking. In addition, MIT also developed the Signal Processing Language and Interactive Computing Environment (SPLICE) for DSN data analysis and algorithm development, and Pitch Director's Assistant for interactively estimating fundamental frequency using domain knowledge.

Moving up the processing chain, tracking multiple targets in a distributed environment is significantly more difficult than centralized tracking. The association of measurements to tracks and estimation of target states (position and velocity) given associations have to be distributed over the sensor nodes. In the 1980s, Advanced Decision Systems (ADS), Mountain View, CA, developed a multiple-hypothesis tracking algorithm to deal with difficult situations involving high target density, missing detections, and false alarms, and decomposed the algorithm for distributed implementation. Multiple-hypothesis tracking is now a standard approach for difficult tracking problems.

For demonstration, MIT Lincoln Laboratory developed the real-time test bed for acoustic tracking of low-flying aircraft. The sensors were acoustic arrays (nine microphones arranged in three concentric triangles with the largest being 6 m across). A PDP11/34 computer and an array processor processed the acoustic signals. The nodal computer (for target tracking) consists of three MC68000 processors with 256-kB memory and 512-kB shared memory, and a custom operating system. Communication was by Ethernet and microwave radio. Fig. 1 (extracted from) shows the acoustic array (nine white microphones), the mobile vehicle node with an acoustically quiet generator in the back, and the equipment rack with the acoustic/tracking node and gateway node in the vehicle. Note the size of the system and that practically all components in the network were custom built. That was the state of the art in the early 1980s. The DSN test bed was demonstrated with low-flying aircraft, which was successfully tracked with acoustic sensors as well as TV cameras. The tracking algorithm was fairly sophisticated, since the acoustic propagation delay is significant relative to the speed of the aircraft.

Another test bed in the DSN program was the distributed vehicle monitoring test bed at the University of Massachusetts, Amherst. This was a research tool for empirically investigating distributed problem solving in networks. The distributed knowledge-based problem solving approach used a functionally accurate, cooperative architecture consisting of a network of Hearsay-II nodes (blackboard architecture with knowledge sources). Different local node control approaches were explored.

3) Military Sensor Networks in the 1980s and 1990s

Even though early researchers on sensor networks had in mind large numbers of small sensors, the technology for small sensors was not quite ready. However, planners of military systems quickly recognized the benefits of sensor networks, which become a crucial component of network-centric warfare. In platform-centric warfare, platforms "own" specific weapons, which in turn own sensors in a fairly rigid architecture. In other words, sensors and weapons are mounted with and controlled by separate platforms that operate independently. In network-centric warfare, sensors do not necessarily belong to weapons or platforms. Instead, they collaborate with each other over a communication network, and information is sent to the appropriate "shooters." Sensor networks can improve detection and tracking performance through multiple observations, geometric and phenomenological diversity, extended detection range, and faster response time.[3] Also, the development cost is lower by exploiting commercial network technology and common network interfaces.

An example of network-centric warfare is the Cooperative Engagement Capability (CEC) developed by the U.S. Navy. This system consists of multiple radars collecting data on air targets. Measurements are associated by a processing node "with reporting responsibility" and shared with other nodes that process all measurements of interest. Since all nodes have access to essentially the same information, a "common operating picture" essential for consistent military operations is obtained. Other military sensor networks include acoustic sensor arrays for antisubmarine warfare such as the Fixed Distributed System (FDS) and the Advanced Deployable System (ADS), and unattended ground sensors (UGS) such as the Remote Battlefield Sensor System (REMBASS) and the Tactical Remote Sensor System (TRSS).

4) Sensor Network Research in the 21st Century

Recent advances in computing and communication have caused a significant shift in sensor network research and brought it closer to achieving the original vision. Small and inexpensive sensors based upon microelectro-mechanical system (MEMS) technology, wireless networking, and inexpensive low-power processors allow the deployment of wireless ad hoc networks for various applications.[4] Again, DARPA started a research program on sensor networks to leverage the latest technological advances.

The recently concluded DARPA Sensor Information Technology (SensIT) program pursued two key re-search and development thrusts. First, it developed new networking techniques. In the battlefield context, these sensor devices or nodes should be ready for rapid deployment, in an adhoc fashion, and in highly dynamic environments. Today's networking techniques, developed for voice and data and relying on a fixed infrastructure, will not suffice for battlefield use. Thus, the program developed new networking techniques suitable for highly dynamic adhoc environments. The second thrust was networked information processing, i.e., how to extract useful, reliable, and timely information from the deployed sensor network. This implies leveraging the distributed computing environment created by these sensors for signal and information processing in the network, and for dynamic and interactive querying and tasking the sensor network.

SensIT generated new capabilities relative to today's sensors. Current systems such as the Tactical Automated Security System (TASS) for perimeter security are dedicated rather than programmable. They use technologies based on transmit-only nodes and a long-range detection paradigm. SensIT networks have new capabilities. The networks are interactive and programmable with dynamic tasking and querying. A multitasking feature in the system allows multiple simultaneous users. Finally, since detection ranges are much shorter in a sensor system, the software and algorithms can exploit the proximity of devices to threats to drastically improve the accuracy of detection and tracking. The software and the overall system design supports low latency, energy-efficient operation, built-in autonomy and survivability, and low probability of detection of operation. As a result, a network of SensIT nodes can support detection, identification, and tracking of threats, as well as targeting and communication, both within the network and outside the network, such as an overhead asset.

3. Technology Trends

Current sensor networks can exploit technologies not available 20 years ago and perform functions that were not even dreamed of at that time. Sensors, processors, and communication devices are all getting much smaller and cheaper. Commercial companies such as Ember, Crossbow, and Sensoria are now building and deploying small sensor nodes and systems. These companies provide a vision of how our daily lives will be enhanced through a network of small, embedded sensor nodes. In addition to products from these companies, commercial off-the-shelf personal digital assistants (PDAs) using Palm or Pocket PC operating systems contain significant computing power in a small package. These can easily be "ruggedized" to become processing nodes in a sensor network. Some of these devices even have built-in sensing capabilities, such as cameras. These powerful processors can be hooked to MEMS devices and machines along with extensive databases and communication platforms to bring about a new era of technologically sophisticated sensor nets.

Wireless networks based upon IEEE 802.11 standards can now provide bandwidth approaching those of wired networks. At the same time, the IEEE has noticed the low expense and high capabilities that sensor networks offer. The organization has defined the IEEE 802.15 standard for personal area networks (PANs), with "personal net-works" defined to have a radius of 5 to 10 m. Networks of short-range sensors are the ideal technology to be employed in PANs. The IEEE encouragement of the development of technologies and algorithms for such short ranges ensures continued development of low-cost sensor nets. Furthermore, increases in chip capacity and processor production capabilities have reduced the energy per bit requirement for both computing and communication. Sensing, computing, and communications can now be performed on a single chip, further reducing the cost and allowing deployment in ever larger numbers.

Looking into the future, we predict that advances in MEMS technology will produce sensors that are even more capable and versatile. For example, Dust Inc., Berkeley, CA, a company that sprung from the late 1990s Smart Dust research project at the University of California, Berkeley, is building MEMS sensors that can sense and communicate and yet are tiny enough to fit inside a cubic millimeter. A Smart Dust optical mote uses MEMS to aim submillimeter-sized mirrors for communications. Smart Dust sensors can be deployed using a 310 mm "wavelet" shaped like a maple tree seed and dropped to float to the ground. A wireless network of these ubiquitous, low-cost, disposable microsensors can provide close-in sensing capabilities in many novel applications (as discussed in Section IV).

Table 2 compares three generations of sensor nodes; Figure 1 shows their sizes.

Table 2　Three Generations of Sensor Nodes

	Yesterday(1980's~1990's)	Today (2000~2003)	Tomorrow (2010)
Manufacturer	Custom contractors, e.g., for TRSS	Commercial: Crossbow Technology, Inc. Sensoria Corp., Ember Corp.	Dust, Inc. and others to be formed
Size	Large shoe box and up	Pack of cards to small shoe box	Dust, particle
Weight	Kilograms	Crams	Negligible
Node architecture	Separate sensing, processing and communication	Integrated sensing, processing and communication	Integrated sensing, processing and communication
Topology	Point-to-point, star	Client server, peer to peer	Peer to peer
Power supply lifetime	Large batteries; hours, days and longer	AA batteries; days to weeks	Solar; months to years
Deployment	Vehicle-placed or air-drop single sensors	Hand-emplaced	Embedded,"sprinkled"left-behind

TRSS Node　　Crossbow　Ember　Sensoria　Dust,Inc.

Fig.1　Three generations of sensor nodes

4. New Applications

Research on sensor networks was originally motivated by military applications. Examples of military sensor networks range from large-scale acoustic surveillance systems for ocean surveillance to small networks of unattended ground sensors for ground target detection. However, the avail-ability of low-cost sensors and communication networks has resulted in the development of many other potential applications, from infrastructure security to industrial sensing. The following are a few examples.

1) Infrastructure Security

Sensor networks can be used for infrastructure security and counterterrorism applications. Critical buildings and facilities such as power plants and communication centers have to be protected from potential terrorists. Networks of video, acoustic, and other sensors can be deployed around these facilities. These sensors provide early detection of possible threats. Improved coverage and detection and a reduced false alarm rate can be achieved by fusing the data from multiple sensors. Even though fixed sensors connected by a fixed communication network protect most facilities, wireless ad hoc networks can provide more flexibility and additional coverage when needed. Sensor networks can also be used to detect biological, chemical, and nuclear attacks. Examples of such networks can be found in, which also describes other uses of sensor networks.

2) Environment and Habitat Monitoring

Environment and habitat monitoring is a natural candidate for applying sensor networks, since the variables to be monitored, e.g., temperature, are usually distributed over a large region.

The recently started Center for Embedded Network Sensing (CENS), Los Angeles, CA, has a focus on environmental and habitat monitoring. Environmental sensors are used to study vegetation response to climatic trends and diseases, and acoustic and imaging sensors can identify, track, and measure the population of birds and other species. On a very large scale, the System for the Vigilance of the Amazon (SIVAM) provides environmental monitoring, drug trafficking monitoring, and air traffic control for the Amazon Basin. Sponsored by the government of Brazil, this large sensor network consists of different types of interconnected sensors including radar, imagery, and environmental sensors. The imagery sensors are space based, radars are located on aircraft, and environmental sensors are mostly on the ground. The communication network connecting the sensors operates at different speeds. For example, high-speed networks connect sensors on satellites and aircraft, while low-speed networks connect the ground-based sensors.

3) Industrial Sensing

Commercial industry has long been interested in sensing as a means of lowering cost and improving machine (and perhaps user) performance and maintainability. Monitoring machine "health" through determination of vibration or wear and lubrication levels, and the insertion of sensors into regions inaccessible by humans, are just two examples of industrial applications of sensors. Several years ago, the IEEE and the National Institute for Standards and Technology (NIST) launched the P1451 Smart Transducer Interface Standard to enable full plug-and-play of sensors and networks in industrial environments. Factories have continued to automate production and assembly lines with remote sensing nets, implementing sophisticated on-line quality control tests enabled by the sensors. Remote, wireless sensors in particular can enable a factory to be instrumented after the fact to ensure and maintain compliance with federal safety and guidelines while keeping installation costs low.

Spectral sensors are one example of sensing in an industrial environment. From simple optical devices such as optrons and pH probes to true spectral devices that can function as miniature spectrometers, optical sensors can replace existing instruments and perform material property and composition measurements. Optical sensing is also facilitated by miniaturization, as low-cost charge-coupled device (CCD) array devices and microengineering enable smaller, smarter sensors. The goal of this and other industrial sensing is to enable multipoint or matrix sensing: inputs from hundreds or thousands of sensors feed into databases that can be queried in any number of ways to show real-time information on a large or small scale.

4) Traffic Control

Sensor networks have been used for vehicle traffic monitoring and control for quite a while. Most traffic intersections have either overhead or buried sensors to detect vehicles and control traffic lights. Furthermore, video cameras are frequently used to monitor road segments with heavy traffic, with the video sent to human operators at central locations. However, these sensors and the communication network that connect them are costly; thus, traffic monitoring is generally limited to a few critical points. Inexpensive wireless ad hoc networks will completely change the landscape of traffic monitoring and control. Cheap sensors with embedded networking capability can be deployed at every road intersection to detect and count vehicle traffic and estimate its speed.

The sensors will communicate with neighboring nodes to eventually develop a "global traffic picture" which can be queried by human operators or automatic controllers to generate control signals.

Another more radical concept has the sensors attached to each vehicle. As the vehicles pass each other, they ex-change summary information on the location of traffic jams and the speed and density of traffic, information that may be generated by ground sensors. These summaries propagate from vehicle to vehicle and can be used by drivers to avoid traffic jams and plan alternative routes.

New Words And Expressions

herald	*v.*	宣告，宣布
reconnaissance	*n.*	侦察，观测
surveillance	*n.*	监视
tactical	*adj.*	战术的，战略的
disposable	*adj.*	一次性的，用完可丢弃的
denial	*n.*	否认，拒绝，剥夺
seismic	*adj.*	地震的
global positioning system (GPS)		全球定位系统
ubiquitous	*adj.*	无处不在的，普遍存在的
grid	*n.*	网格，方格
vogue	*v.*	流行，风行
hydrophones	*n.*	水听器
evolve	*v.*	逐渐形成，演化
aerostat	*n.*	浮升器
interdiction	*n.*	禁止，禁用
consecutive	*adj.*	连续不断的
coinventor	*n.*	共同发明者
heuristics	*n.*	启发式，探索法
decompose	*v.*	分解
personal digital assistant (PDA)		个人数字助理
personal area network(PAN)		个人局域网
submillimeter		亚毫米
amazon Basin		亚马逊流域
spectral	*adj.*	光的，光谱的

Notes

1. Even though research was focused on satisfying mission needs, e.g., acoustic signal processing and interpretation, tracking, and fusion, it provided some key processing technologies

for modern sensor networks.

译文：尽管研究仅限于如何满足特定的使用需要，如声音信号的处理、解释、跟踪和综合等，但是它仍然为现代传感网络提供了一些关键的处理技术。

2. Other efforts at CMU included protocols for network inter-process communication to support dynamic rebinding of active communicating computations, an interface specification language for building distributed system software, and a system for dynamic load balancing and fault reconfiguration of DSN software.

译文：卡耐基梅隆大学还有一些研究成果，其中包括编写了支持动态通信计算动态重构的网络内处理通信协议，给出了分布式系统软件的界面描述语言，构建了动态负载平衡系统和 DSN 软件的错误重构等。

3. Sensor networks can improve detection and tracking performance through multiple observations, geometric and phenomenological diversity, extended detection range, and faster response time.

译文：传感网络能够通过多种途径改善检测和跟踪性能，如利用几何学和现象学的多样性进行多种观测，扩大探测范围和加快响应时间等。

4. Small and inexpensive sensors based upon microelectro-mechanical system (MEMS) technology, wireless networking, and inexpensive low-power processors allow the deployment of wireless ad hoc networks for various applications.

译文：由于采用了体积小、价格低的基于微电子－机械系统(MEMS)的传感器、无线网络，以及低价低功耗的处理器，使得无线 ad hoc 网络的应用能推广到多种应用领域。

Exercises

Translate the following sentences into Chinese.

1. Cheap、smart devices with multiple onboard sensors, networked through wireless links and the Internet and deployed in large numbers, provide unprecedented opportunities for instrumenting and controlling homes, cities, and the environment.

2. The network was assumed to have many spatially distributed low-cost sensing nodes that collaborate with each other but operate autonomously, with information being routed to whichever node can best use the information.

3. Since very few technology components were available off the shelf, the resulting DSN program had to address distributed computing support, signal processing, tracking, and test beds.

4. Optical sensing is also facilitated by miniaturization, as low-cost charge-coupled device (CCD) array devices and microengineering enable smaller, smarter sensors.

Text B   Sensor Networks: Evolution, Opportunities, and Challenges (Ⅱ)

1. Hard Problems and Technical Challenges

Sensors networks in general pose considerable technical problems in data processing, communication, and sensor management (some of these were identified and researched in the first DSN program). Because of potentially harsh, un-certain, and dynamic environments, along with energy and bandwidth constraints, wireless ad hoc networks pose additional technical challenges in network discovery, network control and routing, collaborative information processing, querying, and tasking.[1]

1) Ad Hoc Network Discovery

Knowledge of the network is essential for a sensor in the network to operate properly. Each node needs to know the identity and location of its neighbors to support processing and collaboration. In planned networks, the topology of the network is usually known *a priori*. For ad hoc networks, the network topology has to be constructed in real time, and up-dated periodically as sensors fail or new sensors are deployed. In the case of a mobile network, since the topology is always evolving, mechanisms should be provided for the different fixed and mobile sensors to discover each other. Global knowledge generally is not needed, since each sensor node interacts only with its neighbors. In addition to knowledge of the topology, each sensor also needs to know its own location. When self-location by GPS is not feasible or too expensive, other means of self-location, such as relative positioning algorithms, have to be provided.

2) Network Control and Routing

The network must deal with resources-energy, band-width, and the processing power—that are dynamically changing, and the system should operate autonomously, changing its configuration as required. Since there is no planned connectivity in ad hoc networks, connectivity must emerge as needed from the algorithms and software. Since communication links are unreliable and shadow fading may eliminate links, the software and system design should generate the required reliability. This requires research into issues such as network size or the number of links and nodes needed to provide adequate redundancy. Also, for networks on the ground, RF transmission degrades with distance much faster than in free space, which means that communication distance and energy must be well managed. Protocols must be internalized in design and not require operator intervention.

Alternative approaches to traditional Internet methods [such as Internet Protocols (IP)], including mobile IP, are needed. One of the benefits of not requiring IP addresses at each node is that one can deploy network devices in very large numbers. Also, in contrast to the case of IP, routes are built up from geoinformation, on an as-needed basis, and optimized for survivability and energy. This is a way to form connections on demand, for data-specific or application-specific purposes. IP is not likely to be a viable candidate in this context, since it needs to maintain routing tables for the global topology, and because updates in a dynamic sensor network environment incur heavy overhead in terms of time, memory, and energy.[2]

Survivability and adaptation to the environment are ensured through deploying an adequate number of nodes to provide redundancy in paths, and algorithms to find the right paths. Diffusion routing methods, which rely only upon information at neighboring nodes, are a way to address this, although such methods may not achieve the information-theoretic capacity of a spatially distributed wireless network. Another important design issue is the investigation of how system parameters such as network size, and density of nodes per square mile affect the tradeoffs between latency, reliability, and energy.

3) Collaborative Signal and Information Processing

The nodes in an ad hoc sensor network collaborate to collect and process data to generate useful information. Collaborative signal and information processing over a network is a new area of research and is related to distributed information fusion. Important technical issues include the degree of information sharing between nodes and how nodes fuse the information from other nodes. Processing data from more sensors generally results in better performance but also requires more communication resources (and, thus, energy). Similarly, less information is lost when communicating information at a lower level (e.g., raw signals), but requires more bandwidth. Therefore, one needs to consider the multiple tradeoffs between performance and resource utilization in collaborative signal and information processing using microsensors.

When a node receives information from another node, this information has to be combined and fused with local information. Fusion approaches range from simple rules of picking the best result to model-based techniques that consider how the information is generated. Again there is a trade off between performance and robustness. Simple fusion rules are robust but suboptimal while more sophisticated and higher performance fusion rules may be sensitive to the underlying models. In a networked environment, information may arrive at a node after traveling over multiple paths. The fusion algorithm should recognize the dependency in the information to be fused and avoid double counting. Keeping track of data pedigree is an approach used in networks with large and powerful sensor nodes, but this approach may not be practical for ad hoc networks with limited processing and communication resources.

Sensor networks are frequently used in the detection, tracking, and classification of targets . Data association is an important problem when multiple targets are present in a small region. Each node must associate its measurements of the environment with individual targets. In addition, targets detected by one node have to be associated with targets detected by other nodes to avoid duplication and enable fusion. Optimal data association is computationally expensive and requires significant bandwidth for communication. Thus distributed data association is also a trade off between performance and resource utilization, requiring distributed data association algorithms tailored to sensor nets.

Other processing issues include how to meet mission latency and reliability requirements, and how to maximize sensor network operational life. A dense network of cheap sensors may allow spatial sampling without the need for expensive algorithms. These algorithms must be asynchronous, as the processor speeds and communication capabilities may vary or even disappear and reappear. Sensor nodes must determine results with progressively increasing accuracy, and so the processes can be terminated when enough precision is gained.

4) Tasking and Querying

A sensor field is like a database with many unique features. Data is dynamically acquired from the environment, as opposed to being entered by an operator. The data is distributed across nodes, and geographically dispersed nodes are connected by unreliable links. These features render the database view more challenging, particularly for military applications given the low-latency, real-time, and high-reliability requirements of the battlefield.

It is important that users have a simple interface to inter-actively task and query the sensor network. An example of a human-network interface is a handheld unit that accepts speech input. The users should be able to command access to information, e.g. operational priority and type of target, while hiding details about individual sensors. One challenge is to develop a language for querying and tasking, as well as a database that can be readily queried. Other challenges include finding efficient distributed mechanisms for query and task compilation and placement, data organization, and caching.

Mobile platforms can carry sensors and query devices. As a result, seamless internetworking between mobile and fixed devices in the absence of any infrastructure is a critical and unique requirement for sensor networks. For example, an air-borne querying device could initiate a query, and then tell the ground sensor network that it will be flying over a specific location after a minute, where the response to the query should be exfiltrated.

5) Security

Since the sensor network may operate in a hostile environment, security should be built into the design and not as an afterthought. Network techniques are needed to provide low-latency, survivable, and secure networks. Low probability of detection communication is needed for net-works because sensors are being envisioned for use behind enemy lines. For the same reasons, the network should be protected again intrusion and spoofing.

2. Some Recent results

Research sponsored by the DARPA SensIT and other programs has addressed the challenges described previously. The following are examples of some recent research results.

1) Localized Algorithms and Directed Diffusion

As discussed previously, even though centralized algorithms that collect data from multiple sensor nodes can potentially provide the best performance, they are undesirable because of high communication cost and lack of robustness and reliability.[3] In localized (or distributed) algorithms, the sensor nodes only communicate with sensors within a neighborhood. Localized algorithms are attractive because they are robust to network changes and node failures. The communication cost also scales well with increasing network size. However, localized algorithms are difficult to design because of the potentially complicated relationship between local behavior and global behavior. Algorithms that are locally optimal may not perform well in a global sense. How to optimally distribute the computation of a centralized algorithm in a distributed implementation continues to be a research problem.

Estrin et al. developed directed diffusion routing algorithms that belong to the class of localized algorithms. Diffusion is a form of broadcast routing that does not specify a destination node address (such as the IP address in Internet protocols). Packets are forwarded to neighboring nodes, and a direction or gradient is overlaid to control the broadcast or forwarding of the packet, which eventually reaches the destination. The gradient could be based on geographic information or other attributes such as power, congestion, and other resources available in the network nodes. For example, if a user application based at one location is interested in events occurring at and around that location, then the nodes around would forward information packets to neighboring nodes that are in the direction; and intermediate nodes would also forward to their neighbors in the direction.[4] Gradients can also be established intermsofin formation producers and consumers via publish-subscribe mechanisms, and consumer interests in specific information types propagated over the network. Intermediate nodes may cache or transform the data locally to increase efficiency, robustness and scalability.

Research results indicate the efficiency of directed diffusion. It requires considerably less energy than standard routing mechanisms such as flooding and omniscient multicast. For instance, simulation and experimental results of directed diffusion in representative sensor networks indicate that multicast protocols (such as omniscient multicast, which is an IP-based multicast routing technique) requires less than half the energy required for flooding, and diffusion requires only 60% of the energy needed for even multicast.[5] These savings are achieved by eliminating paths spent delivering redundant data, and from in-network aggregation such as through intermediate nodes suppressing duplicate location estimates.

2) Distributed Tracking in Wireless Ad Hoc Networks

Tracking mobile targets is an important application of sensor networks for both military and defense systems. Even though target tracking has been widely studied for sensor networks with large nodes and distributed tracking algorithms are available, tracking in ad hoc networks with microsensors poses different challenges due to communication, processing and energy constraints. In particular, the sensors should collaborate and share data to exploit the benefits of sensor data fusion, but this should be done without sending data requests to and collecting data from all sensors, thus overloading the network and using up the energy supply.

Zhao et al. addressed the dynamic sensor collaboration problem in distributed tracking to determine dynamically which sensor is most appropriate to perform the sensing, what needs to be sensed, and to whom to communicate the information. They developed the information-driven sensor querying (IDSQ) approach, enabling collaboration based upon resource constraints and the cost of transmitting information. Each sensor computes the predicted information utility of a piece of non-local sensor data and uses this measure to determine from which sensor to request data. Information utility functions employed include entropy, Mahalanobis distance, and a measure on expected posterior distribution. This approach was demonstrated with simulations as well as experimental data collected from the field.

As discussed in Section V-C, data association is needed in tracking multiple targets that are close to each other relative to the sensor measurement error. Again, distributed data association algorithms are available for networks with large nodes but are computationally too expensive to implement on ad hoc networks. An approximate approach for cheap data association (called identity management) was proposed and demonstrated in.

3) Distributed Classification in Sensor Networks Using Mobile Agents

In a traditional sensor network, data is collected by individual sensors and sent to (possibly multiple) fusion nodes for processing. Because the bandwidth of a wireless sensor network is typically lower than that of a wired network, a sensor network's communications requirements may exceed their capacities. Mobile agents have been proposed as a solution to this dilemma. In a mobile-agent-based DSN, data stay at each local site or sensor, while the integration or fusion code is moved to the data. Communication bandwidth requirement may be reduced if the agent is smaller in size than the data. If this assumption holds, then the sensor network is more scalable, since the performance of the network is not affected by an increase in the number of sensors. The network can also adapt better to the network load and agents can be programmed to carry specific fusion processes. Distributed target classification has been used to demonstrate the effectiveness of the approach.

3. Conclusion

When the concept of DSNs was first introduced more than two decades ago, it was more a vision than a technology ready to be exploited. The early researchers in DSN were severely handicapped by the state of the art in sensors, computers, and communication networks. Even though the benefits of sensor networks were quickly recognized, their application was mostly limited to large military systems. Technological advances in the past decade have completely changed the situation. MEMS technology, more reliable wireless communication, and low-cost manufacturing have resulted in small, inexpensive, and powerful sensors with embedded processing and wireless networking capability. Such wireless sensor networks can be used in many new applications, ranging from environmental monitoring to industrial sensing, as well as traditional military applications. In fact, the applications are only limited by our imagination. Networks of small, possibly microscopic sensors embedded in the fabric of society: in buildings and machinery, and even on people, performing automated continual and discrete monitoring, could drastically enhance our understanding of our physical environment.

New Words and Expressions

Connectivity	*n.*	连通性，互联性
geoinformation	*n.*	地理空间信息
topology	*n.*	拓扑(结构)
diffusion routing methods		扩散路由算法
tradeoff		协调，平衡
fusion	*n.*	融合，聚合，聚变
seamless	*adj.*	无缝的
exfiltrate	*v.*	过滤出，潜出
intrusion	*n.*	入侵

spoof	n.	电子欺骗(网络术语)，是指一台主机设备冒充另外一台主机的IP地址，与其他设备通信，从而达到某种目的的技术；
directed diffusion		定向扩散
gradient	n.	梯度，斜率
congestion	n.	拥挤度，拥塞度
multicast protocol		组播协议

Notes

1. Because of potentially harsh, un-certain, and dynamic environments, along with energy and bandwidth constraints, wireless ad hoc networks pose additional technical challenges in network discovery, network control and routing, collaborative information processing, querying, and tasking.

译文：由于环境中存在的潜在威胁，环境本身也具有不确定性和动态特性，加上能量与带宽的限制，导致无线 ad hoc 网络在网络恢复、网络控制和路由选择，合成信息处理，查询和任务分配等方面存在一系列的技术难题。

2. IP is not likely to be a viable candidate in this context, since it needs to maintain routing tables for the global topology, and because updates in a dynamic sensor network environment incur heavy overhead in terms of time, memory, and energy.

译文：这种情况下，使用 IP 是不明智的，因为 IP 必须保持全局拓扑的路由表，另外，动态传感网络的升级也会在时间、存储空间和能量方面带来巨大的开销。

3. As discussed previously, even though centralized algorithms that collect data from multiple sensor nodes can potentially provide the best performance, they are undesirable because of high communication cost and lack of robustness and reliability.

译文：如前所述，虽然从多个传感器节点采集数据的集中式算法也可能实现最佳性能，但是其昂贵的通信费用，糟糕的灵活性和可靠性都说明，这种算法并不可取。

4. For example, if a user application based at location, is interested in events occurring at and around location, then the nodes around would forward information packets to neighboring nodes that are in the direction; and intermediate nodes would also forward to their neighbors in the direction.

译文：例如，如果某个用户对某点周围发生的事件感兴趣，那么某点周围的节点就会将信息包沿目标方向传输到临近节点，中间节点也将沿目标方向将信息传送到临近节点。

5. For instance, simulation and experimental results of directed diffusion in representative sensor networks indicate that multicast protocols (such as omniscient multicast, which is an IP-based multicast routing technique) requires less than half the energy required for flooding, and diffusion requires only 60% of the energy needed for even multicast.

译文：例如，通过对典型传感网络的定向扩散算法进行仿真和实验所获得的结果表明，组播协议(如基于 IP 多级路由技术的全向多级方式)所需要的能量比洪泛法少一半多，而扩散算法所需要的能量仅为组播方式的 60%。

6. Even though target tracking has been widely studied for sensor networks with large nodes and distributed tracking algorithms are available, tracking in ad hoc networks with microsensors poses different challenges due to communication, processing and energy constraints.

译文：尽管多节点传感网络的目标跟踪技术已经得到广泛研究，而且 ad hoc 网络也采用分布式算法实现跟踪，但是，由于通信、处理和能量限制，微传感器仍然面临诸多挑战。

Exercises

Translate the last paragraph in the text into Chinese.

Lesson Eight　Cryptology

Text A　Introduction to Cryptology

1. Introduction

We live in an exciting, fast-paced world and nothing is changing faster than the way we deal with information. Using the Internet, we can access and use information in ways that we never even dreamed of just a few years ago. Rather than going to the band and standing in line waiting for a teller, we can pay bills, write checks, and shift money between accounts from home, 24 hours a day, 7 days a week. We can apply for and receive approval for loans without ever leaving home. We can buy books, food, gifts, and just about any-thing else over the Internet. Instead of running a garage sale in our front yard on a week-end, we can sell anything at anytime over the Internet. We can buy and sell stock. We can post information for others to read and find information on just about any subject. With the advent of wireless technology, we can do all this and more from almost any location on earth using a cellular phone.

Sure, these are exiting times, but they also have a down side. The same technology that makes life so much easier has the potential to destroy our lives when used by criminals. For example, identity theft is one of the fastest growing crimes in the United States today. It thrives because the legal penalties have not cauhgt up with the effects of the crime, besides the fact that it is easy to do. This is because most of the information "out there" about individuals is not protected. To enjoy the benefits while avoiding the pitfalls of new technology, this can be done is precisely the subject matter of this book. It is about "secret writing", which has been around for centuries, but has now become a vital force for protecting and nurturing the growth of information technology. The field is called cryptography.

Cryptography is the study of codes and ciphers. David Kahn, in what has to be called the "bible of cryptography", defines it as follows: "Cryptology is protection. It is to that extension of modern man-communications—what the carapace is to the turtle, ink to the squid, camouflage to the chameleon." It is centuries old yet it remains fresh, new, and exiting. It is a field that is constantly changing and discovering new challenges. As a result, this is more than just a dry textbook only covering topic of interest to computer scientists and mathematicians. It is also a book that delves into history, political science, language, military tactics, and even games. It covers a body of knowledge that has secretly shaped the world in which we live.

2. Cryptography

This book is a soap opera in some ways. It is the story of three people: Alice, Bob, and Eve. (These are the three names traditionally used by cryptographers to illustrate the principles of both cryptography and cryptanalysis.) It seems that Alice and Bob are constantly sending message to each other. Eve, on the other hand, for reasons that are clouded in the past, wants to keep tabs on what Alice and Bob are saying to each other. Since both Alice and Bob are aware of Eve's intentions, they try as best they can to prevent Eve from discovering the content of their messages. This little soap opera is pictured in Figure 1.

The messages that Alice and Bob send to each other are called *plaintext* because they are readable by anyone. When they first started their correspondence, Alice and Bob sent each other their plaintext without any protection. However, they quickly discovered that if they did nothing to protect the messages, anyone, including Eve, could read them. So, as a result of Eve's reading their plaintext messages, Alice and Bob decided to hide the message contents in such a way that they could recover the plaintext, but Eve could not. This process of disguising a message in such a way as to hide its substance is called *encryption*. The encrypted version of the message is called the *ciphertext*. The process of recovering the plaintext from the ciphertext is called *decryption*. The encryption and decryption processes are determined by an algorithm and are controlled by a single key that only Alice and Bob share. Alice will use the key to encrypt her plaintext and then send the ciphertext on to Bob. Bob will use the same key to decrypt the ciphertext back into plaintext. If Eve intercepts the ciphertext, it appears meaningless to her because she does not have the key. This new process is illustrated in Figure 2.

Fig.1　Typical communication model　　　　Fig.2　Typical communication model

The problem that Alice and Bob face is that Eve is both intelligent and determined. Once they try a particular encryption method, it is only a matter of time before Eve discovers a method to break the cipher. That is, Eve finds a way to either recover the plaintext without the key or a way to recover the key from the ciphertext. This forces Alice and Bob to try an even more complicated encryption method. So, the story of Alice, Bob, and Eve is a never-ending one. Alice and Bob are always trying to stay one step ahead of Eve, who is becoming increasing clever in her approach to breaking new ciphers. This book will allow you to follow this exciting story and watch as Alice and Bob develop new ciphers and Eve discovers new tools to allow her to break them. Before we can pick up the beginning of this story, however, it is necessary to define some basic terms.

3. Important Terms

Cryptology is the science (and to some extent the art) of building and analyzing different encryption-decryption methods. There are really two parts to this science. Cryptography is the science of building new more powerful and efficient encryption-decryption methods. This is the job of Alice and Bob. Cryptanalysis is the science of discovering weaknesses in existing methods so that the plaintext can be recovered without knowledge of the key. This is Eve's job. This book is about both subjects. You will learn how to protect data and how to discover weaknesses in current data-protection methods. Studying both processes will make you better at each. Understanding the different approaches to encryption will make it easier to detect weaknesses in specific ciphers. In addition, it is only through the understanding of cryptanalysis that you can ultimately judge the usefulness of any proposed encryption method. That is, every good cryptologist must spend some time in Eve's shoes in order to judge the security of their own favorite encryption algorithm.

An initial distinction must be drawn between codes and ciphers because sometimes they are mistakenly used to describe the same process. Both are methods used to hide information, but they do it in distinctly different ways. A code will substitute words, phrases, or numbers for plaintext. That is, the word "bomb" might appear in a message as the number sequence 1508. There is no algorithm or simple key that allows plaintext to be recovered from the codetext. The process of creating codetext or recovering plaintext requires a codebook that lists all the numbers (or substitution symbols) and their corresponding plaintext word, phrase, or letter. A cipher uses an algorithm and a key to hide information.

At one time codes were frequently used, but eventually the size of the codebook made it a weak link in the security of the system. Any changes in the code would require the publication and distribution of a new large codebook. A possible enemy could intercept the distribution and compromise the code. Changing the key of a cipher, however, is more secure. Distribution of a simple key is quite a bit easier and less risky than sending out large codebooks. Hence, codes are rarely used today. This does not mean that the process of managing multiple keys is easy. In fact, the process of key management is an important issue in cipher operation and will be covered in Lesson Nine.

Other than codes or ciphers, another form of hiding information is called steganography. This method involves hiding information in ways that conceal the existence of the ciphertext. That is, the ciphertext may be embedded in a photograph or some other message. Using invisible ink is another from of steganography. Steganography fell out of use because of problems with keys, but it is making a comeback through the use of modern computer-generated image-processing techniques.

4. Cipher Evaluation

Throughout this book, the issue of what actually makes a good cipher will be continually explored. In part, you will learn what makes a good cipher by watching how Alice and Bob discover what works and what doesn't work as they continue to try to stay ahead of Eve. Each success on the part of Eve and each failure on the part of Alice and Bob will expose a weakness that will become a test for cipher quality. Each chapter will end with a summary of the current principles of good cipher design that can be derived from the plight of Alice, Bob, and Eve.

However, any discussion of what makes a good cipher must begin with the First General Principle of Cryptography-that is, it will always be assumed that the eavesdropper has knowledge of the underlying algorithm used to encrypt data.[1] This means that data are never secure just because the algorithm is new or unknown. Data are secure only if the key to the cipher algorithm remains secure. Never count on the hop that the enemy does not know how you encrypt your data. Always assume that they know every detail of the algorithm. This is sometimes called Kerckhoff's law, and it is one of the six requirements of any cipher system that Flemish cryptographer Auguste Kerckhofs listed in his 19'h-century work La Crypthographie Militaire. All six are still considered to be fundamental to any cryptographic algorithm.

(1) The system should be unbreakable in practice if not theoretically unbreakable.

(2) Compromise of the system should not inconvenience the correspondents.

(3) The key should be easy to remember without notes and should be easy to change.

(4) The cryptograms should be transmissible by telegraph.

(5) The apparatus or documents should be portable and operable by a single person.

(6) The system should be easy, neither requiring knowledge of a long list of rules nor involving mental strain.

Claude Shannon devised another general evaluation concept in the late 1940s. He took the position that a good cipher should involve both *confusion* and *diffusion.* The confusion property means that the cipher should hide any local pattern—that is, any identifying characteristics of the language should be obscured by the cipher. The cipher should hide features of language that might give away the key to the cipher.[2] The diffusion property requires that the cipher mix up different segments of the plaintext so that no character is left in its original position. Many of the classical ciphers that we will encounter early in this text fail on one or both of these properties. Often it is their failure to satisfy both of Shannon's conditions that allows them to be broken through the process of cryptanalysis.

As with most technologies, the evaluation of a cipher system all comes down to economics in the end. A cipher does not have to be "unbreakable" to be secure. (With one exception, it is doubtful that any cipher is truly unbreakable.) If the value of the information to be obtained is less than the cost of breaking the cipher, the data are secure. Or, if the time required to break the cipher is longer than the useful lifetime of the information, the data are secure. Hence, the ultimate security of any cipher is based on the principle that it is "more work than it is worth" to try and break it.

5. Cryptanalysis

While Alice and Bob are faced with the challenge of creating a safe and secure cipher, Eve has to come up with ways to compromise their work. Eve will be attacking the intercepted ciphertext using all the tools and auxiliary information she can gather. This book will follow the exploits of Eve and teach you hoe to discover weaknesses in ciphers, which is the goal of cryptanalysis. However, it is important to understand that cryptanalysis is a classical double-edged sword. The knowledge you gain can be used for good or for evil. There are important reasons to learn about cryptanalysis—it is a necessary tool for the evaluation of new ciphers and it plays a vital role in preserving our national security. On the other hand, it can become a tool for compromising the privacy of others.[3] Eve has no business attacking the communications between Alice and Bob. No matter how intelligent or skilled she appears to be, ultimately she is evil. You need to commit yourself to using the knowledge you gain to protect and no to harm.

There are three ways that Eve will attack the ciphers of Alice and Bob. The first is called a *ciphertext-only* attack. When all that Eve can get her hands on is the transmitted ciphertext, she will use any information she can gain form the ciphertext alone to try to produce the plaintext. The second is a *known-plaintext* attack. In this case, Eve has both the ciphertext and all or part of the plaintext available. Perhaps she has discovered that Alice and Bob always start or end their messages with the same sentence. Using this information of plaintext-ciphertext may help her pry into other communications between Bob and Alice. The third is a *chosen-plaintext* attack. In this case, Eve has managed to influence the nature of the message between Alice and Bob. Perhaps she has given Alice some juicy information that she knows Alice will send to Bob. She has chosen the information so that the plaintext and the ciphertext have some important properties that make the job of discovering the key easier. Eve can use the information plus Alice's ciphertext to try and discover Alice's key.

Obviously, the ciphertext-only attack is the most difficult, while the chosen-plaintext attack is the easiest. Throughout this book, different ciphers will be compromised using one or more of these attack methods. As you learn how to break ciphers, it is important that you maintain a moral and ethical perspective. I understand that only a few paragraphs earlier this same subject was broached, but it is too important to leave to just one comment. There are only two good reasons to use cryptanalysis skills to break a particular ciphertext: for reasons of national security or to support law-enforcement efforts. Even then it should be done only with specific and lawful authority. On the other hand, there is very good reason to study the weaknesses of cipher systems in general: to ensure that only the strongest, most secure ciphers are actually used to protect sensitive information.

6. Classical And Contemporary Ciphers

This book divides the subject of ciphers into two broad classes (as indicated by the title): classical and contemporary ciphers. Classical ciphers are ciphers that work with individual letters, while contemporary ciphers are those that work with the binary representation of plaintext. Drawing the distinction in this way makes it clear that classical ciphers are of historical (and foundational) interest, while contemporary ciphers are of more practical use today. Each class of ciphers can be further subdivided based on the nature of the algorithm used to generate the ciphertext. One such breakdown is shown in Figure 3.

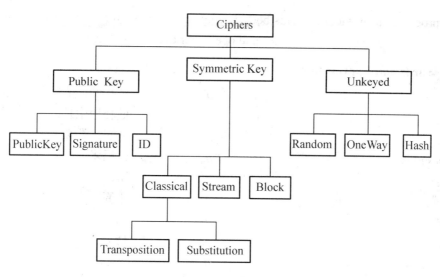

Fig.3   Cipher types

As shown in Figure 3, there are two basic categories of classical ciphers that have been used throughout history. One consists of *substitution* ciphers in which each plaintext letter is replaced by another letter—that is, every plaintext "a" might be replaced by a ciphertext "c". This was the approach of the Hebrews. The other is a *transposition* cipher in which the letters in the plaintext are not changed, but their order is rearranged in the ciphertext much like the Spartan skytale—that is, the word "next" might appear as "xent" in such a ciphertext.

What Figure 3 does not show (simply because the chart would become too complicated) is the breakdown of these two types of classical ciphers. In the category of classical substitution ciphers, for example, there are two approaches. One is called a *monoalphabetic* cipher and the other is called a *polyalphabetic* cipher. The characteristic of a monoalphabetic cipher is that each plaintext letter is mapped to exactly one ciphertext letter—that is, if a plaintext "a" is replaced by a ciphertext "n" once, then it is always replaced by "n". On the other hand, in a polyalphabetic cipher, several different ciphertext letters may replace the same plaintext letter. For example, the ciphertext "a" may represent plaintext characters "n", "s" or "y". It appears that a polyalphabetic cipher is more difficult to produce and to break than a monoalphabetic cipher. However, it will become apparent later that even polyalphabetics have their weakness.[4]

7. Summary

The art and science of cryptology have a long and fascinating history. From the early days of writing, we have tried to find ways to communicate thoughts, feelings, and plans in a way that preserves privacy and secrecy. We have also tried to gain an advantage over others by discovering their secrets. The pursuit of these opposing goals has influenced the history of the world.

History aside, cryptology is also fascinating because it is a blend of so many different fields of science. From languages to mathematics to physics to computer science, cryptology borrows ideas and processes from them all. This book is your introduction to a world that has long been shrouded in secrecy. It will unlock the past and open your eyes to the future.[5]

New Words and Expressions

cellular	*adj.*	多孔的；蜂窝状的；泡沫状的
thrive	*v.*	健壮地生长；茂盛地生长
penalty	*n.*	处罚；罚款
cryptography	*n.*	密码术
cipher	*n.*	密码
carapace	*n.*	甲壳
squid	*n.*	乌贼；墨鱼
camouflage	*n.*	伪装
chameleon	*n.*	变色龙
plaintext	*n.*	明文
encryption	*n.*	加密术；密码术
ciphertext	*n.*	密文
decryption	*n.*	解密
cryptanalysis	*n.*	密码分析学
steganography	*n.*	隐写术
eavesdropper	*n.*	偷听者
apparatus	*n.*	器械；设备
auxiliary	*adj.*	辅助的；补助的
compromise	*v.*	妥协；折中；危及……的安全
monoalphabetic	*adj.*	单字符的
polyalphabetic	*adj.*	多字符的
blend	*n.*	混合

Notes

1. However, any discussion of what makes a good cipher must begin with the First General Principle of Cryptography—that is, it will always be assumed that the eavesdropper has knowledge of the underlying algorithm used to encrypt data.

译文：然而任何对于什么是一个好的密码的讨论必须以密码学的第一通用原则开始——也就是说，总是假设偷听者具有加密数据所用算法的所有知识。

2. Claude Shannon devised another general evaluation concept in the late 1940s. He took the position that a good cipher should involve both *confusion* and *diffusion*. The confusion property means that the cipher should hide any local pattern—that is, any identifying characteristics of the language should be obscured by the cipher.

译文：Claude Shannon 在 20 世纪 40 年代发现了另一项通用的评估原则。他认为一个好的密码必须是混乱的和扩散的。混乱特性意味着密码必须掩盖其局部模式，任何个体的局部特征必须被密码所掩盖。

3. This book will follow the exploits of Eve and teach you how to discover weaknesses in ciphers, which is the goal of cryptanalysis. However, it is important to understand that cryptanalysis is a classical double-edged sword. The knowledge you gain can be used for good or for evil. There are important reasons to learn about cryptanalysis—it is a necessary tool for the evaluation of new ciphers and it plays a vital role in preserving our national security. On the other hand, it can become a tool for compromising the privacy of others.

译文：本书将会追随 Eve 的辉煌成就教你如何发现密码的弱点，这也是密码分析的目的。然而，明白密码分析是一个典型的双刃剑是很重要的。你所学到的知识可用于好的地方也可用于坏的地方。学习密码分析有很重要的原因，它是评估一个新的密码的重要工具，在保卫国家安全方面起着至关重要的作用。另一方面，它会成为危及他人隐私的工具。

4. In the category of classical substitution ciphers, for example, there are two approaches. One is called a *monoalphabetic* cipher and the other is called a *polyalphabetic* cipher. The characteristic of a monoalphabetic cipher is that each plaintext letter is mapped to exactly one ciphertext letter—that is, if a plaintext "a" is replaced by a ciphertext "n" once, then it is always replaced by "n". On the other hand, in a polyalphabetic cipher, several different ciphertext letters may replace the same plaintext letter. For example, the ciphertext "a" may represent plaintext characters "n", "s" or "y". It appears that a polyalphabetic cipher is more difficult to produce and to break than a monoalphabetic cipher. However, it will become apparent later that even polyalphabetics have their weakness.

译文：例如，在经典的替换加密法中有两种方法。一种称为单码加密法；另一种称为多码加密法。单码加密法的特征是，每个明文的字母正好映射到一个密文字母，这也就是说，一旦明文的字母"a"被密文的字母"n"替代，那它总是被"n"替代。而在多码加密法中，同一个明文字母可能用多个不同的密文字母来替代。例如，明文字母"a"可能用密文字母"n"、"s"或"y"来替换。显然，多码加密法的生成和破解比单码加密法更困难。但后来发现，即使是多码加密法也有其弱点。

5. History aside, cryptology is also fascinating because it is a blend of so many different fields of science. From languages to mathematics to physics to computer science, cryptology borrows ideas and processes from them all. This book is your introduction to a world that has long been shrouded in secrecy. It will unlock the past and open your eyes to the future.

译文：除了历史的原因之外，密码学如此迷人是因为它是这么多不同领域科学的混合。从语言学到数学到物理学到计算机科学，密码学从它们中汲取思想和过程。本书是你到一个被秘密隐藏了很久的世界的指引。它会开启过去的锁并且让你看到未来。

Exercises

Comprehension questions.

1. What is the First General Principle of Cryptology?

2. What is the difference between a code and a cipher, and why are codes rarely used today?

3. What is the definition of cryptology?

4. Bob and Alice decide that because Eve can break a simple shift cipher they will use in twice—that is, they will create ciphertext by shifting every letter by 3. Then they will encipher the first ciphertext using a shift cipher with a key of 5. Is this a good idea? Why or why not?

Text B Advanced Encryption Standard

Since DES was becoming less reliable as new cryptanalysis techniques were developed, the National Institute of Standards and Technology (NIST) put out a notice in early 1999 requesting submissions for a new encryption standard. The requirements were as follows.

(1) A symmetric block cipher with a variable length key (128,192, or 256 bits) and a 128-bit block.

(2) It must be more secure than triple-DES.

(3) It must be in the public domain-royalty free worldwide.

(4) It should remain secure for at least 30 years.

Fifteen algorithms were submitted from 10 different countries. They were subjected to a long public analysis process before the algorithm was selected.

NIST went about the process of selecting a new block-cipher standard in just the right way. They required public disclosure of the algorithm and solicited comments from the cryptology community. At a series of three public conferences, the algorithms were presented and discussed, and weaknesses were exposed.[1] After the second conference, the list of 15 ciphers was reduced to five finalists: MARS, submitted by IBM; RC6, submitted by RSA Laboratories; Rijndael, submitted by Joan Daemen and Vincent Rijment; Serpent, submitted by Anderson, Biham and Knudsen; and Two Fish, submitted by Schneier, Kelsy, Whiting, Wagner, Hall and Ferguson. All five were reexamined, and after another six months of testing, the winner was announced. It was Rijndael (pronounced "rain-doll").

1. Rijndael Structure

Rijndael is a flexible algorithm with a variable block size (128, 192 or 256 bits), a variable key size (128, 192 or 256 bits), and a variable number of iterations (10, 12 or 14). The number of iterations is dependent on the block-key size and varies from 10 to 14. As a result of its flexible nature, there are really three version of Rijndael: AES-128, AES-192 and AES-256. The general structure of Rijndael is shown in Figure 4. Rather than using just a substitution and a permutation at each stage (as DES does), Rijndael consists of multiple cycles of substitution, shifting, column mixing and a key add operation.[2] In this way, Rijndael is more like IDEA—it does not contain a typical Feistel round involving a permutation. (*Note:* this section will use the terms "AES" and "Rijndael" interchangeably).

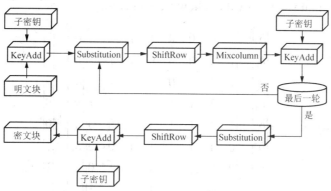

Fig.4   General Rijndael Structure

The process begins by grouping the plaintext bits into a column array by bytes. This is sometimes called the "State within AES". The first four bytes form the first column; the second four bytes form the second column, and so on. The resulting array is shown in Figure 5. If the block size is 128 bits, this becomes a 4×4 array. For larger block sizes, the array has additional columns. The key is also grouped into an array using the same process.

The substitution layer uses a single Sbox (rather than the eight Sboxes used in DES). The Rijndael Sbox is a 16×16 array shown in Figure 6. Each element in the current column array serves as an address into the Sbox: The first four bits identify the Sbox row and the last four bits identify the Sbox column. The Sbox element at that location replaces the current column-array element.[3]

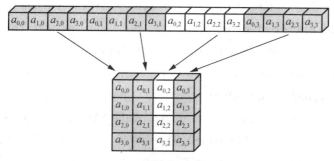

Fig.5   Rijndael grouping

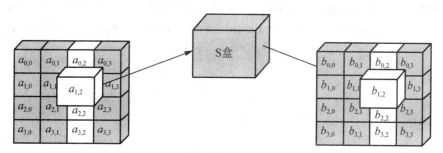

Fig.6   Rijndael substitution operation

The Rijndael Sbox actually performs an algebraic transformation on the input to produce the output. In matrix form, it is given by the following expression.

$$
\begin{vmatrix} b_0 \\ b_1 \\ b_2 \\ b_3 \\ b_4 \\ b_5 \\ b_6 \\ b_7 \end{vmatrix} = \begin{vmatrix} 1 & 0 & 0 & 0 & 1 & 1 & 1 & 1 \\ 1 & 1 & 0 & 0 & 0 & 1 & 1 & 1 \\ 1 & 1 & 1 & 0 & 0 & 0 & 1 & 1 \\ 1 & 1 & 1 & 1 & 0 & 0 & 0 & 1 \\ 1 & 1 & 1 & 1 & 1 & 0 & 0 & 0 \\ 0 & 1 & 1 & 1 & 1 & 1 & 0 & 0 \\ 0 & 0 & 1 & 1 & 1 & 1 & 1 & 0 \\ 0 & 0 & 0 & 1 & 1 & 1 & 1 & 1 \end{vmatrix} \begin{vmatrix} a_0 \\ a_1 \\ a_2 \\ a_3 \\ a_4 \\ a_5 \\ a_6 \\ a_7 \end{vmatrix} + \begin{vmatrix} 1 \\ 1 \\ 0 \\ 0 \\ 0 \\ 1 \\ 1 \\ 0 \end{vmatrix}
$$

Byte a is multiplied by the given matrix, and the result is added to the fixed vector value 63 (in binary) to produce the output value byte b. This can be expressed in a typical Sbox format as shown in Figure 7. For example, if the input state consists of the array (displayed in Hex), then the output is as shown.

输入					输出			
12	2a	21	0b		c9	e5	fd	2b
45	bd	04	cl		6e	7a	f2	78
23	0a	00	lc		26	67	63	9c
89	11	2a	fc		a7	82	e5	b0

In this example, the first input term 12 is replaced by the Sbox element in Row 1 Column 2 which is c9. The rest of the outputs are determined in the same manner. This Sbox design was selected for a variety of reasons, some of which are the following: it is invertible, it has no fixed points (that is, there are no cases in which Row i Column j contains the value ij), and it is simple to describe yet has a complicated algebraic structure.[4] (Do you believe that?)

A row-shift operation is applied to the output of the Sbox in which the four rows of the column array are cyclically shifted to the left. The first row is shifted by 0, the second by 1, the third by 2, and the fourth by 3, as shown in Figure 8. As is evident from the figure, this has the effect of completely rearranging the columns so that each column contains a byte from each of the previous columns. At this point, the columns are ready for a process that will mix up the bits within the columns.

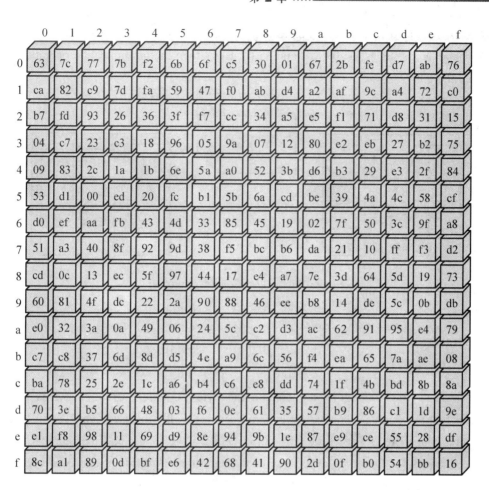

Fig.7   Rijndael Sbox

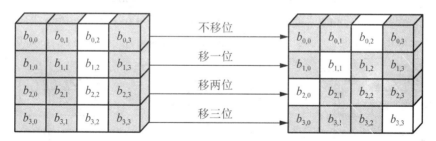

Fig.8   Rijndael Shift Operation

Column mixing is accomplished by a matrix-multiplication operation. The shifted column array is multiplied by a fixed matrix (given in hex) such as

$$
\begin{vmatrix} c_0 \\ c_1 \\ c_2 \\ c_3 \end{vmatrix} = \begin{vmatrix} 02 & 03 & 01 & 01 \\ 01 & 02 & 03 & 01 \\ 01 & 01 & 01 & 03 \\ 03 & 01 & 01 & 02 \end{vmatrix} \begin{vmatrix} b_0 \\ b_1 \\ b_2 \\ b_3 \end{vmatrix}
$$

And is illustrated in Figure 9. For example, if the first column of the current state of the system contained the bytes 11, 09, 01, and 35 (in Hex), then the multiplication operation would look like Figure 9.

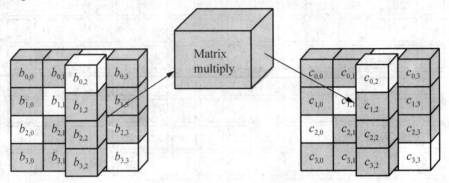

Fig.9　Rijndael MixColumn operation

$$\begin{vmatrix} 73 \\ 6b \\ ba \\ a7 \end{vmatrix} = \begin{vmatrix} 02 & 03 & 01 & 01 \\ 01 & 02 & 03 & 01 \\ 01 & 01 & 01 & 03 \\ 03 & 01 & 01 & 02 \end{vmatrix} \begin{vmatrix} 11 \\ 09 \\ 01 \\ 35 \end{vmatrix}$$

So the new first column would contain the bytes 73, 6b, 6a, and a7. This operation guarantees that the original plaintext bit pattern becomes highly diffused over several founds. It also ensures that there is very little correlation between the inputs and the outputs. Both are important features for the ultimate security of the algorithm. A different matrix is used for the decryption operation.

The final stage of a single iteration XORs a subkey derived from the original key to the current state as shown in Figure 10. This completes one iteration of the algorithm. Each stage was selected for both its simplicity and its ability to create a diffused output—in combination, they do an astounding job.

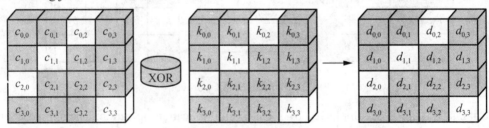

Fig.10　Rijndael KeyAdd operation

It might be helpful now to trace through one iteration of AES to observe the impact of all these operations. Say Alice wants to send Bob this short message: "Bob look at this." Counting the three spaces, this message is exactly 16 characters (or 128 bits in ASCII) long. Rather than look at this at the bit level (you don't want to have to read 128 bits and I don't want to write them), follow the action of AES at the byte level in Hex. In this case, the message is presented to AES as:42 6f 62 20 6c 6f 6f 6b 20 61 74 20 74 68 69 73.

This is written as a 4×4 array

$$
\begin{matrix}
42 & 6c & 20 & 74 \\
6f & 6f & 61 & 68 \\
62 & 6f & 74 & 69 \\
20 & 6b & 20 & 73
\end{matrix}
$$

The array serves as input to the Sbox. The first input is 42, which addresses Row 4 Column 2 of the Sbox. The content of the cell is 2c. Looking up each element in the Sbox produces an output array

$$
\begin{matrix}
2c & 50 & b7 & 92 \\
a8 & a8 & ef & 45 \\
aa & a8 & 92 & f9 \\
b7 & 7f & b7 & 8f
\end{matrix}
$$

This substitution provides the first layer of confusion within AES. This is followed by the next stage, which will rotate the rows

$$
\begin{matrix}
2c & 50 & b7 & 92 \\
a8 & ef & 45 & a8 \\
92 & f9 & aa & a8 \\
8f & b7 & 7f & b7
\end{matrix}
$$

This operation provides the first layer of diffusion within AES by mixing up the order of the rows. This is followed by the multiplication stage, which mixes up and transforms the columns. In this example, the first column is transformed by the relation

$$
\begin{vmatrix} 72 \\ d1 \\ ad \\ 66 \end{vmatrix} = \begin{vmatrix} 02 & 03 & 01 & 01 \\ 01 & 02 & 03 & 01 \\ 01 & 01 & 01 & 03 \\ 03 & 01 & 01 & 02 \end{vmatrix} \begin{vmatrix} 2c \\ a8 \\ 92 \\ 8f \end{vmatrix}
$$

Multiplying each column produces

$$
\begin{matrix}
72 & 19 & 66 & 4b \\
d1 & d1 & be & 91 \\
ad & d0 & d0 & 07 \\
66 & 46 & 23 & 74
\end{matrix}
$$

The subkey is used at this point. For our example, let the subkey (in Hex) be

$$
\begin{matrix}
01 & a3 & 90 & 12 \\
e1 & 44 & 20 & 11 \\
cc & 73 & 04 & a9 \\
59 & 06 & 30 & b4
\end{matrix}
$$

Now XOR the subkey with the current state to produce

$$
\begin{array}{cccc}
72 & 19 & 66 & 4b \\
d1 & d1 & be & 91 \\
ad & d0 & d0 & 07 \\
66 & 46 & 23 & 74
\end{array}
\quad XOR \quad
\begin{array}{cccc}
01 & a3 & 90 & 12 \\
e1 & 44 & 20 & 11 \\
cc & 73 & 04 & a9 \\
59 & 06 & 30 & b4
\end{array}
\quad = \quad
\begin{array}{cccc}
73 & ba & f3 & 59 \\
30 & 95 & 9e & 80 \\
61 & a0 & d4 & a6 \\
3f & 40 & 13 & c0
\end{array}
$$

A quick comparison of the initial input and the first-round output reveals

$$
\begin{array}{cccccccc}
42 & 6f & 62 & 20 & 6c & 6f & 6f & 6b \\
73 & 30 & 61 & 3f & ba & 95 & a0 & 40
\end{array}
\quad
\begin{array}{cccccccc}
20 & 61 & 74 & 20 & 74 & 68 & 69 & 73 \\
f3 & 9e & d4 & 13 & 59 & 80 & a6 & c0
\end{array}
$$

At the bit level, there are 76 bit changes out of 128, and this is just one round—there are 10 more to go.

2. AES Security

During the AES selection process, all the proposed algorithms were subjected to cryptanalysis. In the relatively short time available to the participants, no one was able to come up with a technique to break Rijdael (or the other finalists for that matter). Hence, Rijndael appeared to be secure. Since the adoption of AES, cryptanalysts continue to probe the algorithm searching for weaknesses. They have had varying degrees of success.

It appears that AES is secure against both differential and linear cryptanalysis. This should come as no surprise, since Rijndael was designed with these attacks is mind. However, other attacks have emerged that have been successful against reduced rounds of AES. These are variations on the concept of differential and linear cryptanalysis. The impossible differentials (ID) attack has been used to break a six round version of AES-128. Square attacks have been successful against seven rounds of both AES-128 and AES-192. Collision attacks have also worked on seven round versions of AES-128 and AES-192. All these attacks have failed when applied to the full 10 rounds of AES-128, but they do suggest that there may be an exploitable weakness yet to be found.[5]

In January 2003, a paper was published on the Internet that may have disclosed one of those future exploitable weaknesses. It claimed to have discovered a bias in the AES output bits that could be exploited by what is called a plaintext-dependent repetition-code attack. As should be expected, the paper caused quite an uproar in the cryptographic community. It was not long before a response appeared which claimed that the attack on AES was not valid and that no bias could be found in the AES output bits. While it appears that there were some fundamental errors in the initial paper, the whole process does illustrate the ongoing effort to discover and validate any weaknesses in AES.

New Words and Expressions

reliable	*adj.*	可靠的；可信赖的
disclosure	*n.*	揭露；泄露；公开
solicit	*v.*	恳求
substitution	*n.*	置换
permutation	*n.*	替换
algebraic	*adj.*	代数的
iteration	*n.*	迭代
original	*adj.*	原始的
cyclically	*adj.*	循环的
triple	*adj.*	三倍的
triple-DES	*n.*	三重 DES
block-cipher	*n.*	块加密
simplicity	*n.*	简单性
astounding	*adj.*	使人震惊的
comparison	*n.*	比较
cryptanalysis	*n.*	密码分析法
differential	*adj.*	差分的
linear	*adj.*	线性的
uproar	*n.*	鼎沸；沸腾

Notes

1. NIST went about the process of selecting a new block-cipher standard in just the right way. They required public disclosure of the algorithm and solicited comments from the cryptology community. At a series of three public conferences, the algorithms were presented and discussed, and weaknesses were exposed.

译文：NIST 以非常正确的方式开始了选择一种新的块加密标准的过程。他们公开算法并且请求来自加密社区对该算法的评论。通过连续 3 个公开会议，对算法进行展示和讨论并暴露其弱点。

2. Rather than using just a substitution and a permutation at each stage (as DES does), Rijndael consists of multiple cycles of substitution, shifting, column mixing, and a key add operation.

译文：与 DES 在每个循环仅用一次替换和变换操作不同，Rijndael 包含多轮的替换、移位、列混合及加密钥的操作。

3. The substitution layer uses a single Sbox (rather than the eight Sboxes used in DES). The Rijndael Sbox is a 16×16 array shown in Figure 6. Each element in the current column array serves as an address into the Sbox: The first four bits identify the Sbox row and the last four bits

identify the Sbox column. The Sbox element at that location replaces the current column-array element.

译文：AES 的替换层采用了一个 S 盒（与 DES 中采用 8 个不同）。Rijndael 的 S 盒是一个 16×16 的矩阵，如图 6 所示。当前列数组中的每个元素充当 S 盒的地址：前 4 位确定 S 盒的行而后 4 位确定 S 盒的列。S 盒中对应位置的元素替换当前的列数组元素。

4. This Sbox design was selected for a variety of reasons, some of which are the following: it is invertible, it has no fixed points (that is, there are no cases in which Row *i* Column *j* contains the value *ij*), and it is simple to describe yet has a complicated algebraic structure.

译文：这种 S 盒的设计基于多种原因，其中的一个描述如下：它是可逆转的，它没有固定点（也就是说，不存在行 *i* 列 *j* 处对应值为 *ij* 的点），它描述起来简单，但具有复杂的代数结构。

5. It appears that AES is secure against both differential and linear cryptanalysis. This should come as no surprise, since Rijndael was designed with these attacks is mind. However, other attacks have emerged that have been successful against reduced rounds of AES. These are variations on the concept of differential and linear cryptanalysis. The impossible differentials (ID) attack has been used to break a six round version of AES-128. Square attacks have been successful against seven rounds of both AES-128 and AES-192. Collision attacks have also worked on seven round versions of AES-128 and AES-192. All these attacks have failed when applied to the full 10 rounds of AES-128, but they do suggest that there may be an exploitable weakness yet to be found.

译文：AES 可以抗差分和线性密码分析法的攻击。这并不奇怪，因为 Rijndael 在设计时就考虑了这些攻击法。但是，已经出现了其他一些攻击法，可以成功破解轮数较少的 AES。这些攻击法是差分和线性密码分析法的变体。不可能差分(impossible differential, ID)攻击法已成功破解了 6 轮 AES-128。平方(square)攻击法已成功破解了 7 轮的 AES-128 和 AES-192。冲突(collision)攻击法也已成功破解了 7 轮 AES-28 和 AES-192。所有这些攻击法对于全部 10 轮的 AES-128 都失败了，但这表明，AES 可能有待发现的弱点。

Exercises

Comprehension questions.

1. What is the requirement of AES?
2. Is AES a block-cipher or a stream-cipher?
3. What are the five algorithms submitted to NIST when selecting AES?
4. Please describe the whole structure of AES.
5. Describe the security of AES.

Lesson Nine　Complex Networks and Its Applications

Text A　Exploring Complex Networks(Ⅰ)

Networks are on our minds nowadays. Sometimes we fear their power — and with good reason. On 10 August 1996, a fault in two power lines in Oregon led, through a cascading series of failures, to blackouts in 11 US states and two Canadian provinces, leaving about 7 million customers without power for up to 16 hours. The Love Bug worm, the worst computer attack to date, spread over the Internet on 4 May 2000 and inflicted billions of dollars of damage worldwide.

In our lighter moments we play games about connectivity. "Six degrees of Marlon Brando"[1] broke out as a nationwide fad in Germany, as readers of *Die Zeit* tried to connect a falafel vendor in Berlin with his favourite actor through the shortest possible chain of acquaintances. And during the height of the Lewinsky scandal, the *New York Times* printed a diagram of the famous people within "six degrees of Monica".

Meanwhile scientists have been thinking about networks too. Empirical studies have shed light on the topology of food webs, electrical power grids, cellular and metabolic networks, the World-Wide Web, the Internet backbone, the neural network of the nematode worm. *Caenorhabditis elegans*, telephone call graphs, co-authorship and citation networks of scientists.

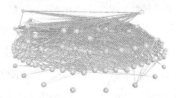

(a) Food web of Little Rock Lake

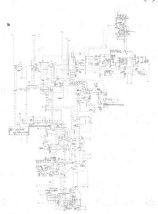

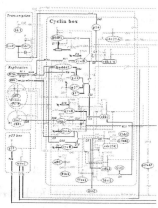

(b) New York State electric power grid　(c) A portion of the molecular interaction map for the regulatory

network that controls the mammalian cell cycle

Fig.1　Wiring diagrams for complex networks

These databases are now easily accessible, courtesy of the Internet. Moreover, the availability of powerful computers has made it feasible to probe their structure; until recently, computations involving million-node networks would have been impossible without specialized facilities.[2]

Why is network anatomy so important to characterize? Because structure always affects function. For instance, the topology of social networks affects the spread of information and disease, and the topology of the power grid affects the robustness and stability of power transmission.

From this perspective, the current interest in networks is part of a broader movement towards research on complex systems. In the words of E. O. Wilson, "The greatest challenge today, not just in cell biology and ecology but in all of science, is the accurate and complete description of complex systems.[3] Scientists have broken down many kinds of systems. They think they know most of the elements and forces. The next task is to reassemble them, at least in mathematical models that capture the key properties of the entire ensembles".

But networks are inherently difficult to understand, as the following list of possible complications illustrates.

(1) Structural complexity: the wiring diagram could be an intricate tangle.

(2) Network evolution: the wiring diagram could change over time. On the World-Wide Web, pages and links are created and lost every minute.

(3) Connection diversity: the links between nodes could have different weights, directions and signs. Synapses in the nervous system can be strong or weak, inhibitory or excitatory.

(4) Dynamical complexity: the nodes could be nonlinear dynamical systems. In a gene network or a Josephson junction array, the state of each node can vary in time in complicated ways.

(5) Node diversity: there could be many different kinds of nodes. The biochemical network that controls cell division in mammals consists of a bewildering variety of substrates and enzymes, only a few of which are shown in Figure.1(c).[4]

(6) Meta-complication: the various complications can influence each other. For example, the present layout of a power grid depends on how it has grown over the years — a case where network evolution (2) affects topology (1). When coupled neurons fire together repeatedly, the connection between them is strengthened; this is the basis of memory and learning. Here nodal dynamics (4) affect connection weights (3).

To make progress, different fields have suppressed certain complications while highlighting others. For instance, in nonlinear dynamics we have tended to favour simple, nearly identical dynamical systems coupled together in simple, geometrically regular ways. Furthermore we usually assume that the network architecture is static. These simplifications allow us to sidestep any issues of structural complexity and to concentrate instead on the system's potentially formidable dynamics.[5]

Laser arrays provide a concrete example. In the single-mode approximation, each laser is characterized by its time-dependent gain, polarization, and the phase and amplitude of its electric field. These evolve according to four coupled, nonlinear differential equations. We usually hope the laser will settle down to a stable state, corresponding to steady emission of light, but periodic pulsations and even chaotic intensity fluctuations can occur in some cases. Now suppose that many identical lasers are arranged side by side in a regular chain or ring, interacting with their neighbours by evanescent coupling or by overlap of their electric fields. Will the lasers lock their phases together spontaneously, or break up into a standing wave pattern, or beat each other into incoherence? From a technological standpoint, self-synchronization would be the most desirable outcome, because a perfectly coherent array of N lasers would produce N^2 times as much power as a single one. But in practice, semiconductor laser arrays are notoriously prone to both spatial and temporal instabilities. Even for a simple ring geometry, this problem is dynamically complex.

The first part of this article reviews what is known about dynamical complexity in regular networks of nonlinear systems. I offer a few rules of thumb about the impact of network structure on collective dynamics, especially for arrays of coupled limit-cycle oscillators.

The logical next step would be to tackle networks that combine dynamical and structural complexity, such as power grids or ecological webs. Unfortunately they lie beyond our mathematical reach — we do not even know how to characterize their wiring diagrams. So we have to begin with network topology.

By a happy coincidence, such architectural questions are being pursued in other branches of science, thanks to the excitement about the Internet, functional genomics, financial networks, and so on. The second part of this article uses graph theory to explore the structure of complex networks, an approach that has recently led to some encouraging progress, especially when combined with the tools of statistical mechanics and computer simulations.

Needless to say, many other topics within network science deserve coverage here. The subject is amazingly rich, and apologies are offered to those readers whose favourite topics are omitted.

New Words and Expressions

complex network		复杂网络
blackout	*n.*	毁灭，出故障
Inflict	*v.*	予以(打击等)；使受(痛苦等)
empirical study		实证研究
courtesy	*vt.*	礼貌，谦恭
intricate	*adj.*	复杂的，难懂的
weight	*n.*	权重

synapse	*n.*	突触
dynamical complexity		动力学复杂性
substrate	*n.*	基质
enzyme	*n.*	酶
sidestep	*v.*	回避

Notes

1. Six degrees of Marlon Brando，这是一个著名的小世界网络实验，俗称"六度分离"。它是社会学家在研究社交网络(social networks)时提出的一个概念。该问题源于社会学家、哈佛大学的心理学教授 Stanley Milgram(1934～1984)在 1967 年做的实验："追踪美国社交网络中的最短路径"。他要求每个参与者设法寄信给一个住在波士顿附近的"目标人物"，规定每个参与者只能转发给一个他们认识的人。Milgram 发现完整的链平均长度为 6 个人。

2. Moreover, the availability of powerful computers has made it feasible to probe their structure; until recently, computations involving million-node networks would have been impossible without specialized facilities.

译文：而且，强大的计算机的使用使我们有可能探明它们的结构；至今，百万节点网络的计算仍旧离不开专业设备的辅助。

3. The greatest challenge today, not just in cell biology and ecology but in all of science, is the accurate and complete description of complex systems.

译文：当今最大的挑战是对复杂系统做精确、完整的分析，这不只存在于细胞生物学和生态学，而是整个科学领域。

4. The biochemical network that controls cell division in mammals consists of a bewildering variety of substrates and enzymes, only a few of which are shown in Figure.1(c).

译文：正如图 1(c)所示的，控制着哺乳动物细胞分裂的生化网络就包含各种各样的基质和酶。

5. These simplifications allow us to sidestep any issues of structural complexity and to concentrate instead on the system's potentially formidable dynamics.

译文：这些简化使我们能够回避结构上的复杂性，从而将重点放在系统潜在的强大的动力学行为上。

Exercises

Translate the following paragraph into Chinese.

One of the main reasons behind complex networks popularity is their flexibility and generality for representing virtually any natural structure, including those undergoing dynamic changes of topology. As a matter of fact, every discrete structure such as lists、trees or even lattices, can be suitably represented as special cases of graphs. It is thus of little surprise that several investigations into complex networks involve the representation of the structure of interest as a network, followed by an analysis of the topological features of the obtained representation performed in terms of a set of informative measurements. Another interesting problem consists of measuring the structural properties of evolving networks in order to characterize how the connectivity of the investigated structures changes along the process.

Both such activities can be understood as directed to the topological characterization of the studied structures. Another related application is to use the obtained measurements in order to identify different categories of structures, which is directly related to the area of pattern recognition . Even when modeling networks, it is often necessary to compare the realizations of the model with real networks, which can be done in terms of the respective measurements. Provided the measurements are comprehensive (ideally the representation by the measurements should be one-to-one or invertible), the fact that the simulated networks yield measurements similar to those of the real counterparts supports the validity of the model.

Text B   Exploring Complex Networks(Ⅱ)

1. Complex Network Architectures

All the network topologies discussed so far — chains、grids、lattices and fully-connected graphs — have been completely regular (Fiure.2(a),(b)). Those simple architectures allowed us to focus on the complexity caused by the nonlinear dynamics of the nodes, without being burdened by any additional complexity in the network structure itself. Now I take the complementary approach, setting dynamics aside and turning to more complex architectures. A natural place to start is at the opposite end of the spectrum from regular networks, with graphs that are completely random.[1]

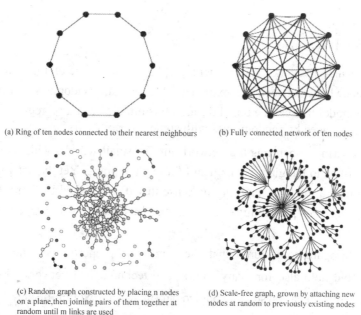

(a) Ring of ten nodes connected to their nearest neighbours   (b) Fully connected network of ten nodes

(c) Random graph constructed by placing n nodes on a plane,then joining pairs of them together at random until m links are used

(d) Scale-free graph, grown by attaching new nodes at random to previously existing nodes

Fig.2   Schematic illustration of regular and random network architectures

2. Random Graphs

Imagine $n \gg 1$ buttons strewn across the floor. Pick two buttons at random and tie them together with thread. Repeat this process m times, always choosing pairs of buttons at random. (If m is large, you might eventually select buttons that already have threads attached. That is certainly allowed; it merely creates clusters of connected buttons.) The result is a physical example of a random graph with n nodes and m links (Figure.2(c)). Now slowly lift a random button off the floor. If it is tied to other buttons, either directly or indirectly, those are dragged up too. So what happens? Are you likely to pull up an isolated button, a small cluster or a vast meshwork?

Erdös and Rényi studied how the expected topology of this random graph changes as a function of m. When m is small, the graph is likely to be fragmented into many small clusters of nodes, called components. As m increases, the components grow, at first by linking to isolated nodes and later by coalescing with other components. A phase transition occurs at $m = n/2$, where many clusters crosslink spontaneously to form a single giant component. For $m > n/2$, this giant component contains on the order of n nodes (more precisely, its size scales linearly with n, as $n \to \infty$), while its closest rival contains only about $\log n$ nodes. Furthermore, all nodes in the giant component are connected to each other by short paths: the maximum number of "degrees of separation" between any two nodes grows slowly, like $\log n$.

In the decades since this pioneering work, random graphs have been studied deeply within pure mathematics. They have also served as idealized coupling architectures for dynamical models of gene networks, ecosystems and the spread of infectious diseases and computer viruses.[2]

3. Small-world Networks

Although regular networks and random graphs are both useful idealizations, many real networks lie somewhere between the extremes of order and randomness. Watts and Strogatz studied a simple model that can be tuned through this middle ground: a regular lattice where the original links are replaced by random ones with some probability $0 \leqslant \phi \leqslant 1$. They found that the slightest bit of rewiring transforms the network into a "small world", with short paths between any two nodes, just as in the giant component of a random graph. Yet the network is much more highly clustered than a random graph, in the sense that if A is linked to B and B is linked to C, there is a greatly increased probability that A will also be linked to C (a property that sociologists call "transitivity").

Watts and Strogatz conjectured that the same two properties — short paths and high clustering — would hold also for many natural and technological networks. Furthermore, they conjectured that dynamical systems coupled in this way would display enhanced signal propagation speed, synchronizability and computational power, as compared with regular lattices of the same size. The intuition is that the short paths could provide high-speed communication channels between distant parts of the system, thereby facilitating any dynamical process (like synchronization or computation) that requires global coordination and information flow.

Research has proceeded along several fronts. Many empirical examples of small-world networks have been documented, in fields ranging from cell biology to business. On the theoretical side, small-world networks are turning out to be a Rorschach test — different scientists see different problems here, depending on their disciplines.

Computer scientists see questions about algorithms and their complexity. Walsh showed that graphs associated with many difficult search problems have a small-world topology. Kleinberg introduced an elegant model of the algorithmic challenge posed by Milgram's original sociological experiment — how to actually find a short chain of acquaintances linking yourself to a random target person, using only local information — and he proved that the problem is easily solvable for some kinds of small worlds, and essentially intractable for others.[3]

Epidemiologists have asked how local clustering and global contacts together influence the spread of infectious disease, with implications for vaccination strategies and the evolution of virulence. Neurobiologists have wondered about the possible evolutionary significance of small-world neural architecture. They have argued that this kind of topology combines fast signal processing with coherent oscillations, unlike either regular or random architectures, and that it may be selected by adaptation to rich sensory environments and motor demands.

4. Scale-free Networks

In any real network, some nodes are more highly connected than others are. To quantify this effect, let p_k denote the fraction of nodes that have k links. Here k is called the degree and p_k is the degree distribution.

The simplest random graph models predict a bell-shaped Poisson distribution for p_k. But for many real networks, p_k is highly skewed and decays much more slowly than a Poisson. For instance, the distribution decays as a power law $p_k \sim k^{-\gamma}$ for the Internet backbone, metabolic reaction networks, the telephone call graph and the World-Wide Web (Figure.3(a)). Remarkably, the exponent $\gamma \approx 2.1$–2.4 for all of these cases. Taken literally, this form of heavy-tailed distribution would imply an infinite variance. In reality, there are a few nodes with many links (Figure.2(d). For the World-Wide Web, think Yahoo; for metabolic networks, think ATP. Barabási, Albert and Jeong have dubbed these networks "scale-free", by analogy with fractals, phase transitions and other situations where power laws arise and no single characteristic scale can be defined.

The scale-free property is common but not universal. For coauthorship networks of scientists, p_k is fit better by a power law with an exponential cutoff (Figure.3(b)); for the power grid of the western United States, p_k is an exponential distribution (Figure.3(c)); and for a social network of Mormons in Utah, p_k is gaussian (Figure.3(d)).

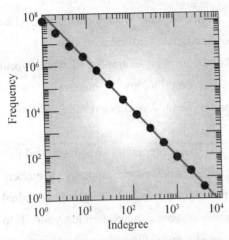

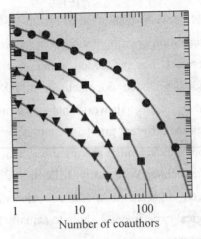

(a) World-Wide Web. Nodes are web pages; links are directed URL hyperlinks from one page to another. The log–log plot shows the number of web pages that have a given in-degree (number of incoming links)

(b) Coauthorship networks. Nodes represent scientists; an undirected link between two people means that they have written a paper together

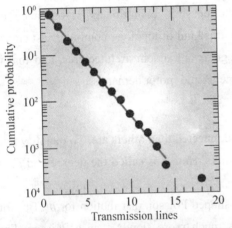

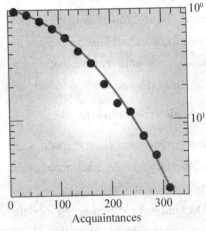

(c) Power grid of the western United States and Canada. Nodes represent generators, transformers and substations; undirected links represent high-voltage transmission lines between them

(d) Social network. Nodes are 43 Mormons in Utah; undirected links represent acquaintances with other Mormons

Fig.3　Degree distributions for real networks

Nevertheless, the scale-free case has stimulated a great deal of theorizing. The earliest work is due to Simon in 1955, now independently rediscovered by Barabási, Albert and Jeong. They showed that a heavy-tailed degree distribution emerges automatically from a stochastic growth model in which new nodes are added continuously and attach themselves preferentially to existing nodes, with probability proportional to the degree of the target node. Richly connected nodes get richer, and the result is $p_k \sim k^{-3}$. More sophisticated models include the effects of adding or rewiring links, allowing nodes to age so that they can no longer accept new links, or varying the form of preferential attachment. These generalized models predict exponential and truncated power-law p_k in some parameter regimes, as well as scale-free distributions.

Could there be a functional advantage to scale-free architecture? Albert, Jeong and Barabási suggested that scale-free networks are resistant to random failures because a few hubs dominate their topology (Figure.2(d)). Any node that fails probably has small degree (like most nodes) and so is expendable. The flip side is that such networks are vulnerable to deliberate attacks on the hubs. These intuitive ideas have been confirmed numerically and analytically by examining how the average path length and size of the giant component depend on the number and degree of the nodes removed. Some possible implications for the resilience of the Internet, the design of therapeutic drugs, and the evolution of metabolic networks have been discussed.

5. Outlook

In the short run there are plenty of good problems about the nonlinear dynamics of systems coupled according to small-world、scale-free or generalized random connectivity. The speculations that these architectures are dynamically advantageous (for example, more synchronizable or error-tolerant) need to be sharpened, then confirmed or refuted mathematically for specific examples. Other ripe topics include the design of self-healing networks, and the relationships among optimization principles、network growth rules and network topology.

In the longer run, network thinking will become essential to all branches of science as we struggle to interpret the data pouring in from neurobiology, genomics, ecology, finance and the World-Wide Web. Will theory be able to keep up? Time to log back on to the Internet...

New Words and Expressions

regular network	*n.*	规则网络
cluster	*n.*	团簇
spontaneously	*adv.*	自然地；本能地
empirical study	*n.*	实证研究
ransitivity	*n.*	传递性
cquaintance	*n.*	交往；相识
accination strategy	*n.*	疫苗接种策略

Notes

1. A natural place to start is at the opposite end of the spectrum from regular networks, with graphs that are completely random.

译文：一个很自然的出发点就是从规则网络图谱到完全随机的图谱。

2. They have also served as idealized coupling architectures for dynamical models of gene networks、ecosystems and the spread of infectious diseases and computer viruses.

译文：它们还为动态基因网络、生态网络、传染病及计算机病毒传播提供了理想的耦合模型。

3. Kleinberg introduced an elegant model of the algorithmic challenge posed by Milgram's original sociological experiment — how to actually find a short chain of acquaintances linking yourself to a random target person, using only local information — and he proved that the problem is easily solvable for some kinds of small worlds, and essentially intractable for others.

译文：为了解决 Milgram 的原始社会学实验中所存在的算法难题，(如何仅仅根据本地信息找到自己和一个随机目标人物之间的最短人际关系链？)Kleinberg 引入了一个可靠的模型，而且他还证明尽管大多数情况下这个问题难以处理，但对于一些小世界而言是易于解决的。

Exercises

Translate the following paragraph into Chinese.

Particular attention has recently been focused on the relationship between the structure and dynamics of complex networks, an issue which has been covered in two excellent comprehensive reviews . However, relatively little attention has been given to the equally important subject of network measurements . Indeed, it is only by obtaining informative quantitative features of the networks topology that they can be characterized and analyzed, and particularly, their structure can be fully related to the respective dynamics. The quantitative description of the networks properties also provides fundamental subsidies for classifying theoretical and real networks into major categories. The present survey's main objective is to provide a comprehensive and accessible review of the main measurements which can be used to quantify important properties of complex networks.

Lesson Ten   Cloud Computing

Text A   An Introduction to Cloud Computing(I)

1. Executive Summary

Cloud computing is a consequence of economic, commercial, cultural and technological conditions that have combined to cause a disruptive shift in information technology (IT) towards a service-based economy. The underlying driver of this change is the commoditization of IT.[1]

While there are many well-documented benefits of cloud computing from economies of scale to acceleration of speed to market, there are also three main groups of risks associated with it; the risk of doing nothing, transitional risks related to this disruptive change in our industry and the general risks of outsourcing.

Canonical's view is that open source technology will help solve many of these latter concerns by not only enabling enterprises to deploy, experiment and test cloud computing concepts behind the firewall, but also by encouraging the formation of competitive marketplaces based around standards.

Canonical is therefore launching Ubuntu Enterprise Cloud, an open source system, based on Eucalyptus, that enables our users to build their own private clouds that match the popular emerging standard of Amazon's Elastic Compute Cloud (EC2).[2]

By using Ubuntu Enterprise Cloud, an enterprise can gain and experiment with many of the benefits of cloud computing while keeping the service behind the firewall and running on its own infrastructure. It's cloud computing that the enterprise controls. By matching emerging industry standards, Canonical aims to simplify any future migration to an external provider. By providing an open source system, Canonical intends to foster an ecosystem so that when the enterprise chooses to move outside the firewall, it will have a choice of service providers.

In summary, Canonical aims to give Enterprise IT a mechanism to prepare for a future life in the clouds along with a simple path for migration between clouds.[3]

Ubuntu Enterprise Cloud is currently provided as a technology preview in the Ubuntu 9.04 Server Edition distribution.

2. Introduction

Today it feels as though IT is under assault from a heady mix of terminology such as utility computing, disruptive technologies, innovation, network effects, open source, agile development, software as a service (SaaS), mashups, web 2.0,web 3.0 and commoditization … the list goes on. It's easy to start drowning as wave after wave of new concepts crash onto the scene. The latest wave is cloud computing.

To some, cloud computing is a future where you won't host your own infrastructure. To others, the cloud is an electricity grid of utility software. While there has been much debate over what cloud computing means, the reality is the term generic. It describes a combination of business and technological factors that are causing a change to our industry and is no more precise than the term "industrial revolution".

Sorting through the tangled mess of today means first getting a clear understanding of what is causing this change. This article is an explanation of the underlying processes behind this onslaught. It aims to provide the reader with a simple pattern to help make sense of the maelstrom. We will examine the fundamental forces behind change, what cloud computing really is, the benefits and disadvantages of cloud computing and why open source matters. Finally, we will also cover how Canonical plans to help you safely navigate this storm.

3. The fundamental forces behind change

Back in the 1990s, Paul Strassmann demonstrated that there was no link between IT spending and business value. While there has been some argument over the validity of the research, Strassmann's work created an idea that rapidly spread. This idea was that not all IT is the same, not all IT has value and some IT has commoditised.

Commoditisation is a neologism that describes how a rare and poorly-understood innovation becomes well-defined and ubiquitous in the eyes of the consumer. In other words, it's a transition that describes how a once-exciting and new activity (an innovation) becomes commonplace and standardized (more of a commodity).[4]

The most often-quoted example of this is the electricity industry and how this innovation led to the formation of national grids in the 1930s.Today, to most consumers, electricity is something you get from a plug and few companies describe their use of electricity as a source of competitive advantage.

In Figure 1, we plot business activities against an axis of ubiquity (how common something is) and certainty (how well-defined and understood something is). The data is derived from the TV, radio and telephony industries and it suggests that an S Curve relationship exists between the ubiquity and certainty of an activity.

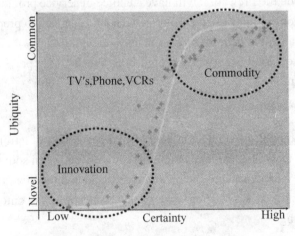

Fig.1　A path for how a rare and poorly-understood innovation becomes a common and well-defined commodity

All business activities are somewhere on that path and all of them are moving-commoditisation never stops and IT activities are no exception. However, the journey of an innovation to ubiquity is not an easy one and some of the changes can be disruptive to an existing industry. This is especially true as any activity moves from the product to the services stage of its journey.[5]

Such a disruptive change is occurring in IT today. A quick glance at the current list of hot topics brings up subjects such as service-oriented architecture (SOA), web services and mashing-up services. All of these contain a strong service theme. The computing stack, which for brevity I'll characterize into the three layers of application, platform and infrastructure, is slowly shifting away from products towards standard components provided as Internet services.

This shift requires 4 simultaneously occurring factors.

(1) The suitability of activities to change (for example, an activity that is widespread and well-defined).

(2) The technology to support such a change.

(3) The concept of service provision to spread in the industry.

(4) The willingness of consumers to adopt such a shift (for example, more of IT being seen and treated as a commodity).

The last thing to note is that you have no choice when it comes to commoditisation. If you treat an activity as an innovation while everyone else uses standard services, then you are only likely to create a competitive disadvantage for yourself. Any company needs to continuously adapt to changes in the surrounding market just to retain its competitive position. Doing nothing is a risk in itself.[6]

Commoditisation is a continual process that can be highly disruptive. You have to continuously adapt to this change and it is happening in IT today.

4. What is cloud computing

A combination of business attitude and technology, together with certain activities becoming common and well-defined, has led to a situation whereby some parts of IT are now suitable for service provision through volume operations. This is not confined to one particular layer of the computing stack but across all layers. This transition has given rise to the "as a Service" industry which includes the following.

(1) Infrastructure (or Hardware) as a Service providers such as Amazon and FlexiScale.

(2) Platform (or Framework) as a Service providers like Ning, BungeeLabs and Azure.

(3) Application (or Software) as a Service providers like Salesforce, Zoho and Google Apps.

Supporting this transition is a range of technologies from clustering to virtualization. In essence, these have provided an effective means of balancing the supply of computing resources to match the demand for volume operations.

While the concept of offering computing resources through utility-like service providers dates back to John McCarthy in the 1960's, many early attempts were unsuccessful as they tried to apply such ideas to activities that lacked both ubiquity and definition.[7] Over the years, as numerous IT activities were widely adopted, they became more suitable for outsourcing to service providers. Managed hosting led the second wave of change and the new breed of volume operations specialists such as Amazon are leading this third wave.

The disruptive transition of the computing stack from a product to a service economy, the growth of a new breed of volume-based service providers and the underlying technologies supporting this change have been grouped together under the heading of cloud computing.

New Words and Expressions

commoditization	n.	商品化
outsourcing	n.	外包；外购；外部采办
marketplace	n.	市场；市场环境；商场；市集
foster	vt.	培养；养育，抚育；抱（希望等）
mechanism	n.	机制；原理，途径；进程；机械装置；技巧
migration	n.	迁移；移民；移动
mashup	n.	混搭程式；混搭网站；混合；聚合；糅合技术
infrastructure	n.	基础设施；公共建设；下部构造
maelstrom	n.	大漩涡；极度混乱；不可抗的破坏力
validity	n.	有效性；正确；正确性
neologism	n.	新词；新义；新词的使用
ubiquity	n.	普遍存在；到处存在
cluster	n.	群；簇；丛；串
	vi.	群聚；丛生
	vt.	使聚集；聚集在某人的周围
virtualization	n.	虚拟化 虚拟化技术
stack	n.	堆；堆叠
	vt.	使堆叠；把……堆积起来
	vi.	堆积，堆叠
disruptive shift		剧变
economies of scale		规模经济
Ubuntu Enterprise Cloud		乌班图企业云
open source system		开源服务系统
emerging industry		新兴产业
derived from		来源于
volume operation		卷操作；并联工作；批量操作
in essence		本质上；其实；大体上

Notes

1. Cloud computing is a consequence of economic、commercial、cultural and technological conditions that have combined to cause a disruptive shift in information technology (IT) towards a service-based economy. The underlying driver of this change is the commoditisation of IT.

译文：当今经济、商业、文化和工艺条件等因素联合起来导致信息技术（IT）不断向以服务业为基础的经济转变，这种剧变导致了云计算的产生。而这种变化的根源则是信息技术产业的商品化。

2. Canonical is therefore launching Ubuntu Enterprise Cloud, an open source system, based on Eucalyptus, that enables our users to build their own private clouds that match the popular emerging standard of Amazon's Elastic Compute Cloud (EC2).

译文：因此，Canonical 正在开设乌班图企业云服务，一种基于 Eucalyptus 技术的开源服务系统。他可以允许用户建立自己的私人云端以便匹配亚马逊弹性计算云（EC2）的新服务标准。

3. In summary, Canonical aims to give Enterprise IT a mechanism to prepare for a future life in the clouds along with a simple path for migration between clouds.

译文：总之，Canonical 的目的在于，为信息技术企业提供一种机制，这种机制可以作为在未来云环境中进行简单云端资源切换的准备。

4. Commoditisation is a neologism that describes how a rare and poorly-understood innovation becomes well-defined and ubiquitous in the eyes of the consumer. In other words, it's a transition that describes how a once-exciting and new activity (an innovation) becomes commonplace and standardized (more of a commodity).

译文：商品化在用户的眼中被赋予了一种新义，即一种罕见的、鲜为人知的创新技术变得无处不在、人人皆知。换句话说，是一种技术（革新）从新鲜刺激、不断升级到普遍应用、标准完备的转变（不仅仅作为一种商品存在）。

5. However, the journey of an innovation to ubiquity is not an easy one and some of the changes can be disruptive to an existing industry. This is especially true as any activity moves from the product to the services stage of its journey.

译文：然而，新兴产业走向普及化的道路并不平坦，一些变革对于已经存在的产业来说可能是破坏性的，这一点在任何产业从产品生产阶段到企业服务阶段的转变过程中尤为凸显。

6. Any company needs to continuously adapt to changes in the surrounding market just to retain its competitive position. Doing nothing is a risk in itself.

译文：对于公司企业而言亦是如此，他们都需要不断地适应周围市场的变化来维持自己的竞争地位，而无为本身就是一种风险。

7. While the concept of offering computing resources through utility-like service providers dates back to John McCarthy in the 1960's, many early attempts were unsuccessful as they tried to apply such ideas to activities that lacked both ubiquity and definition.

译文：然而通过使用服务供应商来提供计算资源的观念要追溯到 20 世纪 60 年代，John McCarthy 做出了很多这方面的尝试，但由于他将这种观念赋予了那些既不普及也没有标准规范的产业，所以这些尝试均以失败告终。

Exercises

Translate the following paragraph into Chinese.

Intel Labs has created an experimental "Single-chip Cloud Computer, SCC" a research microprocessor containing the most Intel Architecture cores ever integrated on a silicon CPU chip — 48 cores. It incorporates technologies intended to scale multi-core processors to 100 cores and beyond, such as an on-chip network, advanced power management technologies and support for "message-passing."

Architecturally, the chip resembles a cloud of computers integrated into silicon. The novel many-core architecture includes innovations for scalability in terms of energy-efficiency including improved core-core communication and techniques that enable software to dynamically configure voltage and frequency to attain power consumptions from 125W to as low as 25W.

This represents the latest achievement from Intel's Tera-scale Computing Research Program. The research was co-led by Intel Labs Bangalore, India, Intel Labs Braunschweig, Germany and Intel Labs researchers in the United States.

The name "Single-chip Cloud Computer" reflects the fact that the architecture resembles a scalable cluster of computers such as you would find in a cloud, integrated into silicon.

In a sense, the SCC is a microcosm of cloud datacenter. Each core can run a separate OS and software stack and act like an individual compute node that communicates with other compute nodes over a packet-based network.

Text B   An Introduction to Cloud Computing(Ⅱ)

1. Benefits and risks of cloud computing

The shift of the computing stack provides an opportunity to eliminate complexities、cost and capital expenditure in much the same way that using an electricity provider removes the need for every company to build power generators.[1]

The main benefits of cloud computing are therefore economies of scale through volume operations, pay-per-use through utility charging, a faster speed to market through componentisation and the ability to focus on core activities through the outsourcing of that which is not core(including scalability and capacity planning).[2]

Providing self-service IT while simultaneously reducing costs may be highly attractive but it creates a competitive risk to doing nothing.

However, it should be remembered that we are in a disruptive transition at this moment. This transition creates commonly-repeated concerns covering management、legal、compliance and trust of service providers. A Canonical survey of 7,000 companies and individuals found that, while over 60 percent of respondents thought that the cloud was ready for mission-critical workloads, less than 30 percent are planning to deploy any kind of workload to the cloud.

In addition to these transitional risks, there also exist the normal considerations for outsourcing any common activity, including whether the activity is suitable for outsourcing, what the second-sourcing options are and whether switching between providers is easy.

Though service level agreements (SLAs) can help alleviate some concerns, any fears can only be truly overcome once customers can easily switch between providers through a marketplace. This already occurs in many industries from electricity to telephony and it is this switching, which has created competitive markets with competitive price pressures. Until such markets appear, it is probable that many corporations will continue to use home-grown solutions, particularly in industries that have already expended capital to remove themselves from lock-in, which is widespread in the product world.[3]

While the cloud lacks any functioning marketplaces today, it is entirely possible that ecosystems of providers will emerge based on easy switching and competition through price and quality of service. In such circumstances, many of the common concerns regarding the uncertainty of supply will be overcome.

While the benefits of cloud computing are many and obvious, there exist the normal concerns associated with the outsourcing of any activity, combined with additional risks due to the transitional nature of this change.

2. Why open source matters

Open source companies give away their products freely while competing on services. Hence this disruptive shift of the computing stack is not only beneficial to them, they are also the companies least likely to be held back through a product mentality. Many of the winners in the cloud computing space are likely to come from an open source background.

It is also likely that open source will lead the way in creating defector standards in the cloud in much the same way that Apache became the standard for the web. An open source reference implementation of a potential standard provides a fast means for multiple parties to operationally implement a standard without sacrificing strategic control to a technology vendor.[4] The use of open source also encourages ecosystems to develop around a technology and, while there currently exists a plethora of different cloud offerings for the same activity (such as infrastructure provision), none have created a widespread ecosystem. Successful creation of an ecosystem is the difference between becoming the TCP/IP of the cloud computing world or the Banyan Vines.

As outlined above, the solution to many of the risks of cloud computing depends on the formation of viable ecosystems containing marketplaces of providers with easy switching between them. Such marketplaces depend on standards and understanding this issue is key for any reader wishing to explore the potential future of cloud computing.

In the analogy of the electricity industry, a power plant is used by a provider to create electricity as a standardised output. In the computing industry, while physical hardware is the equivalent of a power plant, the output is the three layers of the computing stack. To standardise this would mean that providers would need to offer the same outputs. For example, a marketplace of application providers would need to consolidate around standardised applications. Competition, in such a marketplace, would be around price and quality of service for the provision of the same application.

For a product-based industry, this creates a fundamental shift in mindset to competition on service rather than feature differentiation. Such a change is inevitable as it is only those activities, which are well-defined and commonplace that are suitable for service provision. The ubiquity and feature-completeness of those activities means there is little advantage to the end consumer through further feature differentiation.

However, standardised output is not in itself enough as the analogy of computing to the electricity industry contains a flaw. In the electricity industry, you have no relationship with your provider. In the case of cloud computing, you do, it's called your data. Hence any future marketplaces will require not only standardised outputs and competition on service, but also freedom of data and, as a result, easy switching.

While many will argue that such effects can be created through agreed and open specifications (known as open standards), the historical problem has always been not what is in the standard but how providers seek to extend beyond it. In the service world, such extensions or feature differentiations are the antithesis of portability and would severely limit the growth of any ecosystem. While a service provider might consider it to be an advantage to lock in a consumer, it is these very same concerns that continue to slow user adoption.

In a service world, it makes little sense for the code that describes an activity to be anything other than open source or at least based on an open source reference implementation that ensures portability between providers. In such a world, service providers will need to seek competitive advantages through operations and not feature differentiation.

As a general rule of thumb, the future of open source and the development of cloud computing appear to go hand in hand. We've already seen the first shoots of this future with the Distributed Management Task Force's (DMTF's) proposals for a standard to enable portability between virtual machines and the creation of open source systems such as Eucalyptus.[5]

Eucalyptus, a system developed by University of California Santa Barbara (UCSB),is an open source environment that enables you to create and build your own cloud that matches the Amazon EC2 application program interface(API).Creating your own internal cloud is a way of testing, deploying and experimenting with the benefits of cloud computing without the need to venture outside of the corporate firewall.

It is Canonical's view that the open source Eucalyptus system will help to create an ecosystem of providers and is likely to develop into a defacto standard for cloud computing at the infrastructure layer of the stack.

Open source is likely to feature strongly in the future of cloud computing and the

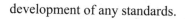

development of any standards.

3. What is Canonical doing about the cloud

Canonical supports and sponsors Ubuntu, the fastest-growing Linux-based operating system with over 10 million users and a huge community of developers. As a service-focused company that specializes in the free provision of software for common activities, Canonical is well positioned to compete in this cloud computing world.

The software we provide is used for everything from customer relationship management (CRM) to databases. We focus on those common workloads and those commodity-like activities, which have become ubiquitous in IT. Our approach of providing standardised open source components is specifically aimed at enabling companies to quickly implement standard services, which can be used to support more innovative activities.

In our recent survey, 85 percent of respondents said they would use Ubuntu on the cloud. For this reason, we have introduced Ubuntu Server Edition onto Amazon EC2 (see www.ubuntu.com/ec2) to enable our users to take advantage of the benefits that cloud computing can create.

While we are aware that as the cloud industry develops, many of the adoption issues will be resolved, we also realize that our users need specific support in this time of transition. We take the view that many of our users and enterprise customers wish to experiment with cloud computing but within the confines of their own environments.

For this reason, we will be releasing Ubuntu Enterprise Cloud, which includes Eucalyptus in the Ubuntu distribution. We will also be working on supporting efforts to ensure the portability of infrastructure between different service providers. This will minimise any future impact on our users due to migration. As part of these efforts, we will be looking to build a consortium of providers and management tools to help promote open source in the cloud computing space.

Our aim is to support the growth of both private and public clouds based around an entirely open source stack, and to provide portability between both environments. Canonical will also be offering commercial support for internal clouds along with technical consultancy for installation.

Canonical will be providing open source cloud computing systems in the Ubuntu distribution. This will give Enterprise IT a mechanism to deal with common workloads while preparing for a life in the clouds.

4. Summary

Cloud computing is a disruptive change, caused by the underlying commoditisation of IT. Canonical expects to see a future dominance of the open source model in cloud computing, which will solve the major adoption concerns for users.[6]

At this moment in time, IT is in transition from "as a product" to "as a service" for common workloads and activities. Unsurprisingly the cloud currently lacks standards and there remain several unresolved legal, management and compliance questions. This is on top of the normal concerns raised by the outsourcing of a common activity including: whether the activity is suitable for outsourcing, whether second-sourcing options exist and whether there is easy switching between providers.

To support our users in this time of transition, Canonical will be launching Ubuntu Enterprise Cloud by including Eucalyptus in the Ubuntu distribution. This will provide our users with an open source system that enables them to build their own private clouds, which match the current emerging standard of the Amazon EC2 API.

Canonical views this system as a stepping stone on the road to a future marketplace of external cloud providers. Hence, we are also providing Ubuntu for use with leading cloud providers and promoting infrastructure portability between clouds.

New Words and Expressions

Componentization	*n.*	构件化；元件化；组件化
scalability	*n.*	可扩展性；可伸缩性；可量测性
simultaneously	*adv.*	同时地；同时发生地
compliance	*n.*	顺从，服从；承诺
respondent	*adj.*	回答的；应答的
	n.	应答者
deploy	*vt.*	配置；展开；使疏开
	vi.	调配；部署；展开
	n.	部署
mentality	*n.*	心态；智力；精神力；心理素质
defacto	*adj.*	事实上的；实际上的
	adv.	事实上
vendor	*n.*	卖主；供应商
plethora	*n.*	过多；过剩
consolidate	*vt.*	巩固，使固定；联合；合并
	vi.	巩固，加强
flaw	*n.*	瑕疵，裂纹；缺点
antithesis	*n.*	对立面；对照
portability	*n.*	可移植性；轻便；可携带；可调动性
consortium	*n.*	联合；结合
pay-per-use		按每次使用计费；付费 ；使用付费；量计价
service level agreements (SLAs)		服务水平协议
easy switching		轻松切换
feature-completeness		功能完整性
make sense		有意义；讲得通；言之有理
as a rule of thumb		根据经验；一般说来
private cloud		私有云；私有云端；私人云端

Notes

1. The shift of the computing stack provides an opportunity to eliminate complexities、cost and capital expenditure in much the same way that using an electricity provider removes the need for every company to build power generators.

译文：IT 产业的转型为企业带来了消除复杂度、成本和基建费用的机遇，这就与每一个企业都有电力供应商而不需要使用电力发电机差不多。

2. The main benefits of cloud computing are therefore economies of scale through volume operations, pay-per-use through utility charging, a faster speed to market through componentisation and the ability to focus on core activities through the outsourcing of that which is not core(including scalability and capacity planning).

译文：云计算服务的主要优势在于，批量业务操作的规模经济、按使用付费、组件化快速投入市场以及通过外包非核心产业使企业能够更加致力于核心产业（包括可扩展性和产能规划）的建设。

3. Until such markets appear, it is probable that many corporations will continue to use home-grown solutions, particularly in industries that have already expended capital to remove themselves from lock-in, which is widespread in the product world.

译文：这样的市场一经出现，很多公司很有可能继续使用自有的服务措施，尤其对于那些已经花费了成本用于解除价格压力的公司来说更会如此，接着这种市场效应就会蔓延到产品生产层面。

4. An open source reference implementation of a potential standard provides a fast means for multiple parties to operationally implement a standard without sacrificing strategic control to a technology vendor.

译文：一项带有潜在标准的开源系统参考运行提供了一种多方在不丧失对技术供应商战略性控制的情况下快速完成操作上执行标准的方法。

5. As a general rule of thumb, the future of open source and the development of cloud computing appear to go hand in hand. We've already seen the first shoots of this future with the Distributed Management Task Force's (DMTF's) proposals for a standard to enable portability between virtual machines and the creation of open source systems such as Eucalyptus.

译文：以一般的经验角度来说，未来开源技术以及云计算服务的发展将会齐头并进。我们已经看到这种未来发展的第一支萌芽，那就是为了实现虚拟机和建立像 Eucalyptus 这样的开源系统之间相互调度而创立的分布式管理任务组建议的提出。

6. Cloud computing is a disruptive change, caused by the underlying commoditisation of IT. Canonical expects to see a future dominance of the open source model in cloud computing, which will solve the major adoption concerns for users.

译文：IT 产业的潜在商品化使得云计算成为颠覆性的变革。Canonical 认为，未来云计算中占据支配地位的将是开源模型，这些模型将解决用户关心的大部分问题。

Exercises

Translate the following paragraph into Chinese.

One of the most important aspects of the SCC's network fabric architecture is that it supports "scale-out" message-passing programming models that have been proven to scale to 1000s of processors in cloud datacenters. Though each core has 2 levels of cache, there is no hardware cache coherence support among cores in order to simplify the design, reduce power consumption and to encourage the exploration of datacenter distributed memory software models, on-chip. Intel researchers have successfully demonstrated message-passing as well as software-based coherent shared memory on the SCC.

Fine-grained power management is a focus of the chip as well. Software applications are given control to turn cores on and off or to change their performance levels, continuously adapting to use the minimum energy needed at a given moment. The SCC can run all 48 cores at one time over a range of 25W to 125W and selectively vary the voltage and frequency of the mesh network as well as sets of cores. Each tile (2 cores) can have its own frequency, and groupings of four tiles (8 cores) can each run at their own voltage.

Intel Labs believes the SCC is an ideal research platform to help accelerate many-core software research and advanced development. Intel researchers have already ported a variety of applications to the SCC, including web servers、physics modeling、and financial analytics. By the middle of 2010, Intel Labs anticipates having dozens of industry and academic research partners conducting advanced software research on the SCC hardware platform.

第3章 科技论文写作的基础知识

3.1 概 述

现代科学技术工作已经趋于综合化、社会化。科技工作与社会各方面的联系十分密切。在某一科学技术领域中往往是一群人在进行各个不同方向(或者是相同方向、相同课题)的研究，这就需要彼此联系、交流和借鉴。这种联系、交流和借鉴主要是通过科技工作者发表论文的形式进行的。论文的写作与发表，是科技工作者之间进行科学思想交流的永久记录，也是科学的历史，它记载了探索真理的过程，记载了各种观测结果和研究结果，而科学技术研究是一种承上启下的连续性的工作，一项研究的结束可能是另一项研究的起点。因此，科技工作者通过论文写作与发表的形式进行学术交流，从而促进研究成果的推广和应用。

不少作者往往把写论文当成课题研究最后阶段的事来做，因而常常听到他们说："等课题完了再写吧！"其实，写论文不是为了"交差"、"还账"，也不只是为了发表。科技论文的写作是科学技术研究的一种手段，是科学技术研究工作的重要组成部分。最好的作法是，课题研究的开始就是论文写作的开始，因为思考一个比较复杂的问题，借助于写作，效果会更好些。如果把写作贯穿在整个研究工作中，边研究，边写作，则可及时发现研究工作的不足，补充和修正正在进行的研究，使研究成果更加完善；同时也还有这样的可能，即写作灵感的突发将导致研究方案的重大改进，从而最终提高研究成果的水平和价值。

科技论文写作水平的高低往往直接影响科技工作的进展。例如，一篇写得好的科研选题报告或建设项目可行性论证报告，可以促进一个有价值的科研项目或建设项目尽快上马；反之，一篇写得不好、表达不规范的论文，也将会妨碍某项科研成果得到公认，妨碍某种新理论、新方法被人们所接受，妨碍某项先进技术得到迅速推广。或者，尽管研究成果具有发表的价值，但由于文稿写作质量太差，有时也不易被期刊编辑部门所接受。因此，作为科技工作者，应当掌握科技论文写作的一般方法，了解编辑出版部门对文稿质量和规格的要求，熟悉有关的国家标准和规定，不断提高自己的写作能力，从而使自己能够得心应手地写出学术价值或实用价值高、科学性强、文字细节和技术细节表达规范性好的科技论文，以此奉献给社会，让它们在促进学术交流和推动科学技术及经济建设的发展中发挥应有的作用。

3.1.1 科技论文的定义及分类

科技论文的定义有很多。简单地说，科技论文是对创造性的科研成果进行理论分析和总结的科技写作文体。比较翔实的定义为科技论文是报道自然科学研究和技术开发创新工作成果的论说文章，它是通过运用概念、判断、推理、证明或反驳等逻辑思维手段，来分析表达自然科学理论和技术开发研究成果的。

从论文的内容这个角度来下定义，将使读者对于什么样的文章才叫做科技论文有一个明确的概念，这个定义也恰恰反映了科技论文区别于其他文体的特点。科技论文是创新性科学技术研究工作成果的科学论述，是某些理论性、实验性或观测性新知识的科学记录，是某些已知原理应用于实际中取得新进展、新成果的科学总结。

科技论文的分类就像它的定义一样，有很多种不同的分法。下面从两个不同的角度对科技论文进行分类，并说明各类论文的概念及写作要求。

1. 从作用上分

科技论文就其发挥的作用来看可分为 3 类：学术性论文；技术性论文；学位论文。

(1) 学术性论文。

指研究人员提供给学术性期刊发表或向学术会议提交的论文，它以报道学术研究成果为主要内容。学术性论文反映了该学科领域最新的、最前沿的科学水平和发展动向，对科学技术事业的发展起着重要的推动作用。这类论文应具有新的观点、新的分析方法和新的数据或结论，并具有科学性。

(2) 技术性论文。

指工程技术人员为报道工程技术研究成果而提交的论文，这种研究成果主要是应用已有的理论来解决设计、技术、工艺、设备、材料等具体技术问题而取得的。技术性论文对技术进步和提高生产力起着直接的推动作用。这类论文应具有技术的先进性、实用性和科学性。

(3) 学位论文。

指学位申请者提交的论文。这类论文依学位的高低又分为以下 3 种：即学士论文、硕士论文、博士论文。

学位论文要经过考核和答辩，因此，无论是论述还是文献综述，或是介绍实验装置、实验方法都要比较详尽，而学术性或技术性论文是写给同专业的人员看的，要力求简洁。除此之外，学位论文与学术性论文和技术性论文之间并无其他严格的区别。就写作方法而论，这种分类并无太大意义，这里仅借分类说明一下它们各自的特点和一般写作要求而已。

2. 从研究方式与论述内容上分

在科学技术研究工作中，人们的研究内容和方式是不同的，有的以实验为研究手段，通过实验发现新现象，寻找科学规律，或验证某种理论和假说，总之，实验结果的科学记录和总结就是研究工作的成果。有的是先提出假说，进行数学推导或逻辑推理，或者借助数学方法作为研究的手段，用实验结果来检验理论，这类论文以论述或论证为中心，或提出新的理论，或对原有的理论作出新的补充和发展，或作出否定。有的研究对象虽然属于自然科学或工程技术范畴，但论述的方式却类似于社会科学的某些论文，即用可信的调查研究所得的事实或数据来论证新的观点；等等。所以，按照研究的方式和论述的内容可对科技论文作如下分类。

(1) 实(试)验研究报告。

这类论文不同于一般的实(试)验报告，其写作重点应放在"研究"上。它追求的是可靠的理论依据，先进的实(试)验设计方案，适用的测试手段，合理、准确的数据处理及科

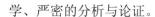

学、严密的分析与论证。

(2) 理论推导。

这类论文主要是对提出的新假说通过数学推导和逻辑推理，得到新的理论，包括定理、定律和法则。其写作要求是数学推导要科学、准确，逻辑推理要严密，并准确地使用定义和概念，力求得到无懈可击的结论。

(3) 理论分析。

这类论文主要是对新的设想、原理、模型、机构、材料、工艺、样品等进行理论分析，对过去的理论分析加以完善、补充或修正。其论证分析要严谨，数学运算要正确，资料数据要可靠，结论除了要准确以外，一般还须经实(试)验验证。

(4) 设计计算。

它一般是指为解决某些工程问题、技术问题而进行的计算机程序设计；某些系统、工程方案、机构、产品的计算机辅助设计和优化设计，以及某些过程的计算机模拟；某些产品(包括整机、部件或零件)或物质(材料、原料等)的设计或调、配制等。对这类论文总的要求是相对要"新"，数学模型的建立和参数的选择要合理，编制的程序要能正常运行，计算结果要合理、准确；设计的产品或调、配制的物质要经试验证实或经生产、使用考核。

(5) 专题论述。

这类论文是指对某些事业(产业)、某一领域、某一学科、某项工作发表议论(包括立论和驳论)，通过分析论证，对它们的发展战略决策、发展方向和道路，以及方针政策等提出新的独到的见解。

(6) 综合论述。

这类论文应是在作者博览群书的基础上，综合介绍、分析、评述该学科(专业)领域里国内外的研究新成果、发展新趋势，并表明作者自己的观点，作出发展的科学预测，提出比较中肯的建设性意见和建议。一篇好的综合论述，对于学科发展的探讨，产品、设计、工艺材料改进的研究，科学技术研究的选题，以及研究生学位论文的选题和青年科技人员及教师进修方向的选择等的指导作用都是很大的。对这类论文的基本要求是资料新而全，作者立足点高、眼光远，问题综合恰当、分析在理，意见和建议比较中肯。

3.1.2 科技论文的突出特点

科技论文同一般的科技文章有共同之处，具有准确、鲜明、生动的特点，但作为科技论文，它又有自身的特殊性。

1. 创新性或独创性

科技论文报道的主要研究成果应是前人(或他人)所没有的。没有新的观点、见解、结果和结论，就不称其为科技论文。对于某一篇论文，其创新程度可能大些，也可能很小，但总要有一些独到之处，总要对丰富科学技术知识宝库和推动科学技术发展起到一定的作用。"首次提出"，"首次发现"，当然是具有重大价值的研究成果，这毕竟为数不多。在某一个问题上有新意，对某一点有发展，应属于创新的范围。基本上是重复他人的工作，尽管确实是作者自己"研究"所得的"成果"，则不属于创新之列。在实际研究中，有很多课题是在引进、消化、移植国内外已有的先进科学技术，以及应用已有的理论来解决本地区、本行业、本系统的实际问题，只要对丰富理论、促进生产发展、推动技术进步有效果，有作用，报道这类成果的论文也应视为有一定程度的创新。

由于创新性的要求，科技论文的写作不应与教科书(讲义)和实验报告、工作总结等同。科技论文报道的是作者自己的研究成果，因而与他人相重复的研究内容，基础性的知识，某些一般性的、具体的实验过程和操作或数学推导，以及比较浅显的分析等都应删去，或者只做简要的交代和说明，同时应对原始材料有整理、有取舍、有提高，要形成新观点、新认识、新结论。

2. 理论性或学术性

理论性指一篇科技论文应具有一定的学术价值，它有两个方面的含义。

(1) 对实验、观察或用其他方式所得到的结果，要从一定的理论高度进行分析和总结，形成一定的科学见解，包括提出并解决一些有科学价值的问题。

(2) 对自己提出的科学见解或问题，要用事实和理论进行符合逻辑的论证与分析或说明，总之要将实践上升为理论。

3. 科学性和准确性

所谓科学性，就是要正确地说明研究对象所具有的特殊矛盾，并且要尊重事实，尊重科学。具体说来，包括论点正确，论据必要而充分，论证严密，推理符合逻辑，数据可靠，处理合理，计算精确，实验反复，结论客观等。所谓准确性，是指对客观事物即研究对象的运动规律和性质表述的接近程度，包括概念、定义、判断、分析和结论要准确，对自己研究成果的估计要确切、恰当，对他人研究成果(尤其是在做比较时)的评价要实事求是，切忌片面性和说过头话。

4. 规范性和可读性

撰写科技论文是为了交流、传播、储存新的科技信息，让他人利用，因此，科技论文必须按一定格式写作，必须具有良好的可读性。在文字表达上，要求语言准确、简明、通顺，条理清楚，层次分明，论述严谨。在技术表达方面，包括名词术语、数字、符号的使用，图表的设计，计量单位的使用，文献的著录等都应符合规范化要求。科技论文规范表达的要求来自科学技术期刊编排的标准化和规范化。科技论文表达规范，不仅能提高论文本身的水平，而且可以反映出作者具有严谨的治学态度和优良的写作修养。这为论文被期刊编辑部门选中发表提供了极为有利的条件。诚然，一篇论文能否被期刊采用，主要决定于论文报道的研究成果是否有发表价值，但是，表达规范与否也是不能忽视的因素。尤其是对于稿源丰富的期刊，当在两篇都有发表价值的论文中只能选用一篇时，被选中的肯定是表达比较规范的那一篇，因为它的编辑加工量小，或者不必要经过作者再修改，从而可以保证出版质量，缩短发表周期。因此，为了使确有发表价值的论文能得到及时发表，避免因表达不规范被退稿或推迟发表，作者应努力提高论文的写作质量，使之达到规范表达的要求。

科技论文的规范表达涉及如下主要内容。

(1) 编写格式的标准化。

(2) 文字细节和技术细节表达的标准化或规范化，主要包括名词名称、数字、量和单位、数学式、化学式等的规范表达，以及插图和表格的合理设计。

(3) 科技语言和标点符号的规范运用。

3.1.3 科技论文的结构及编写格式

科技论文一般由引言、方法、结果和讨论等主要部分构成。在引言中回答研究什么问题，问题的位置；在方法中回答怎样研究这个问题；在结果这一部分阐述新的发现；对于新发现的意义可在讨论部分回答。

科技论文的基本格式为：题名(Title)、作者(Authors)、联系地址(Address)、摘要(Abstract)、关键词(Keywords)、引言(Introduction)、方法(Methodology)、结果和讨论(Results and Discussion)、结论(Conclusion)、附录(Appendix)、致谢(Acknowledgement)、参考文献(References)等。

题名(Title)是科技论文的必要组成部分。它要求用最简洁、恰当的词组反映文章的特定内容，把论文的主题明白无误地告诉读者，并且使之具有画龙点睛，启迪读者兴趣的功能。一般情况下，题名中应包括文章的主要关键词。题名像一条标签，切忌用冗长的主、谓、宾语结构的完整语句逐点描述论文的内容，以保证达到"简洁"的要求；而"恰当"的要求应反映在用词的中肯、醒目、好读好记上。当然，也要避免过分笼统或哗众取宠的所谓简洁，缺乏可检索性，以至于名实不符或无法反映出每篇文章应有的主题特色。

著者署名(Authors)是科技论文的必要组成部分。著者系指在论文主题内容的构思、具体研究工作的执行及撰稿执笔等方面的全部或局部上做出主要贡献，能够对论文的主要内容负责答辩的人员，是论文的法定主权人和责任者。合写论文的各著者应按论文工作贡献的多少顺序排列。著者的姓名应给出全名。同时还应给出著者完成研究工作的单位或著者所在的工作单位或通信地址(address)，以便读者在需要时可与著者联系。

摘要(Abstract)是以提供文献内容梗概为目的，不加评论和补充解释，简明确切地记述文章重要内容的短文。学位论文等文章具有某种特殊性，为了评审，可写成变异式的摘要，不受字数的限制。摘要的编写应该客观、真实，切忌掺杂编写者的主观见解、解释和评论。

为了便于读者从浩如烟海的书刊中寻找文献，特别是适应计算机自动检索的需要，GB3179/T-92 规定，现代科技期刊都应在学术论文的摘要后面给出 3～8 个关键词(Key words)。

引言(前言、序言、概述)(Introduction)经常作为论文的开端，主要回答"为什么研究(why)"这个问题。它简明介绍论文的背景、相关领域的前人研究历史与现状(有时亦称这部分为文献综述)，以及著者的意图与分析依据，包括论文的追求目标、研究范围和理论、技术方案的选取等。引言应言简意赅，不要等同于摘要，或成为摘要的注释。引言中不应详述同行熟知的，包括教科书上已有陈述的基本理论、实验方法和基本方程的推导；除非是学位论文，为了反映著者的学业等，允许有较详尽的文献综述段落。如果在正文中采用比较专业化的术语或缩写词时，最好先在引言中定义说明。

正文是科技论文的核心组成部分，主要回答"怎么研究(how)"这个问题。正文应充分阐明论文的观点、原理、方法及具体达到预期目标的整个过程，并且突出一个"新"字，以反映论文具有的首创性。根据需要，论文可以分层深入，逐层剖析，按层设分层标题。一般应包括材料、方法、结果和讨论等几个部分。

　　结论(Conclusion)是整篇文章的最后总结。尽管多数科技论文的著者都采用结论的方式作为结束，并通过它传达自己欲向读者表述的主要意向，但它不是论文的必要组成部分。结论不应是正文中各段小结的简单重复，主要回答"研究出什么(what)"。它应该以正文中的试验或考察中得到的现象、数据和阐述分析作为依据，由此完整、准确、简洁地指出以下内容。

　　(1) 对研究对象进行考察或实验得到的结果所揭示的原理及其普遍性。

　　(2) 研究中有无发现例外或本论文尚难以解释和解决的问题。

　　(3) 与先前已经发表过的(包括他人或著者自己)研究工作的异同。

　　(4) 本论文在理论上与实用上的意义与价值。

　　(5) 对进一步深入研究本课题的建议。

　　致谢(Acknowledgement)一般单独成段，放在文章的最后面，但它不是论文的必要组成部分。它是对曾经给予论文的选题、构思或撰写以指导或建议，对考察或实验过程中做出某种贡献的人员，或给予过技术、信息、物质或经费帮助的单位、团体或个人致以谢意。

　　文后参考文献(References)是现代科技论文的重要组成部分，但如果撰写论文时未参考文献也可以不写。它是反映文稿的科学依据和著者尊重他人研究成果而向读者提供文中引用有关资料的出处，或为了节约篇幅和叙述方便，提供在论文中提及而没有展开的有关内容的详尽文本。

3.2　科技论文写作

　　科技论文(research paper)是在科学研究、科学实验的基础上，对自然科学和专业技术领域里的某些现象或问题进行专题研究，分析和阐述，为揭示这些现象和问题的本质及其规律而撰写成的文章。也就是说，凡是运用概念、判断、推理、论证和反驳等逻辑思维手段，来分析和阐明自然科学原理、定律和各种问题的文章，均属科技论文的范畴。

　　科技论文是作者用科学思维，将通过科学实践所获得的科研成果进行总结归纳后，按论点和论据所写成的论证性文章。一篇优秀论文既要求内容丰富新颖、科学性强，又要富有理论性、实践性和创新性，且文字通顺，层次清楚，逻辑性强。

　　为了写一篇科技论文，必须进行很多带有评判性的阅读并对获得的材料进行评估。这些经历对大学学习和大学毕业以后的工作都有益处。写作的过程也给了学生学习如何使用图书馆，如何使用文献的机会。这个过程也会使学生熟悉一篇科技论文的结构和写作要素，并学习到一些从前不了解的知识。

3.2.1　科技论文写作步骤

　　任何两个人的写作过程都不会相同。但是在写作的时候，每一位作者都可以遵从一定的写作步骤。这里给出了这些步骤。要注意这些步骤都不是相互排斥的，有时当处于某一阶段时，很可能又要回头进行早已完成的阶段。

　　1. 选择一个能够研究下去的主题

　　所有的研究论文写作都是从确定一个主题开始的，因此确定主题是写作论文的第一个

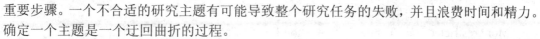

重要步骤。一个不合适的研究主题有可能导致整个研究任务的失败，并且浪费时间和精力。确定一个主题是一个迂回曲折的过程。

选择主题是件非常困难的事情。选择的主题是不是太大？是不是太窄？能不能找到足够的材料来写一篇研究性论文，必须找一个感兴趣的并且能够进行下去的主题。建议按照下述过程选择主题。

(1) 选择一个方向。

选择一个感兴趣的方向。然后到图书馆或者其他地方，查找是否有足够多的相关材料，如果找不到就放弃。

选择主题的时候，不要为了方便就自动选择一个早已经熟悉的方向，但也不要放弃某些你已经很熟悉的方向。应该选择一个感到好奇并且认为如果研究下去，能够学习到一些新知识的主题。

(2) 阅读并思考。

在选择主题的过程中，不能忽略的一件事情就是到图书馆查找一些参考资料。阅读尽可能多的资料，并进行深入的思考。也可以通过网络查找一些适合于该主题的材料。在读的过程中，考虑该主题是否已经被研究透，是否可以进一步进行研究，从而发现一些新的东西。如果已经被研究透，不能发现新的东西就放弃该主题。

(3) 细化主题。

选择的主题不要太宽，以至于必须写一本书才能完成。一定要把主题限制在某个特殊的方面，以在有限的时间内完成论文。

把选择的主题用问题的形式给出。例如：媒体是否影响到选举？使用主题词来描述主题。在这个例子中，明显的主题词是 media 和 elections，但是也有其他可能。

television	AND	elections
press	AND	politics
press	AND	influence

太宽的主题可能检索到太多的材料，而太窄的主题有可能检索到资料太少或者检索不到资料。如果主题太宽，可以尝试重新表述问题。对上面提到的例子，可以重新表示为电视覆盖率对 2008 年美国总统选举有什么影响？

下面给出适用于论文主题的一些标准。

① 主题必须是有意义的和严肃的。一篇研究论文必须使人思考和学习。译文不是告知听众已有的信息、数据和分析，而是创造新的知识！

② 必须是一个能够操作的主题。不能处理一些没有进行过必要训练的主题。例如，你主修英语，但是却想写一篇有关核物理方面的论文。

③ 选择的主题必须是可以获得足够多材料的主题。

④ 选择的主题必须能够被客观对待，不能有个人喜恶。

⑤ 选择的主题不能太热门。

如果选择的主题符合以上的标准，就可以进入到下一阶段，否则必须修改主题直到符合上述标准。

下面看一个如何选择和细化科技论文主题的例子。

Sample 2

General topic: Channel Equalization

Restricted: Channel Equalization for IEEE 802.16

More restricted: Channel Equalization for IEEE 802.16 Single-Carrier System

Topic chosen: MLSE equalization algorithm for IEEE 802.16 Single-Carrier System

2. 收集材料

确定一个研究主题后，就可以开始收集相关材料了。到图书馆标出所有需要的书籍、杂志，然后对这些材料进行复印。如果有电子版材料，可以马上打印出来。

这里的材料指的是与研究相关的材料。不可能没有任何材料就能把论文写出来，所参考材料的数量和质量反映了研究的深度。应该从决定写作论文的时候就开始收集材料。

收集材料的时候注意：需要多少信息？这取决于需要信息的理由；写论文的目的是什么？论文需要多少页？需要一些深层次的信息还是仅仅是一些背景信息？需要什么类型的信息？什么级别的，学术的还是大众的？

可以找到材料的地方很多，下面列举一些。

(1) Internet：有很多搜索工具，如 Google、Dog Pile、Yahoo 等。当使用 Web 搜索工具时，注意以下事项。

① 仔细阅读搜索工具的使用帮助。例如，Google 的高级搜索可以使搜索结果仅仅限于教育性的，非营利性的，或者政府网站。

② 不要期望能从搜索结果中直接获得相关期刊、杂志、报纸详细的内容。很多材料是受版权保护的，不能免费获得这些材料。

③ 不要期望一种搜索工具能够搜到所有的信息。同样，不要期望两种搜索工具搜索的结果是一样的。

④ 不要认为搜索结果中的材料顺序就显示了材料的价值顺序。每一个搜索工具都有自己的搜索策略。

⑤ 不要随意相信所读的信息，特别是在 Web 上的信息。

(2) 图书馆的在线目录。

(3) 期刊杂志。

大部分原始材料来自书籍、杂志、期刊或网络。收集信息的主要方法就是阅读这些原始材料。在阅读的时候，应该在最短的时间内，发现阅读的内容是不是有用的信息。要快速并带有评判性地阅读原始材料。对一篇论文和一本书籍，不总是需要从头到尾进行阅读。首先看看目录或者索引，来发现哪些章节有可能成为有用的材料。应该忽略一些不相关的内容。

当发现一些有用材料时，必须考虑它是否可靠。如果材料来源可疑，则没有任何价值。因此必须知道有哪些人对该文进行了评价，并且评价内容是什么。如果是书籍，最好找到该书的最新版本，并且同其他具有相同主题的书籍进行比较。必须保证你的材料不是过时的或者带有偏见的。

评价材料来源的标准有如下几条。

① 权威性：看看该来源是出自何处，并且他/它的信用等级如何。从书、期刊、Web 上查找该出处的所有信息。作者是一个自由作者还是一个研究者？他隶属于某个协会还是某个组织？出版社或者期刊是否权威？

② .精确性：考虑材料是否前后一致，是否被其他资源证实或引用。如果是一本书或者一篇论文，查找它是否被引用过。对 Web 上的材料，一定要从其他地方得到证实。记住，没有人对 Web 上的内容进行管理和限制。

③ 客观性：考虑提供该材料的作者或者组织的最终目的是什么，其目的是告知性的，劝说性的，还是纯粹为了卖产品。

④ 实时性：检查来源是不是最新更新过的。要记住书籍从写作到发行，至少要一年。因此，即使最新的书籍，其内容也有一两年是"过时"的。期刊杂志往往能提供实时性信息。

⑤ 全面性：考虑收集的材料在深度上和广度上是否适合你的主题。

一旦确定了主题，并且收集到一些必要的材料后，你应该开始做笔记。没有人能够记住他所读过的所有材料，也没有人不做笔记就能写出好的研究论文。做笔记的最好时刻是在阅读的时候。阅读时信息在你的脑子里是最清晰的。不要说你会在阅读完一分材料后马上回过头来做笔记。你不会记住所有你想记住的内容，也不会记住在哪里再找到它们。

在做笔记时应该注意以下事项。

① 使用自己的字词。用自己的字词总结材料也是为了防止剽窃他人成果。

② 引用时要使用引用标记。这提醒你这是一个引用，并且需要进行解释。

③ 使用较短的句子，避免使用长的句子。

④ 记住所记录内容的出处和页码。

3. 明确你的论点或研究问题

选定主题并阅读了一些材料后，必须为论文确定一个论点或研究问题，也就是你的论文的最终目的是什么。不同性质的论文有不同的确定方式，以下分别叙述分析性论文和辩论性论文两种研究性论文。

(1) 分析性论文：分析就是把一个主题或概念进行分解，并按照自己的想法进行重组。在一篇分析性论文中，你会在该主题上成为一个专家，并按照自己的观点对该主题进行重组和表述。在没有完成论文之前，你对该主题还没有任何结论。你的任务是调查并研究，这需要评判性的思考和阅读，并对材料进行评估。当论文写作结束时，你会在该主题上有自己的想法，并得出一些结论。

(2) 辩论性论文：辩论是用事实或者逻辑来维护一个论点或者驳斥某个论点。同分析性论文相比，辩论性论文就某个主题摆出一个论点，并使用证据来支持这个论点，而不是对该主题进行研究，从而提出一个新的论点。

对辩论性论文，重点是论点陈述；对分析性论文来说，重点是一个没有解决的问题，也就是研究问题。

这里没有给出一些抽象的定义，而是给出一个例子来说明二者的不同。

假设你被要求就"现代媒体技术对个人的影响"写作一篇论文。可以选择写成分析性论文或者辩论性论文，也没有给定论点或者研究问题。但是你知道无线电是一种现代媒体，并对个人有影响。经过一些阅读和思考，并细化主题后，你决定写一篇有关"听音乐对学生影响"的论文。

如果选择写辩论性论文：经过阅读和思考，你决定论文的论点陈述可能是："Contrary to

popular, parental, and librarian opinion, 'quiet study time' does not in fact enhance but instead impairs students' productivity. Listening to music while studying is in fact a beneficial activity to add to a study regime for better grades because of the way music motivates students and keeps them alert."

如果选择写分析性论文：你的研究问题可能是"What is the ultimate effect of music-listening while studying on grades?"这篇论文就会对该问题进行分析，并给出一些答案。

4. 写出一个提纲

有了一个比较满意的论点或者研究问题后，下一步就是为论文写出一个提纲。

提纲是论文的计划。到这个阶段，知道了出发点，也就是论文的论点或者研究问题；也知道目的地，即一些总结或者结论。但是如何从出发点到达目的地？提纲不但给出计划想说的内容，也给出了在两段之间进行过渡的方法。

提纲无疑是很重要的。如果到现在还不能写出一个提纲，根本就不能写出一篇论文。如果在写提纲的时候发现文章结构问题，就比较容易进行纠正。这总比在写第三稿或第四稿的时候进行纠正要容易得多。提纲也告诉了在什么地方该叙述或论述什么。

假如确定的论文主题是：Performance Analysis of the IEEE 802.11a Protocol at the Physical Layer，写出的提纲如下。

I. Introduction.

    A. 802.11a MAC and PHY PDUs.

    B. OFDM PHY Layer.

II. Motivation.

    Cross Layer Interaction.

III. Experimental Analysis.

    A. Model.

    B. Parameters.

    C. Metrics

    D. Indoor

    E. Outdoor

IV. Conclusion

    A. WLAN Performance highly dependant on the ability of the PHY layer to equalize the channel

    B. Significant dual effect of TCP Layer

V. Future Work

    A. Proposed Multi-rate switching algorithm

    B. Cross Layer Interaction

    C. Improved PHY layer

1. MIMO antenna systems for improved bandwidth efficiency at low SNR values.

2. Improved channel equalization techniques such as adaptive semi-blind equalization.

5. 写初稿

写初稿是写论文过程中耗时最少的阶段。写初稿可以分为以下几个部分。

1) 写引言

引言很重要，它引起读者的兴趣。引言同时介绍主题。简而言之，引言是论文的第一印象。不论论文是什么风格，一般会把论点或问题放在段落的末尾，而把一些重要的背景信息放在它们的前面。引言的第一句话可以是一个引用、一个问题、一个简短的叙述、一个有趣的事实、一个定义或者对术语的解释、一句反话或者自相矛盾的话等。

2) 写文章主体

文章主体是论文最重要的部分，没有它们，论点是没有意义的，研究问题仍然是没有解决的问题。

写一篇论文应该像在陡峭的山上行走。在山顶上，用比较概括抽象的话向读者介绍最全面的景观。然后从山顶下行到山谷，也就是从概括到具体。在这个过程中用具体的内容来论述论点。最后又返回到山顶，读者可以从中看到很多例子。也就是论文应该做到从上到下，然后从下到上；从概括到具体，再从具体到概括。如果山谷变成巨大的草原，读者就会对原来的概括陈述感到疑惑。如果山顶变成平原，读者就会感到混乱，就会希望有具体的例子。因此，论文必须在一般性和特殊性两个方面得到平衡。

文章主体段落的数目依赖于论文的长度和主题的复杂度。段落有 3 个要素，分别是统一、一致和充分发展。"统一"就是从一个主题句开始，段内其他每一句话都是该主题句的发展、论证或说明。"一致"就是段内内容的前后一致性。有很多方法来获得一致性。

(1) 重复关键词。

(2) 对一些重要的名词使用代名词。

(3) 使用类似于"This policy…，""that event…，"or "… these examples"等句子。

(4) 段内句子要有逻辑顺序。

(5) 使用一些连接词。"therefore，""moreover，""however，"等词不但是句子的过渡词，更表明了语句之间的关系。"充分发展"就是履行你在主题句中的承诺。如果你想讨论一些商店的不平常条款，那么就举出几种，给你的读者足够的材料进行思考。

把材料整合到文章主体中是一件艰苦的工作。但是如果做得好，论文就会比较出色。

(1) 使用材料来支持你的论点，而不是作为论文的支柱。材料的拼凑永远不是一篇研究论文。

(2) 要经常使用总结(用自己的话来对一段话进行压缩)和解释(用不同的方式来说明同一件事情)，而不是总是使用直接引用。

(3) 不要使用直接引用，除非原作者的话是非常经典和非常适宜的。

(4) 如果使用了直接引用，那么对此解释的长度要大于引用语的长度。即使用自己的话对材料进行总结和解释。读者要知道为什么要包含这些材料。

(5) 如果多个材料说明了同样一件事情，总结它们所说的，并对此进行注释。这增加了材料的可信度，也节省了文章的篇幅。

3) 写总结

如同引言，总结也没有什么固定的模式。总结的内容依赖于文章的内容。注意以下几点。

(1) 不要依靠总结来对文章各段落进行总结。

(2) 应该行文流畅，从正文平滑过渡到总结部分。

(3) 总结很重要，但要注意总结应该是简洁的。

(4) 不要仅仅是对引言的重复。试着用另外一种方式叙述主题。

(5) 指出所陈述论点的重要性。

(6) 对分析性论文，可以提到结论的不足。这也表明理解了该主题的复杂性。

(7) 不要用引用来进行总结，也不要用可能是另外一篇论文的论点来总结。

6. 对草稿进行修改

应该反复地、带有评判性地阅读草稿，并进行修改。即使是非常专业的写作者也不会用键盘第一次就能写出完美的论文。现在要反复进行阅读，看看有什么错误、缺陷。一开始，应该把注意力集中在高层次方面上(如论文的各段是否合理)，然后是低层次上(句子，词的选择，技巧等)。

在修改的时候应该注意以下内容。

(1) 论文标题是否能够说明论文主要讨论的内容。

(2) 论点或者研究问题是否明确。

(3) 引言中是否有足够的篇幅对论点和问题进行了说明，来表示它们的重要性。这些说明是太多了还是太少了。在引言的末尾，读者是否能够清楚论文后面部分会有什么内容。

(4) 文章段落是否逻辑清楚。也就是引言的结尾，文章主体的开始及结尾，结论的开始都要清楚！

(5) 文章各节和段的衔接是否流畅。

(6) 主体各段是否都有一个主题句。把各段的主题句和论文的论点/问题都抽出来，看看它们是否是你想在论文中表达的内容。如果不是，必须修改论点/问题，或者各段的主题句。

(7) 各段的主题句应该做到与论点/问题相联系。同时同上一段的主题句有某种联系(也许是某种顺序，也许是一种比较和对比)。还要注意能否给读者以足够的信息，让读者猜知该段的主要内容。

(8) 各段是否有一个正式的结尾句。在各段的末尾部分，是否提到了该段与文章主题的某种联系/关系，以提醒读者为什么要写该段。

(9) 各段的顺序是不是有意义的? (例如，各段的顺序是否符合逻辑)。

(10) 段落是否太短，是否太长，各段是否可以合并，某些段是否可以拆分，是否需要对内容进行增加或删减。

(11) 举例是否可信、有代表性、有说服力，举例是否太多或者太少。

(12) 材料来源是否可信，自己的观点与专家的观点是否平衡。

(13) 是否还有些内容需要给出出处。

(14) 是否有内容脱离主题，或者不是必要的。

(15) 结论是否与引言有所不同，是否给人印象深刻。

在修改的时候，有可能会出现 4 种操作。

(1) 添加：插入必须的词、句、段。

(2) 删除：去掉脱离主题的，或者重复的内容。

(3) 替代：如果需要，用新的词、新的句子、新的段进行内容更替。

(4) 移动：改变材料的顺序，以使它们符合逻辑。

这些操作在计算机上可以很容易地进行。但是，为了修改进展顺利，最好在"屏幕"和"纸"上交替进行。

7. 用一种可行的风格和格式完成你的论文

论文的风格取决于个人爱好。每个人的风格都有所不同，但必须让论文容易被阅读和理解。语言必须简单、清楚、易懂。尽量避免复杂的句子。华而不实的语言和结构复杂的句子不会凑成好的研究论文。使用引言时要尽量自然，以使文章顺畅和风格一致。

根据论文的写作目的，可能会有不同的格式要求。具体内容，可以参考本书 3.2.2 节。

最后，必须保证文章中没有标点符号、语法、拼写错误，没有参考文献等格式上的错误。仔细阅读最终版本，如果没有上述错误，论文写作就结束了。

3.2.2　风格

科技论文主要是摆事实、讲道理。出色的研究不一定就能写出出色的论文。出色的论文应该精确、清楚、直截了当，不要使用一些诡辩、夸大的词语，从而使论文让人糊涂。

1. 清晰(clarity)

论文写作的一个重要品质就是清晰。最重要的任务就是把思想清楚地表达出来，并用一种读者可以理解的方式来表达。

(1) 说你想表达的内容。

写作的内容应该很清楚地表达出你所想表达的内容。如果做不到这一点，你就有可能像下面这些话一样名垂千古了。

在一个希腊旅馆：Visitors are expected to complain at the office between the hours of 9 and 11 a.m. daily.

在一个苏黎世旅馆：Because of the impropriety of entertaining guests of the opposite sex in the bedroom it is suggested that the lobby be used for this purpose.

在一个罗马洗衣店：Ladies, leave your clothes here and spend the afternoon having a good time.

在一个瑞士山间小酒店：Special today—no ice cream.

在一个挪威鸡尾酒会：Ladies are requested not to have children in the bar.

在布达佩斯动物园：Please do not feed the animals. If you have any suitable food, give it to the guard on duty.

在一个巴黎旅馆：Please leave your values at the front desk.

(2) 要用准确的语言来写作。

科技论文最忌讳使用含糊不清的语言。形容词、副词的含义多半是含糊不清的，因为它们涉及作者的印象和判断，而不是事实本身。例如，The efficiency of that algorithm is high. 这句话中的 high 是一个相对的概念，因为效率达到什么程度才算是高效的？并没有一个客观的标准。也许对某一个目的来说，这种算法就是高效、满足要求的。The efficiency of that algorithm is high enough to deal with the coming data from the port. 但是这还不够确切，因为应用该算法的程序是否能够及时处理数据，与运行该程序的主机性能及数据的速率有关。所以应该说明算法的处理速度与数据数目的关系。We have given an algorithm with expected running time $O(n^2)$, and now improve it to be $O(n\log_2 n)$.

这并不是说作者不能在科技论文中对事实做任何定性判断，相反，作者在很多场合需要对事实做出判断，但同时应该给出一些定量的数据。

2. 简洁(Concision)

简洁与清晰(clarity)密切相关。简洁应该是每一位作者努力的目标。写作是一个过程性、发散性的活动，伴随着一定的紧张和一定程度的混乱。思想在脑子当中打转，必须要使得这些思想能够以一定的顺序、一定的简洁性、还有一定的活力表达出来。

作者都有种想对写作内容进行填充材料的冲动。一定的字数要求是很多人写废话的一个理由。写废话的另外一个理由就是，通过废话可以进行一定的伪装，来掩盖由于作者本身对某些内容的不理解。

对比下面两个例子可以看出，B 句不但比 A 句用词少，而且比 A 句更容易看懂。

(1) A. Experimentations are being done on the communication system. These experimentations strive to make the communication efficiency in that system more efficient, thus minimizing the resource and financing waste in the telecom company.

B. For reducing the waste in resource and financing, experiments are being done to improve the efficiency in the communication system.

(2) A. Some changes are expected to be made in the organization of this department but no one as yet knows what changes are going to take place.

B. No one can anticipate the changes that will be made in the organization of this department.

3.2.3 几个问题

在科技论文中，图、表、符号、单位、缩写语和标点符号会大量出现。本节就这些问题给出一些必要的信息，以便给遇到这类问题的读者以帮助。

1. 使用表格

表格常用来简化统计数字的表达。如果表格的内容可以用一句话来总结，使用表格没有任何意义。如果使用得当，表格能比文字更有效、清楚地表达信息。一个好的表格应该提供有意义的数据。表中数据应该是明确的，能有效地传递信息。

数据是否有意义取决于数据是否和正在分析、论述的内容密切相关。数据及包含在数据中的关系用于帮助论文得出结论。当然，这个结论应该是重要的结论，是正在分析的内容所不可或缺的部分。

表格中表达的内容是否明确取决于表格中所包含的文字是否说明清晰、明确。表格中包含的信息有数据、标题、脚注、参考文献等。这些内容应该自我包含、自我解释，不需要从正文中获取支持。标题和表格中的文字应该定义确切。参考文献应该使读者相信数据的有效性和可靠性。

有效的表格表示，可让读者从中得出很多重要的结论。读者能否从表格中快速得出结论，能否从中发现数据之间的重要关系，得出多少有意义的结论都取决于表格是否安排得合理有效。Table 1 和 Table 2 是两个表格例子。

Table 1　Network Operators and Licensing

Company	Fixed Line	Cellular	Paging	VoIP	Data	Int'l Gateways	Satellite
China Telcom	△		△	△	△	△	
Unicom	△	△	△	△	△	△	
CMCC		△		△	△	△	
CNC				△	△		
Jitong	△			△	△	△	△
Railcom				△	△		△
China Sat							△

Source: Compiled by authors, 2001

Table 2　CT International Long-distance rates

Destination Country	Previous(RMB/minute)	Current(RMB/minute)	Percentage Change (as result of latest reduction)
Australia	4.8	3.6	25%
Canada	4.8	2.4	50%
Italy	4.8	3.6	25%
Japan	4.8	3.6	25%
USA	4.8	2.4	50%

Source: China Telecom, 2000

2. 使用数据图

一张图片胜过千言万语。同样地，一张数据图可以总结成百上千的数字。某些统计信息，如果用表格的形式来表示就不易读，也很难理解。但是如果使用图的形式，则比较容易读懂。数据图用图片的方式而不是数字或者文字来传递信息。

表格表示数据的 3 个标准：有效性、有意义、明确性，同样适应于数据图。如同表格，对于用数据图的形式表示数据，选择有意义的数据、清楚地定义数字代表的内容、使用一种有效的方式让读者快速明白数据表达的含义都是至关重要的。

设计好的数据图表示要比设计好的表格需要更多的科学和艺术才能。要知道和理解自己的数据，但同时也要预测读者会如何理解图表内容。好的数据图会比表格告知读者更多的信息。相反，差的数据图会破坏或隐藏应该告诉读者的意义。

下面介绍几种常见的图表形式。

(1) 饼图。

饼图(Pie Chart)表示变量频率或者百分比上的差异。它把一个圆分成几块面积与变量所占百分比相对应的扇形。饼图应该尽量少用，因为它不如柱形图能够清楚地表示各个数据之间的相互关系，如 Figure 1 所示。

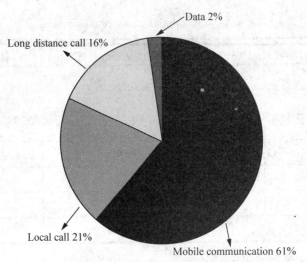

Source: Compiled by authors, 2006

Fig.1　Telecom service revenue of China,2005

(2) 柱形图。

柱形图(Bar graph)表示变量在频率或者百分比上的差异。它用相同宽度、不同高度的矩形来表示数据的差异。可以垂直或水平放置矩形，如 Figure 2 所示。

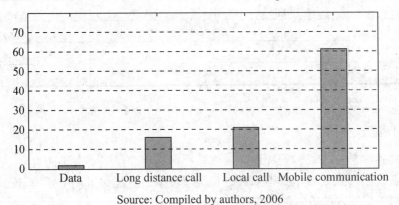

Source: Compiled by authors, 2006

Fig.2　Telecom service revenue of China,2005

(3) 直方图。

直方图(Histogram)用来表示一定时间间隔上的变量在频率或者百分比上的差异。但是直方图的矩形是连续的，宽度与变量的时间间隔成正比，高度与变量的频率或百分比成正比。直方图与柱形图类似，只是矩形之间是连续的、相互接触的，如 Figure 3 所示。

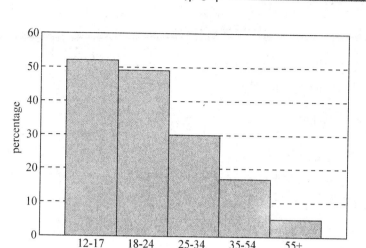

Source: Compiled by authors, 2006

Fig.3　The percentage of downloading color ring back tone in
various age groups in American, 2005

(4) 多边形图。

多边形图(The frequency polygon)也用于表示一定时间间隔上的变量在频率或者百分比上的差异。注意观察 Figure 4 的特点。

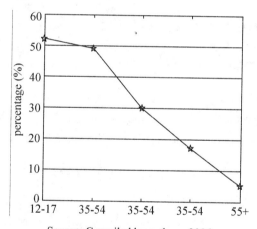

Source: Compiled by authors, 2006

Fig.4　The percentage of downloading color ring back tone
in various age groups in American, 2005

(5) 时间序列图。

时间序列图(Time series chart)用于表示不同时间点上变量的变化。横坐标表示时间，纵坐标表示变量值。注意观察 Figure 5 的特点。

various age groups in American,2005

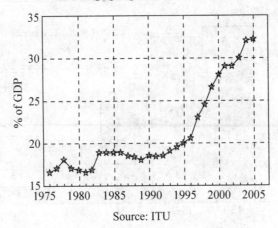

Source: ITU

Fig.5　Telecom service revenues, worldwide

3. 标点

标点可以把文章分成符合逻辑的单元，使读者容易读下去。标点包括所有用于分开词的符号、空格、每段第一句的缩排、空白行、大写字母，以及各种标记或停顿符(逗号，分号，冒号等)。使用标点是传统的，并且随时间演化。最早的写作语言是没有标点的，现在的正式写作中，标点必不可少。

标点符号的选择影响着意思的表达。如果使用不同的标点符号组合，有可能使表达的意思完全相反。请阅读下面的例子。

Dear John,

　　I want a man who knows what love is all about. You are generous, kind, thoughtful. People who are not like you admit to being useless and inferior. You have ruined me for other men. I yearn for you. I have no feelings whatsoever when we're apart. I can be forever happy—will you let me be yours?

Gloria

Dear John,

　　I want a man who knows what love is. All about you are generous, kind, thoughtful people, who are not like you. Admit to being useless and inferior. You have ruined me. For other men, I yearn. For you, I have no feelings whatsoever. When we're apart, I can be forever happy. Will you let me be?

Gloria

幸运的是，标点符号不会总是造成这么戏剧性的后果。但是适当的标点法仍然是写作的重要部分。

(1) 逗号和句号。

逗号(Comma)用于连接两个独立从句。

Planck's ideas seemed incredible, many scholars simply ignored him.

句号(Period)用在很多场合。最方便的是把两个独立从句分成独立的句子。

Planck's ideas seemed incredible. Many scholars simply ignored him.

此句也可以使用分号。

Planck's ideas seemed incredible; many scholars simply ignored him.

破折号有时也用于两个独立从句的连接，特别是当第二个从句较短时。

Planck's ideas seemed incredible—many scholars simply ignored him.

并列连词也能完成这个任务。

Planck's ideas seemed incredible, and many scholars simply ignored him.

或者用主从句。

Since Planck's ideas seemed incredible, many scholars simply ignored him.

(2) 分号。

分号(Semicolons)可以把两个独立从句连接成一个句子。分号也可以告诉读者，当分号出现的时候，他遇到了一个语义上的完整停顿，但是后面的从句与前面的从句具有紧密的联系。另外，当使用逗号来分割几个从句，有可能造成混淆时，也用分号来替代逗号。

Hobbes's Leviathan has many memorable passages: his audacious view of human beings as mere mechanical constructions, his evocation of a brutish, savage state of nature, his establishment of a binding, permanent social contract to protect individuals, and his refusal to place any limits on the power of a duly established ruler.

使用分号进行修改。

Hobbes's Leviathan has many memorable passages: his audacious view of human beings as mere mechanical constructions; his evocation of a brutish, savage state of nature; his establishment of a binding, permanent social contract to protect individuals; and his refusal to place any limits on the power of a duly established ruler.

(3) 冒号。

冒号(Colons)用于连接两个具有直接逻辑关系的独立从句。

This form of social organization creates habits that are carried into the business world: Chinese companies are literally families.

也可以使用冒号来连接句子的具有紧密关系的两个部分，而不一定是独立从句。

The data point to only one conclusion: fraud.

(4) 破折号。

破折号(Dashes)的使用比较灵活。如果不过分使用，破折号可以使文章生机勃勃。破折号也可以用来连接独立从句。

During Machiavelli's lifetime, Italy as a single political entity did not exist—instead, there was a patchwork of little city-states, petty kingdoms, republics, duchies, and ecclesiastical states, constantly at war with each other.

请注意，连字符 Hyphens(-) 和破折号 dashes(—) 是不同的。连字符连接多个词以组成复合词(shoo-in, a run-of-the-mill transaction)。

错误：In Coriolaznus, Sicinius and Brutus are the tribunes of the people-the voice of the people.

正确：In Coriolanus, Sicinius and Brutus are the tribunes of the people—the voice of the people.

(5) 括号。

括号(Parentheses)包括()、[]、{}。注意在括号的外部添加空格，而不是在括号的内部添加。不是 not(this)，而是 not (this)。

(6) 问号和惊叹号。

在论文写作当中，很多场合可以使用问号(Question marks)和惊叹号(exclamation marks)。事实上，尖锐的问题和感叹可以带来活力和能量，引起读者的注意。

How might this anomaly be explained?

Does Beatrice's decision make sense?

4. 数词

科技英语写作中常常涉及数字，因此多写成阿拉伯数字的形式。具体写法如下。

(1) 10 及 10 以上的数字写成阿拉伯数字。

(2) 10 以下的数字拼写出来，如 5 写成 five。但是如果数字后面带单位，则仍然写成阿拉伯数字，如 8 inches 等。

(3) 如果 21 到 99 间的数字要拼写出来，十位与个位之间需加连字号。如 22 写成 twenty-two，99 写为 ninety-nine。

(4) 当数字频繁出现时则仍然写成阿拉伯数字。

He used a crew of 3 carpenters, 1 plumber, 6 laborers, 1 foreman, and 1 timekeeper.

(5) 仅作为估计数的数字一般都拼写出来。

The communication system can be used for twenty years.

(6) 一个句子不要以阿拉伯数字开始。遇到这种情况时，应该将数字拼写出来或者采用一些变通的方法。

错误：105 television stations are in this country.

变通为：There are 105 television stations in this country.

(7) 对于整数，3 位以内的没有特殊要求。4 位数时，可以写成 1234 或者 1,234。

超过四位时，每向左增加 3 位加一个逗号，如 54,251,000。

(8) 带小数时，小数点前多带有 0，如 0.0256。对于算法语言产生的结果或者有很多数据时，也可以不带 0，如 .0256。

(9) 数字和文字间有连字号时，一位数字多用文字拼写表达，如 five-wire circuit；多位数字用拼写或阿拉伯表示都可以，如 50-channel system 或 fifty-channel system。

5. 单位

对外交流的科技写作当中，都应该采用国际单位制(简称为 SI 制)。国际单位制分为两大系统，一个为基本单位系统，一个为导出单位系统，见 Table 3。

Table 3   Table SI Units 国际单位制单位

In English [en]		Symbol 符号	Names used in People's Republic of China	
Quantity	Name		量	名称
SI Base Units			基本单位	
length	meter	m	长度	米
mass	kilogram	kg	质量	千克(公斤)
time	second	s	时间	秒
electrical current	ampere	A	电流	安[培]
thermodynamic temperature	kelvin	K	热力学温度	开[尔文]
amount of substance	mole	mol	物质的量	摩[尔]
luminous intensity	candela	cd	发光强度	坎[德拉]
Examples of SI derived units in terms of base units			以基本单位表示的导出单位举例	
area	square meter	m^2	面积	平方米
volume, capacity	cubic meter	m^3	体积	立方米
speed, velocity	meter per second	m/s	速度	米每秒
acceleration	meter per second squared	m/s^2	加速度	米每秒平方
density, mass density	kilogram per cubic meter	kg/m^3	密度, 质量密度	千克(公斤)每立方米
SI derived units with special names			具有专门名称的导出单位	
plane angle	radian	rad	平面角	弧度
solid angle	steradian	sr	立体角	球面度
frequency	hertz	Hz	频率	赫[兹]
force	newton	N	力; 重力	牛[顿]
pressure, stress	pascal	Pa	压力, 压强; 应力	帕[斯卡]
energy, work, quantity of heat	joule	J	能量; 功; 热	焦[耳]
power, radiant flux	watt	W	功率; 辐射通量	瓦[特]
electric charge, quantity of electricity	coulomb	C	电荷量	库[仑]
electric potential difference, electromotive force	volt	V	电位; 电压; 电动势	伏[特]
capacitance	farad	F	电容	法[拉]
electric resistance	ohm	Ω	电阻	欧[姆]
electric conductance	siemens	S	电导	西[门子]
magnetic flux	weber	Wb	磁通量	韦[伯]
magnetic flux density	tesla	T	磁通量密度, 磁感应强度	特[斯拉]
inductance	henry	H	电感	亨[利]
Celsius temperature	degree Celsius	°C	摄氏温度	摄氏度
luminous flux	lumen	lm	光通量	流[明]

6. 缩写语

英语中缩写语的使用极为广泛，随着科学技术的飞速发展，科技领域中缩写语的使用日益广泛。除了常见的一些各专业通用的缩写语以外，不同专业对同一形状的缩写语可能有不同的含义。作者也可以根据自己的需要在文章或者著作中创造一些缩写语。这种创作的缩写语一般只能在它出现的文章或著作中有效，但也不排除日后广为流传的可能性。

缩写语分为 4 种。第一种是由一个词组的各个单词的首字母组成，称为首字母词。第二种为一个词的缩写，即缩写词。第三种是由几个词各取出一部分组成，称作拼写词。这类词有些已经演变为新词汇，而不按缩写语对待。第四种为姓名的首字母组成，即姓名首字词。

(1) 首字母词。

当需要将一个词组写成首字母词(acronym)时，需要在文章或书籍第一次出现时写成它的全称，并把收入到 acronym 的单词的首字母大写，以示醒目。一些众所周知的 acronym 可以直接写出而不必写出全称。

BASIC：Beginner's All-Purpose Symbolic Instruction Code

TOEFL：Test of English as a Foreign Language

VLSI：Very Large-Scale Integration

有时将介词的首字母也列入 acronym，如 DoD—Department of Defense。

外来语种取首字母构成 acronym 时，往往不能和英译名相对应。

CCITT (取自法语)：国际电报电话咨询委员会—The International Telegraph and Telephone Consultative Committee。

(2) 缩写词。

缩写词(abbreviation)可以有很多形式，其构成没有什么规律。

ad. —advertisement 广告　sync—synchronization 同步　info—information 信息

Ltd. —Limited 有限公司　No—number 号码　　　　Xformer—transformer 变压器

(3) 缩拼词。

科技英语中常将两个技术名词缩拼起来构成一个新词，称为缩拼词(contraction)如：

Heliport—helicopter airport 直升飞机机场　telecast—television broadcast 电视广播

Televiewer—television viewer 电视观众　　　　petrodollar—petrol dollar 石油美元

(4) 姓名的首字母。

在某些场合下，常常使用姓名的首字母(initials)，如 G. B. S. 是萧伯纳(Grorge Bernard Shaw)姓名的首字母。

缩写语有以下一些注意事项。

(1) 缩写语的含义。同一形式的缩写语可能有多种含义，如 RMS，可以表示 root mean square—均方根，也可以表示 Railway Mail Service—铁道邮政，还可以是自由软件奠基人理查德·马修·斯托曼(Richard Matthew Stallman)的英文首字母缩写(该缩写比他本人的姓名更出名)。又如 OTC，可以是 Office of Technical Cooperation 技术合作处(联合国)，Office of Transport and Communications 交通运输处[美]，Officers' Training Corps 军官训练团，Overseas Telecommunications Commission 海外电信委员会[澳]，Oxytetracycline(药)氧四环素，土霉素。

(2) 缩写语的大小写。该问题没有统一的规定，一般来说，作者临时创造的缩写语最好加以说明并采用大写。对于一些已经转化为常规英语词的缩写语则应符合它自身的大小写习惯。

(3) 缩写语的复数形式。许多缩写词有自己的复数形式，有的有一定的规律，有的就没有什么规律。比如 p. 表示 page，但是 pages 用 pp. 表示。有的单复数形式相同，如 foot 或 feet 的缩写都是 ft。

3.2.4 学位论文

学位论文(thesis，dissertations)是作者为获得某种学位而撰写的科技论文。Theses 通常指硕士毕业论文，而 Dissertations 通常指博士毕业论文。其中博士论文具有较高的参考价值，它内容丰富，一般侧重于理论。硕士论文一般侧重于工程。

学位论文包括 4 个主要部分：摘要(abstract)，前言(preliminaries)，正文(text)以及参考材料(references)。有些 thesis 或 dissertations 还包括附录(appendix)。Table 4 是一篇论文通常包含的主要部分，以及它们先后出现的顺序。

Table 4　论文包含内容

Parts of a Theses	Status
I) Abstract	Required
II) Preliminaries	
a) Title Page	Required
b) Dedication	Optional
c) Biography	Required
d) Acknowledgements	Optional
e) Table of Contents	Required
f) List of Tables	Required
g) List of Figures	Required
h) List of Symbols or Abbreviations	Optional
i) Preface	Optional
III) Text	Required
IV) Reference Materials	Required
V) Appendices	Optional

1. ABSTRACT (Required)

摘要在学位论文中很重要，它告诉了读者论文讨论的范围以及论文的主题。通常研究者在查找材料的时候，只读一篇论文的摘要部分，来判断该论文是不是与自己的主题相关。因此摘要中必须把重要的发现和方法等叙述清楚。关于如何写摘要？详细内容请参阅 3.3.1 节。

2. TITLE PAGE (Required)

题目页应该包含关键词，来反映研究的独特方面，以便与其他人的工作分开。题目应避免使用诸如 "A Study of" 等表达形式。

同摘要一样，各种组织，各个学校，各个学科，甚至不同的导师对题目页的具体格式、字数等具体规范都可能有不同的要求。Table 5 是一个题目页的具体例子。

Table 5　题目页

Performance Analysis of the IEEE 802.11a Protocol at the Physical Layer
by
KOGER KEITH BALLARD
A theses submitted to the Graduate Faculty of
North Carolina State University
in partial fulfillment of the
requirements for the Degree of
Master of Science
MASTERIALS SCIENCE AND ENGINEERING
Raleigh
1993
APPROVED BY:

_____

Chair of Advisory Committee

3. DEDICATION (Optional), PERSONAL BIOGRAPHY (Required) AND ACKNOW LEDGMENTS (Optional)

这一部分与作者个人有关，可以包含任何作者想同读者分享的内容。没有字数要求和限制。致谢等内容可有可无，但是必须有作者个人信息。

4. TABLE OF CONTENTS (Required)

目录标出论文所有的章节、部分，可以包括论文中所出现的图、表格的目录。注意所有标题应该与其在论文中完全一致。Table 6 是一个例子。

Table 6　目录

TABLE OF CONTENTS

5. LIST OF TABLES AND LIST OF FIGURES (Required)

如果在论文中出现表格和图片，需要给出它们的索引。在索引中出现的图表名称应该与论文中相一致，见 Table 7。

Table 7　索引

6. LIST OF SYMBOLS, ABBREVIATIONS OR NOMENCLATURE (Optional)

当出现很多符号、缩写词或命名时，应该给出一个单独的符号表、缩写词表、命名表等。

7. TEXT (Required)

论文正文的组织和格式应该符合一定的规范。一般来说，正文应该包含以下内容。

(1) 一个导言或绪论，有时二者都可以包含。

(2) 一个明确的目标陈述。

(3) 适当的前期研究回顾。

(4) 对研究中所使用的方法进行描述。

(5) 记录研究所获得的结果，并讨论所获得的结果对其他研究的意义。

(6) 研究中所有重大有意义发现，并进行总结。

(7) 对未来研究的建议。

8. LIST OF REFERENCES, LITERATURE CITED OR BIBLIOGRAPHY (Required)

论文中应该包含适当的材料，也就是论文所参考的原始文献。在人文科学和社会科学论文中，使用脚注(footnotes)或尾注(endnotes)，通常称为参考书目(bibliography)；在自然科学、工程技术类论文中，通常使用参考文献(Cited References)的方式。

原始文献可以在某种程度上使得其他研究者能够架构或重现所做的研究。没有原始文献，读者不能相信所提供的信息是否可信。原始文献也可以直接引用其他研究者的研究成果，而不需要对他们的研究工作做详细的论述。

参考书目或参考文献必须包括直接引用的，或者对论文提供了很多信息的材料。对论文影响很小的材料不要包括。注意不要仅仅为了使得这一部分足够长而随意添加原始文献材料。

不同的导师、不同的学校、不同类型的杂志都可能会有不同的参考书目或参考文献格式要求。因此，要根据所提交论文的要求，正确安排参考书目或参考文献的格式。

在研究论文中，通常有 4 种参考格式。

(1) MLA 格式：由 the Modern Language Association 制定，广泛用于英语写作、文学等。

(2) APA 格式：由 the Publication Manual of the American Psychological Association 制定，广泛用于社会科学。

(3) CMS 格式：用于人文科学(不是文学)，使用传统的脚注和尾注。

(4) CBE (Council of Biology Editors, 现在称为 the Council of Science Editors)格式：广泛用于医学、物理学、数学等学科。在 CBE 格式中，还分为两种不同的格式。一种称作 Citation-Sequence (CS) system，用于化学、计算机、数学、物理、医学、电子信息等学科；另外一种称为 the Name-Year system，用于生物、地球、考古、农业等学科。

本节只介绍 CBE 格式中的 CS 格式的使用。这种格式需要在文章中使用数字，而不是年代。在文章的末尾要有一个参考文献表(Cited References，或 References)。可以用以下两种方式安排参考文献。

(1) 按照参考文献的字母进行排序，并依次数字标记。

(2) 按照文献在文章中出现的先后顺序进行数字标记。

下面给出了参考文献的一些注意事项。

(1) 在文章正文中使用数字标记。

数字用圆括号(1)或方括号[2]括起，也可以进行上标，如 [3]。不需要也不鼓励使用名称。

It is known (1) that the DNA concentration of a nucleus doubles during Interphase.

A recent study [1] has raised interesting questions related to photosynthesis, some of which have been answered [2].

In particular, a recent study[1] has raised many interesting questions related to photosynthesis, some of which have been answered.[2]

如果在文章中提及了作者的名字，在作者名字后加注数字。

Additional testing by Cooper (3) includes alterations in carbohydrate metabolism and changes in ascorbic acid incorporation into the cell and adjoining membranes.

如果需要，可以添加页码等数字信息。

"The use of photosynthesis in this application is crucial to the environment" (Skelton,[8] p. 732).

The results of the respiration experiment published by Jones (3, Table 6, p. 412) had been predicted earlier by Smith (5, Proposition 8).

(2) 参考文献表中的格式。

参考文献表放在文章的末尾。表的标题是 "Cited References"，或 "Reference"，居中。

表中各条使用缩进格式。

① 参考的书籍。首先是数字，然后是作者，书籍的名称、出版地点、出版商、年分和参考的页数范围。

[1] Gehling E. The family and friends'guide to diabetes: Everything you need to know. New York: Wiley; 2000.

[2] Schwartz, M., Information Transmission, Modulation and Noise, Second Edition, McGraw Hill, New York, 1970, pp. 105~160.

[3] L.J.Mordell. Diophantine Equations[M], Academic Press. New York, 1969.

② 期刊。数字、然后是作者、文章的题目、期刊名、年月、卷数，如果需要还可以添加出版期号、参考页码。

[4] Bolli GB, Owens DR. Insulin glargine. Lancet 2000; 356:443-444.

[5] S.L. Ariyavisitakul and G.M. Durant, "A Broadband Wireless Packet TechniqueBased n Coding, Diversity and Equalization", IEEE Communications, Vol. 36, No. 7, July 1998, pp. 110-115.

[6] H. Sari, G. Karam and I. Jeanclaude, "Transmission Techniques for Digital Terrestrial TV Broadcasting", IEEE Comm. Mag., Vol. 33, No. 2, Feb. 1995, pp. 100-109.

③ 杂志和报纸。加上日期，如果是报纸，注明是第几版。

[7] Schlosberg S. The symptoms you should never ignore. Shape 2000 Aug:136.

[8] [Anonymous]. FDA approval of drug gives diabetics a new choice. Los Angeles Times 2000 Aug 2; Sect A:4.

④ 网络文章和其他电子出版物。添加访问的日期和现在是否在线。

[9] [Anonymous]. Diabetes insipidus. Amer Acad. Of Family Physicians [online] 2000. Available from: http://www.aafp.org/patientinfo/insipidu.html. Accessed 2000 Aug 8.

[10] Roberts S. The diabetes advisor. Diabetes Forecast [serial online] 2000;53: 41-42. Available from: http://www.diabetes.org/diabetesforecat/00August/default.asp. Accessed 2000 Aug 8.

⑤ 报告。除了作者、报告名称等，还需添加报告号、发布报告的组织、地点和日期。

[11] Bogusch, R. L.,Digital Communication in Fading Channels: Modulation and Coding, Mission Research Corp., Santa Barbara, California, Report no. MRC-R-1043, March 11, 1987.

[12] Holmes-Siedle, A. G. (1980). *Radiation effects in the Joint European Torus experiment: guidelines for preliminary design.* Report No. R857/2 Fulmer Research laboratories, Stoke Poges UK.

(3) 参考文献表的安排。

Table 8 是一个使用 CS 格式的参考文献表的例子。

Table 8　CS 格式参考文献表

REFERENCES

[1] Guthrie DW, Guthrie RA. Nursing management of diabetes mellitus. New York: Springer, 1991.

[2] [Anonymous]. Diabetes insipidus. American Academy of Family Physicians. Available from: http://www.aafp.org/patientinfo/insipidu.html. Accessed 2000 Aug 10.

[3] Clark CM, Fradkin JE, Hiss RG, Lorenz RA, Vinicor F, Warren-Boulton E. Promoting early diagnosis and treatment of type 2 diabetes. JAMA 2000;284:363-5.

[4] Nurses' Clinical Library. Endocrine Disorders. Springhouse, PA: Springhouse, 1984.

9. 附录 APPENDICES (Optional)

附录中包含一些必需的，但不适宜出现在正文中的材料。可以包含研究中获得的数据、计算机程序、调查数据、详细的程序流程图，以及一些特别的文献。有可能其他学者希望以此为基础进行更进一步的研究。注意附录部分必须同正文分开，新起一页，并标以用"Appendix"或者"Appendices"，居中显示。

3.2.5　科技期刊文章

著名物理、化学家法拉第有一句名言"科学研究有三个阶段，首先是开拓，其次是完成，第三是发表"。很多研究成果都发表在各自的行业期刊上。科技期刊论文既具有一般议论文的特点，论点、论证、结论构成，又具有与一般议论文不同的特点，而科学性和准确性；学术性或理论性；创新性与独创性；规范性与人工语言符号(图表、照片、公式、化学等)的应用。

一篇发表在期刊上的科技论文通常包括以下几项：(1) 题目(title)；(2) 作者姓名；(3) 作者单位名称地址；(4) 摘要(abstract)；(5) 关键词(keywords)；(6) 正文，包括：① 引言；② 正文论述正文部分；③ 结论；(7) 致谢(acknowledgments)，该项可选，可有可无；(8) 参考文献(references)等。

期刊论文的写作与上面一节讨论的学位论文的写作有很多相似之处，在此不再对各个部分作详细的讨论，仅给出一篇科技论文例文，其参考文献为 CS 格式。

Multirate Performance in Multiuser MMSE and

Decorrelating Detectors using Random

Spreading Sequences for AWGN Channels.

Gustavo Fraidenraich, Renato Baldini F. and Celso de Almeida

DECOM - FEEC - UNICAMP

Abstract—This paper presents simplified expressions for the bit error probability for multirate MMSE and decorrelating multiuser detectors. The multiple data rates are achieved by the variations of the processing gain. It is assumed random spreading sequences and AWGN channel.

Keywords—Multiuser, CDMA, multirate, MMSE, decorrelating.

I. INTRODUCTION

THE new third generation mobile system will allow multirate schemes. There will be different modulations schemes supporting multiple data rates. The aim of this paper is to unveil simplified expressions for the bit error probability for multirate MMSE and decorrelating multiuser detectors. Those expressions are obtained for the AWGN channel where random spreading sequences are considered.

II. SINGLE BIT RATE PERFORMANCE ON AWGN CHANNELS

It is possible to devise a good approximation for the exact performance expression for synchronous CDMA system, using single bit rate, with N users, processing gain G, perfect power control and BPSK modulation. This approximation can be made by assuming that the multiple access interference is Gaussian distributed with zero mean and variance proportional to the number of users. Thus, the bit error probability can be written as:

$$P_b = Q\left(\sqrt{\frac{1}{\frac{1}{\frac{2E_b}{N_0}} + \frac{N-1}{G}}}\right) \tag{1}$$

where $Q(.)$ is the complementary Gaussian error function and $\frac{E_b}{N_0}$ is the signal-to-noise ratio.

III. MULTI PROCESSING GAIN SYSTEMS

Distinct users using different data rates can be allocated in the same bandwidth B, if the processing gain is variable. Thus, high data rate implies low processing gain for a given user.

It is going to be assumed a multi processing gain system with N users and rates $r_1 > r_2 > ... > r_n$, with no loss of generality. All users have the same energy per bit to noise ratio $\frac{E_b}{N_0}$ and the processing gain is defined as $G_i = B / r_i$, where r_i is the bit rate for the i-th group with N_i users. The system is defined in such way that $\sum_{i=1}^{n} N_i = N$, where n is the number of groups with distinct bit rates. It is also assumed that random spreading sequences are utilized for all users. The performance of user k with rate r_k in a synchronous CDMA system using matched filter detector can be expressed as [1]:

$$P_b = Q\left(\sqrt{\frac{1}{\frac{1}{\frac{2E_b}{N_0}} + \frac{1}{G_j}\left(\sum_{i=1}^{n}\frac{r_i}{r_j}N_i - 1\right)}}\right) \tag{2}$$

IV. BIT ERROR PROBABILITY OF DECORRELATING AND MMSE DETECTORS IN A SINGLE BIT RATE SYSTEM ON AWGN CHANNELS

The result given in (2) can be extended to the multiuser MMSE and decorrelating detectors. In [2, 3, 4], equivalent expressions to (1) were derived as a function of the processing gain and the number of users. The bit error probability in any linear multiuser detector can be evaluated by the expression:

$$P_b = Q\sqrt{\frac{2E_b}{N_0}\bar{\eta}} \tag{3}$$

where $\bar{\eta}$ is the near-far resistance[2]. In the case of the decorrelating detector $\bar{\eta}$ can be expressed by:

$$\bar{\eta} = E\left[\frac{1}{R_{k,k}}\right] \tag{4}$$

where R is the spreading sequences crosscorrelation $N \times N$ matrix and $E[.]$ is the average operator. The result in (4) applied to random spreading sequences can be simplified to:

$$\bar{\eta} = 1 - \frac{N-1}{G} \tag{5}$$

Thus the bit error probability P_b for the decorrelating detector with perfect power control in a synczhronous system on AWGN channel can be expressed by:

$$P_b = Q\left(\sqrt{\frac{2E_b}{N_0}\left(1 - \frac{(N-1)}{G}\right)}\right) \tag{6}$$

For the MMSE detector, a similar procedure as for the decorrelating detector case can be made to achieve P_b which is given by [2], [4]

$$P_b = Q\left(\sqrt{\frac{2E_b}{N_0} - \frac{1}{4}F\left(2\frac{E_b}{N_0}, \frac{(N-1)}{G}\right)}\right) \tag{7}$$

with

$$F(x,y) \overset{\Delta}{=} \left[\sqrt{x\left(1+\sqrt{y}\right)^2 + 1} - \sqrt{x\left(1-\sqrt{y}\right)^2 + 1}\right]^2 \tag{8}$$

V. MULTIUSER PERFORMANCE IN A MULTIRATE SYSTEM ON AWGN CHANNELS

Based on the above assumptions it is possible to devise the bit error probability for the decorrelating detector in a multirate synchronous CDMA system using random spreading sequences with multi processing gain on AWGN channel:

$$P_b = Q\left(\sqrt{\frac{2E_b}{N_0}\left(1 - \frac{\left(\sum_{i=1}^{n} \frac{r_i}{r_j}N_i - 1\right)}{G}\right)}\right) \tag{9}$$

For the MMSE detector it can be shown that P_b can be evaluated by:

$$P_b = Q\left(\sqrt{\frac{2E_b}{N_0} - \frac{1}{4}F\left(2\frac{E_b}{N_0}, \frac{\left(\sum_{i=1}^{n}\frac{r_i}{r_j}N_i - 1\right)}{G}\right)}\right) \tag{10}$$

Equation (9) and (10) are tight approximations of the real bit error probabilities for the decorrelating and the MMSE detectors, respectively, in a multirate system.

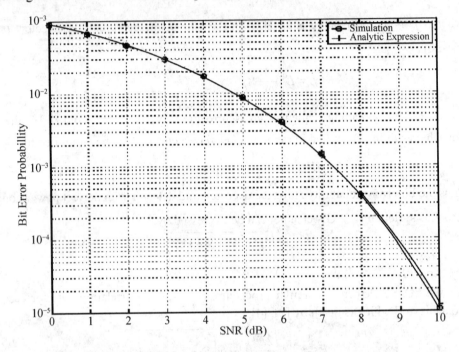

Fig.6　Decorrelating on AWGN channel with 5 users with G=64 and 5 users with G=128.

VI. NUMERICAL RESULTS AND COMPARISONS

Simulations were carried out in order to validate the approximations (9) and (10). The results of the comparisons are shown in Figure 6 and Figure 7. All the simulations were made using N=10 users. The system was subdivided into two subgroups, the first with five users and processing gain $G = 64$ and the other with five users and $G = 128$. The results show that this system is equivalent to a system with 15 users and a processing $G = 128$ or to a system with a fictitious 7.5 users and processing gain $G = 64$.

Figure 6 shows the comparison between the simulation and the analytic expression (9) for the decorrelating detector. Figure 7 shows the comparison between the simulation and the analytic expression (10) for the MMSE detector. Notice that in both figures the simulations and the analytic expressions match perfectly. Note also that it is possible to define the parameter *equivalent number of users*, which allows to represent a multirate system by its equivalent single rate system. For instance, for the parameters used in this paper the equivalent number of users is 15.

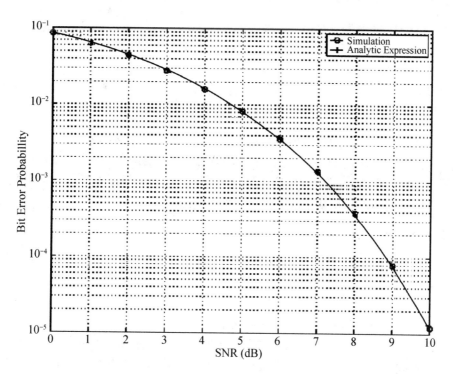

Fig.7   MMSE on AWGN channel with 5 users with G=64 and 5 users with G=128.

VII. CONCLUSIONS

Approximated expressions for the bit error probability with random spreading sequences on AWGN channel using the multiuser MMSE and decorrelating detectors in multirate systemswere presented. Those analytic expressions have shown to be a very good approximation when compared to those obtained by simulation.

ACKNOWLEDGMENTS

This work is supported by ERICSSON and FAPESP under the grant number 00/07633-9.

REFERENCES

[1] T. Ottosson, and A. Svensson, "Multi-rate performance in DS/CDMA systems," Tech. Report no. 14, ISSN 0283-1260, Dept. of Information Theory, Chalmers University of Technology，Gothenburg，Sweden，March 1995.

[2] S. Verdu, Multiuser Detection, Cambridge Press 1998.

[3] Celso de Almeida and Gabriel M. da Silva. On the performance of CDMA Systems with multiuser Decorrelating Detectors for Random Sequences on AWGN channels. Master Thesis, UNICAMP, 2002.

[4] G. Fraidenraich, R. Baldini F. and C. de Almeida - On the Performance for MMSE Detection of Direct Sequence CDMA Signals with Random Spreading in Multipath Rayleigh Fading Channels. Ericsson Report no. 2, Unicamp, Fev. 2002.

[5] J. G. Proakis, Digital Communications, 2nd ed. New York: McGraw-Hill, 1995.

3.3　科技写作实例

3.3.1　摘要

对于会议报告、科技文章、学位论文等，通常要求写一篇摘要(Abstract)。要记住的主要一点是摘要必须短，因为它给出研究的一个概述。事实上，不仅摘要短，而且通常是一个给定的、特别的长度。所以在开始写之前，必须知道摘要应该是多长(比如，硕士论文的摘要通常是 200 字)，那么写摘要时应接近这个数字，而不应超出。超出最大字数限定的摘要经常被否定，因为这种摘要不能被数据库检索使用。

1. 什么是摘要

摘要是对"论文的内容不加注释和评论的简短陈述"。其作用主要是为读者阅读、信息人员及计算机检索提供方便。摘要显示了读者如果继续阅读，要寻找的东西和期望得到的东西。一篇好的摘要可能是文章最重要的段落，也可能是这篇文章值得看与否的原因所在。人们通常是通过快速阅读摘要来决定这篇文章是否是自己需要的。摘要不宜太详尽，也不宜太简短，应将论文的研究体系、主要方法、重要发现、主要结论等，简明扼要地加以概括。

摘要有不同的种类，可以使用描述性 (discriptive) 文体或信息性 (informative) 文体。

(1) 描述性文体：简要叙述(大约 120 字，一段)原始文档讲的内容。

① 告诉读者这篇论文所包含的信息是什么。

② 包括了文章中研究的目的、方法和研究领域。

③ 不提供结果、结论或建议等。

④ 把该论文的主题介绍给读者，文中可以找到作者的结论或建议。

(2) 信息性文体：提供了原始文档更多的信息(200～300 字)；总结了主要的论点和主要数据等。

① 从这篇论文中交流特殊的信息。

② 包括了文章中研究的目的、方法和研究领域。

③ 提供该论文的结论、结果或建议等。

④ 篇幅短，从一个段落到一页或两页不等，长度决定于被摘要的原始研究工作。通常信息性文体摘要占原始工作量的 10%或更少。

2. 写摘要时存在的通病

(1) 太长。如果摘要太长，它也许会被否定掉。摘要要进入数据库，因此常常规定最大字数。

(2) 太详细。太长的摘要经常是包含了一些无用的细节。摘要不是用来详细地叙说研究工作所用的方法，而是只需说出研究的主要点。

(3) 太短。太短的摘要也不是所需要的。如果字数限制为 200 字，但仅写了 95 个字，有可能写得不够详尽。应该重新审读这篇摘要，看看在什么地方应该写得更详细。在许多情况下，读者通过看摘要来决定是否读这篇研究论文，而许多作者却对他们的发现成果没有给出充足的信息。

(4) 没有包括重要信息。作者经常是用太多的空间来解释有关研究工作采取的手段和方法，而没有表达出研究的最终结果。

3. 摘要与引言的比较

初一看，摘要和引言非常相似，因为二者都包含了研究问题、研究目标；简要回顾了方法、主要发现和主要结论。然而，它们有两点重要差别。

(1) 引言应该短，但没有字数限制。写引言的主要目的是通过上下文或背景知识的介绍来阐述研究的主要目的。引言通常是从一般到特殊，介绍研究问题如何被发现。

(2) 摘要有一个最大字数限制，是整篇研究报告的概述。写摘要的主要目的是概括研究工作(尤其是目标和主要发现及结论)，而不是介绍研究领域。

4. 如何写摘要

(1) 带着写摘要的目的去重读整篇文章。

① 重点看论文的这些主要部分，包括目的、方法、研究领域、结果、结论和建议等。

② 用标题、提纲性标题、内容列表来指导写摘要。

③ 如果你正在写另外一个作者文章的摘要，最好的开始地方在引言和概要部分，因为这些地方通常覆盖了论文的重点。

(2) 在看完了这篇论文之后，写草稿，但不要回头看正在写的摘要。

① 不要仅仅复制文章中的关键句。

② 不要依赖于文章中的材料组织方式，而是以一种新的组织方式来概括信息。

(3) 修改草稿，改正文中组织的缺陷，一点一点地改进文中信息的自然过渡。剔除不必要的信息，增加忽略的重要信息。消减重复的单词使用。修正语法、拼写和标点符号的错误。

(4) 打印最后的文稿，再看一遍，做到摘要写得尽善尽美。

5. 写一篇好摘要的几点建议

(1) 易读，语句组织得好，简明而自成一体。

(2) 摘要中包含有许多的关键词，以便用户通过图书馆系统能找到主题。

(3) 不要附加原始文章中不包含的信息。

(4) 以第三人称作主语，因为第一人称作主语常带有强烈的个人感情色彩。主题句可用主动语态，主语为"作者、本人或本论文的目的，等……"；也可用被动语态，主语为"本文、本报告，等……的实质……"。

(5) 众所周知的国家、机构、专用术语尽可能用简称或缩写。

(6) 要采用规范化的名词术语；不使用图、表或化学结构式，以及相邻专业的读者尚难于清楚理解的缩略语、简称、代号。如果确有必要，在摘要中首次出现时必须加以说明。

(7) 定义特殊的专业术语。要求使用法定计量单位以及正确的书写规范字和标点符号。

(8) 保持主语和动词紧密联系。

(9) 使用现在时态。仅在描述试验和特殊变量时用过去时态。

6. 文章摘要实例之一

PASM: A partitionable SIMD/MIMD System for Image Processing and Pattern Recognition

PASM, a large-scale multimicroprocessor system being designed at Purdue University for image processing and pattern recognition, is described. This system can be dynamically reconfigured to operate as one or more independent SIMD and/or MIMD machines. PASM consists of a parallel computation unit, which contains N processor, N memories, and an interconnection network; Q microcontrollers, each of which controls N/Q parallel secondary storage devices; a distributed memory management system; and a system control unit, to coordinate the other system components. Possible values for N and Q are 1024 and 16, respectively. The control schemes and memory management on PASM are explored. Examples of how PASM can be used to perform image processing tasks are given.

7. 文章摘要实例之二

The Center for Technology in Government worked with the Adirondack Park Agency to develop a prototype system that combines document records and geographic data into a unified workstation or "electronic reference desk." This report presents the finding of the technical staff responsible for developing the prototype system. It covers the gathering of geographic data and the development of the database as well as the data conversion process. Hardware and software configurations are included as well as lessons learned from the process and recommendations for other GIS system developers.

8. 文章摘要实例之三

ABSTRACT

TOM, PHILIP HILL

Low-Complexity Equalization of OFDM in
Doubly Selective Channels

(Under the direction of Worner Akaiwa Aldrich.)

Orthogonal frequency division multiplexing(OFDM)systems may experience significant inter-carrier interference (ICI)when used in time- and frequency-selective, or doubly selective, channels. In such cases, the classical symbol estimation schemes, e.g., minimum mean-squared error (MMSE) and zero-forcing(ZF)estimation, require matrix inversion that is prohibitively complex for large symbol lengths. An analysis of the ICI generation mechanism leads us to propose a novel two-stage equalizer whose complexity (apart from the FFT) is linear in the OFDM symbol length. The first stage applies optimal linear preprocessing to restrict ICI support, and the second stage uses iterative MMSE estimation to estimate finite-alphabet frequency-domain symbols. Simulation results indicate that our equalizer has significant performance and complexity advantages over the classical linear MMSE estimator in doubly selective channels.

9. 文章摘要实训之四

以上 3 例都属于描述性摘要，接下来看一个信息性摘要的例子。

"The Effects of Power, Knowledge and Trust on Income Disclosure in Surveys," by Catherine E. Ross and John R. Reynolds (1996. Social Science Quarterly 77:899-911).

ABSTRACT

Why do some social groups report income less often than others? We propose that powerlessness in the household and in society decrease the likelihood of reporting income because they decrease knowledge and trust. (研究目的)Knowledge of household finances affects the ability to report household income. Trust affects the willingness to report it. (研究主题)We analyze the reporting of exact or approximate income in a national U.S. probability sample of 2,031 respondents interviewed by telephone in 1990. (研究范围)Mistrust reduces the probability of reporting income, whether exactly or approximately. Homemakers and those with little household power report income as often as others if allowed to report approximate rather than exact amounts. The same applies to African Americans, the poorly educated, the unmarried, and people who feel powerless. Older persons and those in larger households report income less often than others and tend to give approximate amounts. (报告结论)The results confirm that knowledge and trust affect the reporting of income in surveys. (总结)

3.3.2 实验报告

实验报告(Laboratory reports)是为了与其他人交流做了什么；解释为什么这么做；描述是怎么做的；表达出发现了什么；叙说认为这个实验结果有何含义等内容。

撰写实验报告，一般有一个通用的格式：包括题目(Title)，摘要(Abstract)，引言(Introduction)，方法(Method)，结果(Results)、讨论(Discussion)、参考文献(References)等。

题目(Title)，应该简洁但清楚的给予读者有关实验者主要关心的内容，即反映出这篇报告的确切含义。

摘要(Abstract)是一段自成一体的短文，又是整篇报告主要观点的概述。它包含了被观察问题的简要表述、所使用的设计、被观察的主题、所包含的实验材料及任何重要仪器、得到的重点结果及其分析、最后的主要结论等。摘要通常有 100 字左右。一个快速写摘要的原则是从报告的每个部分摘取主题句。

引言(Introduction)，表达出研究的原因，这意味着已阅读了整个引言的读者应该能够揣测到实验将要做什么。引言包括以下内容。

(1) 与研究相关的背景材料的回顾(已存在的发现和理论)。

(2) 概括选用以研究的准确问题及采用的方法。

(3) 概括研究推测出来的结果等。

方法(Method)必须包含有足够的信息，使读者能重复该项实验。它分成以下几个子部分：设计(Design)、实验人员(Subjects)、仪器及材料(Apparatus & Materials)、过程(Procedure)等。

(1) 设计(Design)部分必须表示出所用的设计类型。非相关变量包括所选择的条件以表征实验不同等级；相关变量包括测量单位的详细内容(如秒、微秒或正确响应数)。还有实验的假设。

(2) 实验人员(Subjects)包括人员数量；他们是如何被选拔出来的；其他重要特征，如平均年龄、年龄范围、男女比例、受教育程度、职业等。

(3) 仪器及材料(Apparatus & Materials)包括仪器清单，如果用到复杂的仪器，如正在运行特殊软件的计算机，应该详细地描述。另外对选用的特殊材料，应该描述选用的一般准则。

(4) 过程(Procedure)描述设计是如何实现的，而且应该确切地描述参加的实验人员及实验在什么仪器和材料下进行的；应包含足够的信息使其他人能正确地重复实验。

结果(Results)这个部分提供给读者一个清晰的、准确的使所收集的数据概述及通过任何统计测试过程之后得到的结果；这个部分报告了实验数据及其分析。它不是对结果进行翻译，而结果应放在讨论部分。图表都应被注有标题，而且要被仔细清楚地标号。报告中必须包括有一些解释文本以描述什么数据出现在表格中。

讨论(Discussion)，在这部分中可以解释翻译实验的结论及对此进行进一步讨论。很重要的一点是讨论应与引言中提到的论点相关。讨论部分也应给进一步的实验提出一些建议，当然也可以讨论实验中还不是很明朗的一些限制因素。撰写讨论(Discussion)的步骤如下。

(1) 表述出所得结论，以摘要的形式列出。

(2) 统计所有的发现。

(3) 挖掘这些发现中隐含的东西。在表述结论时，应该通过概述结论的主要特征来放开讨论。例如，实验条件之间有否明显差别？如果有，则在什么样的条件下？这些发现是否与实验假设相关联等。接下来就是讨论这些发现的含义。如果已经摒弃了不合理的假设，则有必要建立这是否真正是非相关变量的操作所导致的；有必要确保不是其他的易混淆的变量或实验加工产品而导致的实验结果。如果不能摒弃这不合理的假设，则让读者相信这种近乎合理的解释是因果的缺乏并影响相关与非相关变量之间的关系。

当写参考文献(References)时，应区分原始资料(即确已看过)和第二手资料(即引用但没有看过)。可以通过互联网查找到与所写实验报告相关联的进一步信息。

实验报告实例如下。

Title: Laboratory Report on Control System Design for Hang Motion

Abstract: Based on microcontroller mega 16, the control system can control an object to motion, including line motion, circle motion and any assigned motion. The system can also control the object identify route, judge the setover from assigned track and adjust its route automatically. The object is driven by walking beam engineer, the engineer controlled by PWM mode.

Introduction: The motion control system ensures that the requirements are met:

(1) Setting the parameter of coordinates at discretion by keyboard or other means.

(2) The automatic operation to limit in 80cm*100cm and the length of motion track should more than 100cm, the object draws its motion track on the board and all of these are finished in 300s.

(3) The object can be the centre of a circle at discretion and the circle motion of diameter of 50cm completes in 300s.

(4) The object motion is finished in 150s from the origin of the coordinates at lower left to

certain coordinates(the length should more than 40cm).

This paper mainly tells about the design of the motion control system. The first part is the modules consisting of the control system and the method of implementing of modules. The main body of this paper is the design detail of every module and some test results.

Testing Procedures & Testing Results:

Design Project: the module of project; the choosing and argumentation of modules of project (content omitted).

(1) Unit Circuit Design: control module circuit design; motor driving module circuit design; LCD display module design; (content omitted).

(2) System Software Design: seeking mark subroutine design (taking the air line subroutine; taking the circle subroutine; taking willfully assigns the drop procedure from the zero point subroutine; taking the free curve subroutine.); system flow chart; (content omitted).

(3) System Test: measuring instruments；the target tests(the status of motor driving circuit test; the hanged object walks the straight line determines; the hanged object walks the circle determines; the hanged object walks the zero point as the beginning to the determination end point movement determines); (content omitted).

Discussion and Conclusions:

The error of this system mainly exists in the following several aspects:

(1) The hanged object moves from one to another. Although the distance between two points obtains quite slightly, the actual path between two points has the certain determinism. And when prearranging the track, it has some displacements, thus creates the error.

(2) The line and hanging point with the paint brush central position isn't superposition, the electronic contact of paint brush with leaned board and the pulley center line is not parallel with leaned board, all of these will create the error.

3.3.3 技术指南

技术指南(Technical Manuals)是帮助专业技术人员和消费者适当使用和维护产品的说明。这些产品包括从顾客购买的简单装置到制造厂家、企业和政府部门购买的高级尖端系统。技术指南要提供具体的技术信息，如产品如何使用，机器如何操作，设备如何维修、保养，系统如何安装或设置。所以技术指南可分为产品说明(书)，用户手册，操作指南，管理入门，维修保养手册等。各类指南的内容可能分别包括：产品介绍、应用、功能特点、故障检修、零部件浏览、设计参数、标准符号、注意事项中的一项或几项内容。

技术指南通常被厂家看成是重要的销售工具，消费者可以从中判别哪一类的设备更易操作或维修。技术指南一般由专业从事科技写作的人撰写，但有些单位也可让该产品的制造工程师和技术人员来写，因为他们对产品的性能、特点、用途、理论等方面都很熟悉。技术指南的作者喜欢使用常用的词汇，语法结构简洁，语言浅显易懂，确切明了，注意表达的科学性和逻辑性，多使用祈使句、简单句、短句和省略句。避免过多使用被动语态和比喻语言。

技术指南实例如下。

DESIGN AND OPERATION OF AUTOMATIC GAIN CONTROL LOOPS FOR RECEIVERS IN MODERN COMMUNICATIONS SYSTEMS

This article is intended to provide insight into the effective operation of variable gain amplifiers (VGA) in automatic gain control (AGC) applications. Figure 1 is a general block diagram for an AGC loop. The input signal passes through the VGA to produce the output level to be stabilized. The detector's output is compared against a setpoint voltage to produce an error signal, which is then integrated to produce a gain control voltage. This is applied to the control input of the VGA. The attenuator shown between the VGA and the detector is used to align the maximum output level of the VGA with the maximum input level of the detector. In the course of this article several key issues will be addressed, including VGA types, loop dynamics, detector types, the operating level of VGA and the operating level of the detector. Then an example application revolving around an AD8367 VGA will be presented for further discussion of the material.

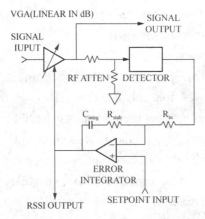

Fig.1　VGA-based AGC loop block diagram

VGA TYPES

There are two major classes of VGA in use today. The first is the so-called IVGA (input VGA), which can be regarded as a passive variable attenuator followed by a fixed-gain amplifier. The second type is the output VGA (OVGA), which is essentially equivalent to a fixed-gain amplifier followed by a passive attenuator.

An IVGA is the preferred choice for a receive AGC system because the available out-put level at low distortion is relatively independent of the gain setting. This is the desired trait for an AGC system, whose very object is to maintain a constant output in the face of varying input signal amplitude.

The OVGA is generally ill suited to AGC applications because of its reduced output signal handling capability at low gain settings and therefore will not be discussed further here.

When a single IVGA is used in a situation in which the VGA sets the system noise floor, the output SNR is essentially independent of the input signal; it does not improve as is often preferred. Occasionally, it is desirable to cascade two VGAs in order to ameliorate this behavior or simply to obtain more gain control range. Doing so requires proper coordination of the gain control inputs of the two devices.

If the gain control of only the second stage VGA is manipulated in the weak signal regime, the signal level to the first stage VGA's amplifier increases with increasing input level, so the output SNR improves with increasing input level. It is necessary to hand off the gain control from the second stage to the first stage only when overload of the first stage's amplifier is imminent.

Alternatively, the two gain control inputs may simply be driven in parallel, in which case the output S/N (expressed in dB) improves at half the rate at which the input level (also expressed in dB) rises. In cases where the VGAs used have residual ripple in their gain control functions, an additional benefit of this approach can be obtained if the two gain control input signals are intentionally offset by half the period of the ripple. This can provide considerable reduction of the ripple.

One of the benefits of using an IVGA in an AGC loop is that the VGA's gain control voltage bears an accurate logarithmic relationship to the input signal level when the loop is in equilibrium. This means that the gain control voltage may also be used as an excellent received signal strength indicator (RSSI).

LOOP DYNAMICS

Response time is an important issue when designing any AGC loop. There is usually a compromise between having the loop respond to undesired input level fluctuations as rapidly as one would like, and having it undesirably modify amplitude modulation on the signal. Additionally, large and/or abrupt changes in the input level may lead to unacceptable recovery behavior, necessitating further adjustments of the response time. The issue of excessive loop bandwidth deserves a bit more explanation. If the loop responds too quickly, it will introduce undesired gain modulation arising from the loop's efforts to stabilize the output level of a signal containing legitimate amplitude modulation. This is referred to as "gain pumping." In the context of digital modulation, the presence of appreciable gain pumping can result in significant modulation errors and perhaps even noticeable spectral re-growth in extreme cases. A tolerable value of gain pumping would generally be only a fairly small fraction of 1 dB.

DETECTOR TYPES (DETECTOR LAW)

One convenient aspect of an AGC loop is that the detector need not necessarily have a very wide dynamic range over which it obeys any particular law. This is because the detector operates at a constant average level when the AGC loop is in equilibrium; thus, the detector should only need to cope accurately with the level range associated with a modulated signal. However, as mentioned earlier, the detector's response law (that is linear, log, square law, etc.) can play a significant role in determining the loop's dynamic response during large, abrupt changes in signal level. Perhaps more importantly, the detector's response law influences the dependency of the loop's equilibrium level on the input's waveform or crest factor.

Four detector types will be considered here: envelope detector; square-law detector; true-RMS detector; and log detector.

ENVELOPE DETECTOR (RECTIFIER)

The output voltage of the envelope detector is proportional to the magnitude of the instantaneous RF input voltage. Assuming that sufficient low pass filtering is applied at its output to eliminate RF ripple, this detector produces a voltage proportional to the envelope amplitude of the RF signal.

Assuming that the loop's bandwidth is made sufficiently small as to avoid significant gain pumping, the effect of the loop using an envelope detector is to stabilize the average rectified voltage of the signal. The resulting power is therefore dependent on the RF signal's envelope waveform. Such a loop acting on a constant-envelope signal such as GSM will produce an average output power which is different than that for a heavily-amplitude-modulated signal, such as CDMA or 64QAM.

The output of the envelope detector can not go negative no matter how weak the input signal, but may reach extreme positive values in response to very strong signals. Starting with the AGC loop in equilibrium, a sudden large increase in input amplitude causes a very large initial increase in detector output, which very rapidly drives the loop towards lower gain. On the other hand, an abrupt reduction of the input signal level (no matter by how many dB) cannot reduce the detector output below zero, and the loop's best response is to slew towards equilibrium at a fairly low rate until the detector output begins to change by a significant fraction of the reference voltage, at which point the recovery trends towards an exponential decay. In the slew rate limited region, the gain of the signal path is varying at a constant number of dB per second.

Figure 2 shows the behavior of such a loop for a large input level step (note that curves for all four detector types are superimposed on this plot). These results were obtained from simulations in which the VGA has representative limits on the gain range and on the maximum output level. The detectors contrived for these simulations have no particular limits, on the grounds that in most practical situations the designer will scale the circuit so that the detector does not limit appreciably before the VGA does.

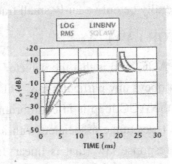

Fig.2　Simulated response of AGC loop to large amplitude steps for various detectors

SQUARE-LAW DETECTOR

This type of detector has an instantaneous output which is proportional to the square of the instantaneous RF input voltage, which is equivalent to say that its output is proportional to input power. This behavior, when incorporated into an AGC loop of sensible bandwidth, makes the loop's equilibrium average output power independent of the input waveform. As with the envelope detector, the output can never go negative, resulting in the loop having a similar tendency towards slew rate limited behavior when reacting to abrupt decreases in input amplitude. The response to large abrupt increases in input amplitude can be even more striking, however, because the square-law detector characteristic exaggerates the effect of the input increase. The extent to which this happens depends on the clipping level of either the VGA or the detector, whichever appears at a lower level.

TRUE-RMS DETECTOR

This detector comprises a square-law detector followed by a low pass filter followed by a square-root function. The low pass filter performs the "mean" operation associated with the root-mean-square (RMS) function, and it should have a sufficiently long time constant to smooth the output variations of the squaring detector that would otherwise arise from the legitimate modulation of the signal.

Because of the square-root element in this detector, the average output is proportional to the signal voltage, not power, so the loop's response to small abrupt decreases or increases of signal level should essentially be the same as that for an envelope detector, provided that the added filter pole within the RMS detector is correctly compensated for elsewhere in the loop. The fact that the added pole is located in a region of the signal path that is square law brings forth the possibility of the large-step response being different from that of the simple envelope detector, which can indeed be seen in the figure. Note that the RMS detector has a slightly slower recovery from a large downward amplitude step than does the standard envelope detector, but a slightly faster recovery (and a bit of overshoot) from a step up in input amplitude. In common with the square-law detector, the true-RMS detector will make the AGC loop's equilibrium point independent of the RF signal waveform.

It should be noted that the presence of the long-time-constant low pass filter in this detector may have a marked influence on loop dynamics; indeed, this filter may even provide the dominant pole in some designs. This time constant must therefore be coordinated with the remainder of the loop design.

LOG DETECTOR

This type of detector produces an output proportional to the logarithm of the RF input voltage。Because this behavior is complementary to that of the linear-in-dB VGA in the loop, the resulting loop dynamics are those of a linear system, assuming that signal level fluctuations during transients remain within the measurement range of the log detector. Subject to that assumption， the AGC loop's response to abrupt large changes in input level will not be slew-rate limited，and will often be faster to recover from amplitude decreases.

As with the envelope detector, the equilibrium point of an AGC loop using the log detector will depend on the RF input waveform.

COMPARISON OF RESPONSES WITH DIFFERENT DETECTORS

The AGC loops whose simulation results are shown were designed so that the small-signal response speeds are identical. The results show that the loop's large-step transient response is markedly dependent on the type of detector. At one extreme, the log detector gives the fastest response to large abrupt decreases in input level because the logarithmic curve has a very steep slope for low inputs, which exaggerates the loop's response. However, the log detector has a shallow slope for high input levels, resulting in a diminished response rate to sudden increases in signal level. At the other extreme, the square-law detector's small slope near zero input level gives it a very sluggish response to large decreases in input amplitude. Conversely, the square-law detector exaggerates the response to large signals, giving the fastest response to increasing signals. The envelope and RMS detectors, having intermediate characteristics, give response speeds in between.

OPERATING LEVEL OF DETECTOR

Ideally the operating level of the detector should be set as high as possible in order to minimize the error due to residual DC offsets. However, other considerations often rule. For signals with amplitude modulation, the peak input to the detector when the loop is in equilibrium must be no higher than what the detector will support, and so the average must be lower. Even for constant-envelope signals, the average level must be reasonably lower than the maximum，so that there is room for the detector level to increase if the system input level increases; otherwise, there could be little or no error signal to drive the loop back towards equilibrium. Note that there will generally be unequal amounts of room for the detector output to swing up or down from the design equilibrium level, which will make the apparent attack and decay speeds of the loop differ.

DESIGN EXAMPLE OF A WORKING AGC LOOP

Let's now put the above considerations to work in a practical design. The design assumptions and goals are as follows:

- Signal modulation: W-CDMA (15 users); symbol rate = 3.84 Msymbols/s
- IF frequency: 380MHz
- VGA: AD8367
- Detector: AD8361 (true RMS, for waveform independence)
- Power supply: 5V DC

From these, reasonable constraints will be established for operating levels to maximize the adjacent channel power ratio (ACPR) and AGC loop bandwidth (to avoid excessive gain pumping).

Previous bench measurements on the AD8367 had revealed that the best ACPR at 380MHz occurs with an output level of about 112mVrms, which gives about −12dBm into 200 ..

Detector Operating Level

The peak-to-average power ratio for the chosen signal is about 18 dB. When operating from a 5V supply, the maximum output level of the AD8361 is about 4.8V (from the AD8361 datasheet). The squarer in the detector will be assumed to go into clipping at the same input level that results in maximum output, for a CW signal. Thus, assuming that the peaks of the modulated signal should not drive the detector's squarer into clipping when the loop is in equilibrium, the average output level of the detector must be such that it is at least 18dB below 4.8V; 4.8 × 10–18/20 = 604mV. Since the conversion gain of the detector is 7.5V/Vrms, the loop-equilibrium level at the detector's input should be 604mV/7.5 = 80mVrms.

This level can be obtained from the desired output level of the VGA by adding a series resistor of 90., which combines with the 225. input resistance of the AD8361 to form a voltage divider that achieves the desired result. Note that this loads the output of the VGA with 315, which means that the lowest additional parallel load impedance on the VGA would be 547. in order to satisfy its design minimum load impedance of 200. However, in this case more than half of the VGA's power output is going to be feeding the detector. This could be remedied by driving the VGA end of the 90. resistor with an emitter follower, raising the input impedance of the overall detector by the beta of the transistor used in the follower. This would free up almost all the output current capability of the VGA for use by the useful load.

Estimation of Target AGC Loop Bandwidth

Here a judgment call must be made, based on an empirical measurement, to establish the maximum loop bandwidth that will avoid intolerable gain pumping. For purposes of this design example, it is assumed that up to 0.5dB p-p gain variation is acceptable. An estimate of the desired loop bandwidth will be made by passing a W-CDMA signal through a spectrum analyzer with very wide resolution bandwidth, zero span and linear detector, and observe what video bandwidth results in 0.5dB p-p output variation. The result turns out to be 200Hz, which means the initial design of the AGC loop will have a 200Hz bandwidth.

The simulation and measured results will be used to see how this choice works out.

RMS Detector Filter

The RMS detector's "mean value" filter comprises an internal filter resistance combined with an external shunt capacitance. The effective value of the filter resistance varies with drive level, from about 2000. at very low drive level down to about 500. at maximum drive level. For this example a value of 1.8k. will be used, which was determined empirically for the operating level established earlier.

In general，an AD8361 would be taken into the lab with a W-CDMA signal source in order to ascertain a suitable filter capacitor value. However, the previous measurement for loop bandwidth gives a clue that allows a reasonable estimate of the required value to be made. A loop bandwidth of 200Hz resulted in a 0.5dB p-p (~6 percent) variation of detector output. It so happens that this is just about the maximum amount of variation of RMS filter level that still gives good RMS accuracy. So, the bandwidth of this filter will simply be made equal to 200Hz, which requires a filter capacitor of about 0.44 μF against the 1.8k. filter resistance.

Loop Dynamics Design

A first order loop will be developed, with a small-signal bandwidth of 200Hz. Note that the RMS detector's filter already contributes one pole at 200Hz, so the remainder of the loop will clearly need to take this into account. This will be achieved by choosing Rcomp to create a zero at 200Hz in conjunction with Cinteg (see Appendix A). The response speed of all the other elements in the loop is so much faster than that of the desired loop that all other poles can be safely ignored.

The loop bandwidth designed will apply only for small deviations from the AGC loop's equilibrium level. Large transients will behave differently because of the nonlinear character of the loop, and simulation and/or breadboarding will be relied upon to investigate the large signal behavior.

The next items on the agenda are the determinations of the incremental gains of the VGA and of the detector from the loop dynamics viewpoint. For the VGA, this means the slope of Vout versus control voltage, not the RF gain.

VGA Gain

Vin and Vout will represent RMS values of the VGA's RF input and output, respectively, and Vg will represent the gain control voltage. From examination of the AD8367 performance data in the datasheet for 240MHz, combined with a bit of extrapolation and rounding, 0dB of gain is found to occur at a control voltage of 0.1V and the control slope is 50dB/V. By formulating and then differentiating Vout with respect to Vg at the equilibrium output of 112 mVrms, the incremental slope is evaluated to be 0.6447Vrms/V.

Next the Detector Slope

The nominal conversion gain of the AD8361 is 7.5. However, a 90 . series resistor was added at the input of the detector; this has the effect of reducing the detector's effective gain to 5.357, which is the value that will be used in the loop analysis.

Avoidance of Excessive Recovery Delay

If the loop is left sitting with a very low (or zero) input signal level for a time，the output voltage of the integrator will continue to rise until it reaches saturation of the op-amp as the loop tries to find more gain. When a significant signal does suddenly arrive at the system input, one has to wait for the integrator's output to ramp back down to 1V before the loop can begin reducing the gain. To reduce this "overload delay" a 4.3:1 attenuator is inserted between the integrator and the control input of the VGA so that the positive limit (nearly 5V) of the integrator's output is about equal to the maximum effective control input (1V) to the VGA.

Calculation of Component Values

In the loop, a net gain (excluding the integrator for the moment) of 0.644 (VGA incremental slope) • 5.357 (effective detector slope)/4.3 (for the Vagc atten) = 0.803, is obtained. For a loop bandwidth of 200Hz, the loop gain should be unity at that frequency. If the rest of the loop has a gain of 0.803, the integrator must have a gain of 1.0/0.803 = 1.245, which requires that the reactance of Cinteg at 200Hz be 1.245 times the value of Rin. Mathematically, $1/(2\pi \cdot 200 \cdot Cinteg)$ = 1.245 • Rin; Rin • Cinteg = 639.2μs.

Now another constraint must be also noted, which is that the AD8361 cannot source very much current, and can sink even less. Therefore, 50 k. is chosen for Rin in order to minimize total loading on the AD8361's output, which leads to a value of 12.78 nF for Cinteg. Finally, in order to compensate for the 200Hz pole in the RMS detector, Rcomp is chosen as 62.3 k. to provide a loop zero at 200Hz with Cinteg. A 10 k. pulldown is also added on the AD8361's output to improve its effective sinking capacity.

Lab Tests

A prototype circuit was constructed according to the schematic in Appendix A. Figures 3 and 4 show the prototype loop's response to small and large (30dB) input level steps, respectively. Figure 5 shows the measured gain pumping obtained by capturing the signal at the gain-control input of the VGA with an oscilloscope and scaling into dB.

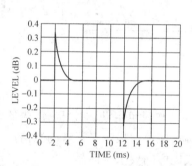

Fig.3   The prototype circuit response to small amplitude stepsis symmetrical and shows exponential recovery

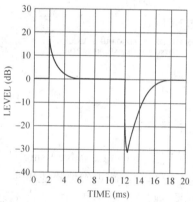

Fig.4   The prototype circuit response to large amplitude steps is asymmetrical and exhibits slow-rate-limited recovery

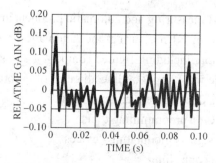

Fig.5   The prototype circuit has about 0.2dB p-p gain pumping

CONCLUSION

Numerous basic and finer points of AGC design have been discussed, and a detailed example of a practical design was worked out. Practical considerations and difficulties encountered along the way were emphasized, as opposed to reiterating textbook loop design equations. Finally, a working circuit was constructed and measurement results presented.

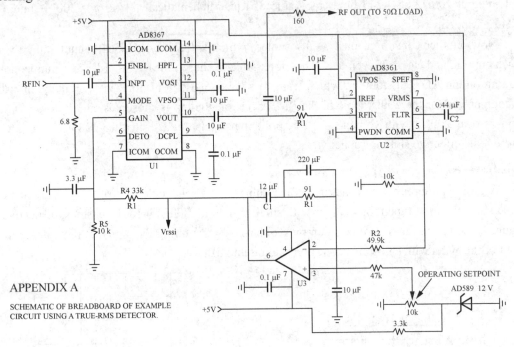

Fig.6   Working Crant

3.3.4   科技广告

科技广告(Technical Advertising)涉及的范围很广，在写作时可用劝诱技巧。广告的感召力必须有逻辑性，即正确地陈述事实、统计数字和实例。应该积极考虑读者的感情，不要偏离主题，避免含混不清的措辞，不要提出无关紧要或虚假的要求。但是，如果读者对广告有怀疑，则需要采用诱导的方法，用有力具体的证据来说服读者。所以，科技广告的遣词造句既有科技性，又有促销宣传之意。

科技广告实例之一。

The gratis catalogue of NI measuring and automatic products in 2005

The brand new catalogue of NI measuring and automatic products in 2005 will display a serious of important information, including figures comparing and structural frame and products features. This annual catalogue will simply outline all kinds of NI products line. This includes:

NI LabVIEW ^{TM} graphics development environment

- Visual Basic and C/C++ programming tools
- Data collecting and signals modulating devices
- Decisional real-time controlling

- Standard hardware platform of measuring and automation—PXI
- Industrial controlling and distributed I/O
- Machine view and dynamical controlling
- GPIB and other instruments controlling of bus

Please visit ni.com/china. If inputting info code (cnkm2c), you will freely take this catalogue

NI in shanghai：the 6th floor at the building of business, 800 Qv Yang Road(200437)

Tel：(021)65557838   FAX: (021)65556244

Email:china.info@ni.com

科技广告实例之二。

Total Solution for Industrial Device Networking

Famous manufacturer of Serial and Network Communication in Asian—Moxa Technologies provides total solution for industrial device networking, including Multiport Serial Board, Serial Device Server, Industrial Ethernet Switch. Moxa Technologies is leader in the field of industrial communication.

NPort multiport serial device networking server.

- RS-232/422/485 having the capability of networking
- Extending COM/tty/ports controlling through Ethernet/Internet
- Providing 1/2/4/8/16 serial number and RS-232/422/485 interface compounding products
- Protecting from surge and magnetic; designing DIN Rail and 19th frame

Industrial Ethernet Switcher

- Eight 10/100 Mbps networking port, selecting Single Mode or Multi Mode (optical mode)
- Supporting Redundant Ethernet Ring
- Working temperature: 0~60℃
- Remotely managing through IE; having the capability of E-mail warning and IP restoring

For detail information, please visit www.moxa.com.cn

附录 1 常用通信与电子信息词汇及注解

A

3GPP(3rd Generation Partnership Project)			第三代伙伴计划

3GPP(3rd Generation Partnership Project)　第三代伙伴计划

AAON(ATM Active Optical Network)　ATM 有源光网络

Abis-interface　GSM BSC 与 BTS 之间的接口

abrasion　[əˈbreiʒən]　n.　磨损

acoustical　[əˈkuːstik(ə)l]　adj.　听觉的，声学的

acoustics　[əˈkuːstiks]　n.　声学

active　[ˈæktiv]　adj.　有源的

active satellite　有源卫星

adaptive control　自适应控制

ADC(analogue-to-digital converter)　模数转换器

Additive printed circuit-board process　印制电路板添加工艺

Ad hoc network　自组织网络

ADM(Add-Drop Multiplexer)　上、下话路复用器

ADSL(Asymmetric Digital Subscriber Line)　非对称数字用户线

A-interface　GSM BSS 与核心网之间的接口

algorithm　[ˈælgəriðəm]　n.　算法

amplifier　[ˈæmpliˌfaiə]　n.　[电工]扩音器，放大器

amplitude　[ˈæmplitjuːd]　n.　振幅

AMPS(Advanced Mobile Phone Service)　高级移动电话业务(北美)

analog　[ˈænəlɔg]　adj.　模拟的

analog signal　模拟信号

ANN(Artificial Neural Network)　人工神经网络

ANSI(American National Standard Institute)　美国国家标准协会

antenna　[ænˈtenə]　n.　天线

aperiodic　[ˌeipiəriˈɔdik]　adj.　不定期的，[物]非周期的

APON(ATM Passive Optical Network)　ATM 无源光网络

approximation　[əˌprɔksiˈmeiʃən]　n.　近似值

arc　[ɑːk]　n.　电弧

argument　[ˈɑːgjuːmənt]　n.　自变量

arithmetic　[əˈriθmətik]　n.　算术

ARPA(Advanced Research Project Agency)   (美国)高级研究计划局

ARPANET(Advanced Research Project Agency Network)   (美国)高级研究计划局通信网

artificial intelligence   人工智能(abbr. AI)

ASCII(American Standard Code for Information Interchange)   美国信息交换标准码

ASICs(application-specific integrated circuits)   专用集成电路

ASR(Automatic Speech Recognition)   自动语音识别

aspect ratio   纵横比，屏幕高宽比

asynchronous transmission   异步传输

ATM(Asynchronous Transfer Mode)   异步传输模式

AT&T(American Telephone and Telegraph)   美国电报电话(公司)

attenuation   [ə,tenju'eiʃən]   *n.*   衰减，衰耗

audio recording   *n.*   唱片

auditory   ['ɔːditəri]   *adj.*   耳的，听觉的

autocorrelation   [ɔːtəukɔri'leiʃən]   *n.*   自相关

auxiliary pilot   辅助导频

auxiliary storage(secondary storage)   辅助存储器

avalanche   ['ævə,lɑːnʃ]   *n.&v.*   雪崩

avalanche-type   雪崩型

B

backbone   ['bækbəun]   *n.*   支撑，(the～支撑网)

bandpass filter   带通滤波器

bandwidth   ['bændwidθ]   *n.*   带宽

baud rate   波特率

Bernoulli distribution   贝努利分布

bias   ['baiəs]   *n.*   偏差，偏置

binary   ['bainəri]   *adj.*   二进位的，二元的

Binomial distribution   二项分布

bipolar   [bai'pəulə]   *adj.*   有两极的，双极的

B-ISDN(Broad band Integrated Service Digital Network)   宽带综合业务数字网

block out   阻断，封闭

BPL(Broadband Over Power Line)   电力线宽带

bps(bits per second)   每秒钟传输的比特

bridge tap   桥式分接头

broadband   *n.*   宽带

buffer   ['bʌfə]   *n.*   缓冲器

bus network   总线形网

C

CAI(Computer-aided Instruction)			计算机辅助教学
calculus	['kælkjuləs]	*n.*	微积分
capacitor	[kə'pæsitə]	*n.*	电容器
Carbon	['kɑ:bən]	*n.*	[化]碳(元素符号 C)
Carrier	['kæriə]	*n.*	载波
CATV(cable television)			有线电视
causal system			因果系统
CCIR(International Radio Communications Consultative Committee)			国际无线通信咨询委员会
CCITT(Consultative Committee in Telegraphy and Telephony)			国际电报电话咨询委员会
CD(Compact Disc)			光盘
CDMA(code division multiple access)			码分多址
CDMA2000			基于 ANSI－41 标准的码分复用接入
CDMA One			码分多路接入
cellular	['seljʊlə]	*adj.*	蜂窝状的，格形的，多孔的
centigrade	['sentigreid]	*adj.*	分为百度的，百分度的，摄氏温度的
chart	[tʃɑ:t]	*n.*	图表(曲线图，略图)
channel	['tʃænl]	*n.*	信道，频道
Channelized receiver			信道接收机
chaotic	[kei'ɔtik]	*adj.*	混乱的，无秩序的，混沌的
chrominance	['krəuminəns]	*n.*	色度
circuitry	['sə:kitri]	*n.*	电路，线路
closed loop gain			闭环增益
CMOS(Complementary Metal Oxide Semiconductor)			互补金属氧化物半导体
CO(Central Office)			中心交换局
coating	['kəutiŋ]	*n.*	涂层，层
coax	[kəuks]	*n.*	同轴电缆
coaxial	[kəu'æksəl]	*adj.*	同轴的，共轴的
code book			码本
coefficient	[kəui'fiʃənt]	*n.*	系数
collision	[kə'liʒən]	*n.*	碰撞，冲突
combinational logic circuit			组合逻辑电路
commutative	[kə'mju:tətiv]	*adj.*	可交换的
communication networks and protocol			通信网络与协议

communication session			通信会话
compact	[ˈkɔmpækt]	adj.	紧密的
Compact disk(CD)			激光磁盘
compatibility	[kəmˌpætiˈbiliti]	n.	兼容性
computability	[kəmˈpjuːtəbiliti]	n.	可计算性
computer-integrated manufacturing(CIM)			计算机集成制造
computer mediated communications(CMC)			计算机中介通信
concentrator	[ˈkɔnsentreitə]	n.	集中器，集线器
conductor	[kənˈdʌktə]	n.	导体
configure	[kənˈfigə]	vi.	配置，设定
congestion	[kənˈdʒestʃən]	n.	拥塞
constant	[ˈkɔnstənt]	n.	常数
contour	[ˈkɔntuə]	n.	轮廓
contrast enhancement			对比度增强
converge	[kənˈvəːdʒ]	v.	收敛(n. convergence)
convolution	[ˌkɔnvəˈljuːʃən]	n.	卷积
coordinate	[kəuˈɔːdinit]	n.	坐标(用复数)
correlation	[ˌkɔriˈleiʃən]	n.	相互关系，相关(性)
cosine	[ˈkəusain]	n.	余弦
criterion	[kraiˈtiəriən]	n.	标准，规范
critical value			临界值
crosscorrelation	[ˈkrɔsˌkɔriˈleiʃən]	n.	互相关
cross talk			串音
cumulative	[ˈkjuːmjulətiv]	adj.	累积的
cursor	[ˈkəːsə]	n.	指针
cut-off frequency			截止频率
Cycling redundancy check (CRC)			循环冗余校验

D

database	[ˈdeitəbeis]	n.	[计]数据库，资料库
database management system (DBMS)			数据库管理信息系统
database transaction			数据库事务
data fusion and mining			数据融合与数据挖掘
data independence			数据独立
data integrity			数据完整性，数据一致性
data management			数据管理
data security			数据安全性
DCS(Digital Communication System)			数字通信系统

DCT(discrete cosine transform)			离散余弦变换
decimal part			小数部分
decision support systems			决策支持系统
derivative	[di'rivətiv]	*n.*	导数
dialing pulse			拨号脉冲
dielectric	[ˌdaii'lektrik]	*n.& adj.*	电介质，绝缘体；电介质的，绝缘的
differentiable	[ˌdifə'renʃiəbl]	*adj.*	可微分的
differential input amplifier			差分放大器
differentiation	[ˌdifəˌrenʃi'eiʃən]	*n.*	微分
diffraction	[di'frækʃən]	*n.*	衍射
diode	['daiəud]	*n.*	二极管
dioxide	[dai'ɔksaid]	*n.*	二氧化物
discipline	['disiplin]	*n.*	学科
discrete	[dis'kri:t]	*adj.*	离散的
Discrete device			分离元件
diskettes(floppy disk)			软盘
disproportionate	[ˌdisprə'pɔ:ʃənit]	*adj.*	不成比例的，不相称的
dissipation	[ˌdisi'peiʃən]	*n.*	损耗
distortion	[dis'tɔ:ʃən]	*n.*	扭曲，变形，失真
Distortion analyzer			失真分析仪
distributed	[dis'tribju:tid]	*adj.*	分布式的
distributive	[dis'tribjutiv]	*adj.*	分配的
disturbance	[dis'tə:bəns]	*n.*	打扰，干扰，骚乱，搅动
dominant	['dɔminənt]	*adj.*	占优势的，支配的
downlink	['daunliŋk]	*n.*	下行线，向下链路
DSL(Digital Subscriber Line)			数字用户线
DSLAM(Digital SUBSCRIBER Line Access Multiplexer)			数字用户线接入多路复用器
duality	[dju(:)'æliti]	*n.*	二元性，对偶性
duration	[djuə'reiʃən]	*n.*	持续时间

E

earth orbit			地球轨道
edge	[edʒ]	*n.*	边缘
EIA(Electronic Industries Association)			电子工业协会
electrocardiogram	[iˌlektrəu'kɑ:diəugræm]	*n.*	心电图(ECG)
electromagnetic	[iˌlektrəumæg'nitik]	*adj.*	电磁的
electromechanical	[iˌlektrəumi'kænikəl]	*adj.*	电动机械的，机电的

emulation	[ˈemjuleiʃ ən]	n.	仿真
encapsulation	[inˌkæpsjuˈleiʃ ən]	n.	包装,封装
entity	[ˈentiti]	n.	实体,存在,本质
entropy	[ˈentrəpi]	n.	熵,平均信息量
envelope	[ˈenviləup]	n.	包络
equalizer	[ˈiːkwəlaizə]	n.	均衡器
equation	[iˈkweiʃ ən]	n.	方程(式);等式
equivalent	[iˈkwivələnt]	adj.	等效的
Ethernet			以太网
ETSI(Europe Telecommunication Standard Institution)			欧洲电信标准学会
evaluation	[iˌvæljuˈeiʃ ən]	n.	赋值,值的计算
exponential	[ˌekspəuˈnenʃ əl]	adj.	指数的,幂数的
expected value			期望值
expert system			专家系统
extraterrestrial	[ˌekstrətəˈrestriəl]	adj.	地球外的,地球大气圈外的

F

fading	[ˈfeidiŋ]	n.	衰落,消失,衰减
fall within			属于
family	[ˈfæmili]	n.	族,一群相似的事物
facsimile	[fækˈsimili]	n.	摹写,传真
fault tolerance			容错
FCC(Federal Communications Commission)			(美国)通信委员会
FEC(Forward Error Correction)			前向纠错
FET(Field Effect Transistors)			场效应管
FDD(Frequency Division Duplex)			频分复用
FDDI(Fiber Distributed Data Interface)			光纤分配数字接口
FDM(Frequency Division Multiplexing)			频分多路复用
feedback	[ˈfiːdbæk]	n.	[无]回授,反馈,反应
fiber optic			光纤
fidelity	[fiˈdeliti]	n.	逼真度,保真度
feedforward	[ˌfiːdˈfɔːwəd]	n.	前馈
field	[fiːld]	n.	磁场,字段,领域
filter	[ˈfiltə]	n.	滤波器,过滤器,滤光器,筛选
		vt.	过滤,渗透,用过滤法除去
Finite Impulse Response			有限冲击响应(abbr.FIR)
fluctuation	[ˌflʌktjuˈeiʃ ən]	n.	波动,起伏
fly-by-light			光控飞行

fly-by-wire			线控飞行
Form factor			波形因数；形状因数
formula	['fɔːmjulə]	n.	公式，规则
forum	['fɔːrəm]	n.	论坛
Fourier series			傅里叶级数
FPGA(Field Programmable Gate Array)			可编程门阵列
fractal	['fræktəl]	n.	(计)分形，分数维
frame	[freim]	n.	(图像)帧
frame rate			帧频率
front-end			前置，前级
full-duplex transmission			全双工传输
fuzzy	['fʌzi]	adj.	模糊的，失真的
fuzzy logic control			模糊逻辑控制

G

gate	[geit]	n.	逻辑门
gateway	['geitwei]	n.	网关
generator	['dʒenəreitə]	n.	发电机，发生器，产生器
genetic algorithm and evolutionary computation			遗传算法与进化计算
gigahertz	['gigəhəːts]	n.	千兆赫
GIS(Ground Instrumentation System)			地面测量系统
GPRS(General Packet Radio Service)			通用分组无线业务
graceful	['greisful]	adj.	平滑的
gray level			(图像的)灰度级
ground	[graund]	vt.	使接地
		n.	接地，地线
ground station			地面站
GSM(Global System for Mobile Communications)			全球移动通信系统
GSM BSC(GSM Base Station Controller)			GSM 基站控制器
GSM BSS(GSM Base Station Subsystem)			GSM 基站子系统
GSM BTS(Base Transceiver Station)			GSM 基站发送接收器
GSM-MAP(GSM-Mobile Application Part)			GSM 移动应用部分

H

half-duplex transmission			半双工传输
half-wave rectified			半波整流
Hamming window			汉明窗

handover	['hændəuvə]	n.	移交，越区切换
handset	['hændset]	n.	手持(移动)设备
hard disk			硬盘
harmonic	[haː'mɔnik]	n.	谐波，谐函数
harmonic distortion			谐波失真
HDSL(High Bit-Rate Digital Subscriber Line)			高比特速率数字用户线
HDTV(High-Definition TV)			高清晰度电视
hexagonal	[hek'sægənəl]	adj.	六角形的，六边形的
HFC(Hybrid Fiber Coaxial Network)			混合光纤同轴网络
hierarchy	['haiəraːki]	n.	层次，层级，分层
High-frequency(HF)			高频
histogram	['histəugræm]	n.	直方图
hologram	['hɔləugræm]	n.	全息摄影，全息图
homogeneity	[,hɔməudʒe'niːiti]	n.	齐次性
hypermedia	['haipəmiːdiə]	n.	超媒体
hypertext			超文本

I

IC(Integrated Circuits)			集成电路
ideal operation amplifier			理想运放(abbr.ideal op amp)
IDLC(Integrated Digital Loop Carrier)			综合数字环路载波
IDSL(ISDN Digital Subscriber Line)			ISDN 数字用户线
IEEE(Institute of Electrical and Electronics Engineers)			电气与电子工程师协会
image	['imidʒ]	n.	图像，镜像
impedance	[im'piːdəns]	n.	阻抗
impurity	[im'pjuəriti]	n.	杂质，混杂物
independent identically distributed			独立同分布(abbr.i.i.d.)
inductive	[in'dʌktiv]	adj.	感应的，电感的，归纳的
in essence			本质上
inference	['infərəns]	n.	推论，推理，推断
Infinite Impulse Response			无限冲击响应(abbr.IIR)
infinitesimal	[in,finə'tesiməl]	adj.	无穷小的，极小的，无限小的
		n.	极小量，极微量，无限小
inflection	[in'flekʃ ən]	n.	变形
infrared	['infrə'red]	adj.	红外线的
		n.	红外线

insulator	['insjuleitə]	n.	绝缘体
instantaneous amplitude			瞬时振幅
integration	[,inti'greiʃən]	n.	积分
intellectual property			知识产权
intelligent network			智能网
INTELSAT(international telecommunication satellite)			国际通信卫星
intended recipient			预定接收机
intensity	[in'tensiti]	n.	亮度，强度
interconnect	[,intə(:)kə'nekt]	vt.	互相连接，互连
interdisciplinary	[,intə(:)'disiplinəri]	adj.	跨学科的
interface	['intə(:),feis]	n.	分界面，接口
interference	[,intə'fiərəns]	n.	干扰
interlace	[,intə(:)'leis]	vi.	隔行扫描
interleaving	[,intə(:)'li:viŋ]	n.	交叉，交错
intermodulation distortion			互调失真
International Journal of Computational Intelligence (IJCI)			国际计算智能期刊
inverse	['in'və:s]	n.	(矩阵的)逆
inverting input			反相输入端
ion	['aiən]	n.	离子
ionosphere	[ai'ɔnəsfiə]	n.	电离层
IPSec(Internet Protocol Security)			互联网安全协议
irrevocably	[i'revəkəbli]	adv.	无法恢复地
ISDN(Integrated Services Digital Network)			综合业务数字网
ISO(International Standards Organization)			国际标准化组织
ITU(International Telecommunication Union)			国际电信联盟
Iu-interface			WCDMA 与核心网之间的接口

J

jamming	['dʒæmiŋ]	n.	干扰台，人为干扰
JPEG(Joint Photographic Experts Group)			联合图像专家组(静止图像数据压缩标准)

K

kilohertz	['kiləhə:ts]	n.	千赫
knowledge base			知识库
knowledge representation			知识表示

L

Large-Scale Integrated (LSI) circuit			大规模集成电路
latency	['leitənsi]	n.	反应时间，等待时间
Leased-line			租用线
LED(light-emitting-diode)			发光二极管
limit	['limit]	n.	极限
limiter	['limitə]	n.	限幅器
line-of-sight			视线，瞄准线
linear	['liniə]	adj.	线性的，线状的(nonlinear 非线性的)
linearity	[ˌlini'æriti]	n.	线性度
linguistics	[liŋ'gwistiks]	n.	语言学
LNA(Low-noise Amplifier)			低噪放大器
LO(Local oscillator)			本地振荡器
logarithmic	[ˌlɔgə'riθmik]	adj.	对数的
logical relationships			逻辑关系
long haul			长途电话，长途运输
LPC(Linear Predictive Coding)			线性预测编码
LSB(Least Significant Bit)			最低有效位
lumped element			集总元件

M

mainstay	['meinsteɪ]	n.	支柱
mainstream	['meinstri:m]	n.	主流
map	[mæp]	n.	映射
M-ary			M 进制
matrix	['meitriks]	n.	矩阵
mean	[mi:n]	n.	平均数
mean square error criteria			均方误差准则
mechanism	['mekənizəm]	n.	机理，机制
megabit	['megəbit]	n.	百万位，兆位，兆比特
membrane	['membrein]	n.	膜，隔膜
mercury	['mə:kjuri]	n.	水银，汞
meteorology	[ˌmi:tjə'rɔlədʒi]	n.	气象学，气象状态
metropolitan	[metrə'pɔlit(ə)n]	adj.	大都市的
Metropolitan Area Network(MAN)		n.	城域网，城市网络

Microelectronic		*n.*	微电子
microprocessor	[maikrəu'prəusesə(r)]	*n.*	[计]微处理器
microwave	['maikrəuweiv]	*n.*	微波
millionfold	['miljənfəuld]	*adj.*	百万倍的
		adv.	百万倍地
minicomputer	['minikəm,pju:tə]	*n.*	小型计算机
misaligned	[,misə'laind]	*adj.*	方向偏离的
mixer	['miksə]	*n.*	混频器
mobile	['məubail]	*adj.*	可移动的，机动的，装在车上的
modem pool			调制解调器(存储)池
modulating signal			调制信号
modulation	[,mɔdju'leiʃən]	*n.*	调制
mold	[məuld]	*n.*	模型
monochromatic	['mɔnəukrəu'mætik]	*adj.*	单色的，单频的，黑白的
monochrome	['mɔnəukrəum]	*n.*	单色，单色的
MOS(metal oxide semiconductor)			金属氧化物半导体
moving average			移动平均(abbr. MA)
MPEG(Moving Picture Expert Group)			活动图像专家组(活动图像数据压缩标准)
MSB(Most Significant Bit)			最高有效位
multi-access			多路存取，多路进入
multi-path			多路，多途径；多路的，多途径的
multi-path fading			多径衰落
multiframe	[,mʌlti'freim]	*n.*	多帧
multiplexing	['mʌltipleksiŋ]	*n.*	多路技术

N

nanometer	['neinə,mi:tə]	*n.*	毫微米，纳米
narrowband			窄带
negative	['negətiv]	*adj.*	负的
neural network			神经网络
neutron	['nju:trɔn]	*n.*	中子
NMT(Nordic Mobile Telephone)			北欧移动电话
NN(Neural Networks)			神经网络
NNI(Network Node Interface)			网络节点接口
nonlinear	['nɔn'liniə]	*adj.*	非线性的
nonsynchronous	['nɔn'siŋkrənəs]	*adj.*	异步的

Normal distribution			正态分布
NTSC(National Television Systems Committee)			全国电视系统委员会制式
nucleus	['njuːkliəs]	n.	原子核
numeral	['njuːmərəl]	n.	数字

O

OFDM(orthogonal frequency division multiplexing)			正交频分多址
offset	['ɔːfset]	n.	偏移量，抵消，
OLT(Optic Line Terminal)			光纤线路终端
one-dimensional			一维的
one order of magnitude			一个数量级
ONU(Optical Network Unit)			光网络单元
operator	['ɔpəreitə]	n.	算子
optical	['ɔptikəl]	adj.	眼的，视力的，光学的
optical disks			光盘
optical computer			光计算机
optically	['ɔptikəli]	adv.	光学地，光地
optic core			纤芯
optimum	['ɔptiməm]	n.	最佳条件，最适宜的
optoelectronic	[ˌɔptəuilek'trɔnik]	adj.	光电子的
Ordinary Differential Equation			常微分方程(abbr. ODE)
orientation	[ˌɔ(ː)rien'teiʃən]	n.	定位，定向
orthogonal	[ɔːˈθɔgənl]	adj.	正交的
orthogonal diversity			正交分集
orthogonality	[ɔːθɔgəˈnæliti]	n.	正交性，正交状态
oscillator	['ɔsileitə]	n.	振荡器
oscilloscope	[ɔ'siləskəup]	n.	示波器
OSI(open-system-interconnection)			开放系统互连
outage	['autidʒ]	n.	停止，运行中断
out-of-band signaling			带外信令
overhead	['əuvəhed]	n.	开销
overlapping	['əuvə'læpiŋ]	n.	重叠
oxygen	['ɔksidʒən]	n.	[化]氧气；氧元素
ozone	['əuzəun]	n.	新鲜的空气，[化]臭氧

P

| PAL(Phase Alternating Line) | | | 逐行倒相制式 |

PAPR(Peak-to-Average Power Ratio)			峰值平均功率比
parallel	['pærəlel]	adj.	平行的，并行的
parameter	[pə'ræmitə]	n.	参(变)数；参量
parasitic	[,pærə'sitik]	adj.	寄生的
passband	['pɑːsbænd]	n.	通频带，传输频带
passive	['pæsiv]	adj.	无源的，被动的
passive satellite			无源卫星
pattern recognition			模式识别
payload	['pei,ləud]	n.	有效载荷
PBX(Private Branch Exchange)			用户小交换机或专用交换机
PCM(pulse code modulation)			脉冲编码调制
PCI(Peripheral Component Interconnect)			PCI 总线
PDC(Personal Digital Cellular)			个人数字蜂窝(日本)
PDH (Plesiochronous Digital Hierarchy)			准同步数字序列
peripheral devices			外设
permissible	[pə(:)'misəbl]	adj.	可允许的
phonetics	[fəu'netiks]	n.	语音学，发音学
photoconductive	[,fəutəukən'dʌktiv]	adj.	光电导的，光敏的
photodiode	[,fəutəu'daiəud]	n.	光敏二极管，光电二极管
pictorial	[pik'tɔːriəl]	adj.	图像的
PIN-type			PIN 型
pixel	['piksəl]	n.	像素
phasor	['feizə]	n.	向量
playback			播放(录音带，唱片)
plesiochronous	['pliːsiəkrənəs]	adj.	准同步的
PLL(Phase locked loop)			锁相环
POH(Path Overhead)			通道开销
Poisson distribution			泊松分布
polarity	[pəu'læriti]	n.	极性
population	[pɔpju'leiʃən]	n.	总体
positive	['pɔzətiv]	adj.	[数]正的
potential	[pə'tenʃ(ə)l]	n.	电势，电位
printed circuit boards			印制电路板
prior	['praiə]	adj.	优先的
probability density function			概率密度函数(abbr. pdf)
product	['prɔdəkt]	n.	乘积
profile	['prəufail]	n.	剖面，侧面，外形，轮廓
progressive scanning			逐行扫描
propagation	['prɔpə'geiʃən]	n.	(声波，电磁辐射等)传播

proportion	[prə'pɔːʃən]	n.	比例，比率，部分
protocol	['prəutəkɔl]	n.	协议
proton	['prəutɔn]	n.	[核]质子
proxy	['prɔksi]	n.	代理
pseudo-random	['psjuːdəu 'rændəm]	adj.	伪随机的
psycho-acoustic			心理(精神)听觉的；传音的

Q

QAM(Quadrature Amplitude Modulation)			正交幅度调制
QoS(Quality of Service)			服务质量
QPSK(Quadrature Phase Shift Key)			正交相移键控
quantization	[ˌkwɔntai'zeiʃən]	n.	量化

R

RAB(Radio Access Bearer)			无线接入承载器
Radar(Radio detective and ranging)			雷达，电波探测器
radio-relay transmission			无线电中继传输
radius	['reidjəs]	n.	半径范围，半径，径向射线
RAN(Radio Access Network)			无线接入网络
RBS(Radio Base Station)			无线基站
random	['rændəm]	adj.	随机的
record	['rekɔːd]	n.	记录
recursive	[ri'kəːsiv]	adj.	递归的
refraction	[ri'frækʃən]	n.	折射
register	['redʒistə]	n.	寄存器
relay	['riːlei]	n.	中继
repeater	[ri'piːtə]	n.	转发器,中继器
resolution	[rezə'luːʃ(ə)n]	n.	分辨率
resonance	['rezənəns]	n.	谐振，共振
resonator	['rezəneitə]	n.	共鸣器
ring network			环形网
RNC(Radio Network Controller)			无线网络控制器
roaming	['rəuming]	n.	漫游
robotics	[rəu'bɔtiks]	n.	机器人技术
robust	[rə'bʌst]	adj.	稳定的, (robustness 鲁棒性, 稳定性)

root mean square (RMS)			均方根
round	[raund]	*vt.*	四舍五入
route	[ru:t]	*n.*	路由
		v.	发送
routing	['ru:tiŋ]	*n.*	路由选择
router			路由器
ruggedness	['rʌgidnis]	*n.*	结实
rule of thumb			单凭经验的方法
run length encoding			行程编码

S

satellite communication			卫星通信
satellite network			卫星网络
sampling	['sɑ:mpliŋ]	*v.*	取样
scalability	[ˌskeilə'biliti]	*n.*	可量测性
S-CDMA(Synchronous-Division Multiple Access)			同步码分多址
SDSL(Symmetric Digital Subscriber Line)			对称数字用户线
SECAM(Sequential Color Avec Memoire)			顺序与存储彩色电视系统
sector	['sektə]	*n.*	扇区
segmentation	['segmən'teiʃ ne]	*n.*	分割
selenium	[si'li:niəm, -njəm]	*n.*	硒
sequence	['si:kwəns]	*n.*	序列
sequential	[si'kwinʃ əl]	*adj.*	顺序的，串行的
sequential logic circuit			时序逻辑电路
serrated	[se'reitid]	*adj.*	锯齿状的，有锯齿的
shift-invariance			时不变特性
silicon	['silikən]	*n.*	硅，硅元素
simplex transmission			单工传输
simultaneous	['siməl'teinjəs]	*adj.*	同时的，同时发生的
sinusoidal	['sainə'sɔidəl]		正弦波的，正弦曲线的
skeletal	['skelitl]	*adj.*	骨骼的，骸骨的
solvent	['sɔlvənt]	*n.*	溶质，溶解
Sonar(Sound detective and ranging)			声呐，声波定位仪
SONET(Synchronous Optical Network)			同步光网络
sophisticated	[sə'fistikeitid]	*adj.*	复杂的，高级的，现代化的
SPC(stored-program control)			存储程序控制
specification	['spesifi'keiʃ nɛ]	*n.*	详述，规格，说明书，规范
spectrum	['spektrəm]	*n.*	光谱，频谱

spectrum analysis			谱分析
splice	[splais]	n.	接头
SSL(Security Socket Layer)			安全套接层
stabilize	['steibilaiz]	vi.	稳定(n. stabilization)
standard normal distribution			标准正态分布(均值为 0，方差为 1)
state-of-the-art facility			现代化设备
statistical	[stə'tistikl]	adj.	统计的，统计学的
statistics	[stə'tistiks]	n.	统计，统计学，统计数字
stereophonic	[,stiəriəu'fɔnik]	adj.	立体声的
stimulate	['stimjuleit]	v.	刺激，激励
stochastic	[stəu'kæstik]	adj.	随机的
strand	[strænd]	n.	多芯电缆绞合线
SU(Speech Understanding)			语音理解
Subscriber	[sʌbs'kraibə]	n.	用户
subsystem	['sʌb,sistim]	n.	次要系统，子系统
successive	[sək'sesiv]	adj.	连续的
sum of unit impulse			单位冲击求和(abbr. SUI)
superposition	['sju:pəpə'ziʃən]	n.	重叠，叠加
surveillance	[sə:'veiləns]	n.	监视，监督
switchboard	['switʃ,bɔ:d]	n.	(电话)交换台
symmetrical	[si'metrikəl]	adj.	对称的，均匀的
synchronous transmission			同步传输
synthesis	['sinθisis]	n.	综合，合成
synthesize	['sinθisaiz]	v.	综合，合成
synthetic	[sin'θetic]	adj.	合成的，人造的，综合的
system identification			系统辨识

T

TACS(Total Access Communication System)			全球接入通信系统(英国)
take over			接管
TDM(Time Division Multiplexing)			时分多路复用
TD-SCDMA(Time Division-Synchronous Code Division Multiple Access)			时分同步 CDMA
telecommunication	['telikəmju:ni'keiʃən]	n.	电信，长途通信，无线电通信，电信学
telephony	[ti'lefəni]	n.	电话学，电话
teleprocessing	[,teli'prəusesiŋ]	n.	远程信息处理

telex	['teleks]	*n.*	电报，电传打字机
template	['templit]	*n.*	模板(=templet)
tensile	['tensail]	*adj.*	张力的，拉力的
terminal	['tə:minl]	*n.*	终端，终端设备
texture	['tekstʃə]	*n.*	(木材，岩石等的)纹理
threshold	['θreʃhəuld]	*n.*	界限，临界值
time slot			时隙
token	['təukən]	*n.*	令牌
tonal	['təunəl]	*adj.*	音调的
topology	[tə'pɔlədʒi]	*n.*	拓扑，布局，拓扑学
track	[træk]	*n.*	磁道
trade-off			权衡，折中
traffic load			通信负载，话务量
traffic throughput			通话能力
transceiver	[træn'si:və]	*n.*	无线电收发机，收发器
			(transmitter + receiver)
transducer	[trænz'dju:sə]	*n.*	传感器，变频器
transient	['trænziənt]	*adj.*	短暂的，瞬时的
transistor	[træn'zistə]	*n.*	[电子]晶体管
trigonometric	[trigənə'metrik]	*adj.*	三角学的，三角法的
truncation	[trʌŋ'keiʃən]	*n.*	截断
trunk line			中继线，干线
two-dimensional			二维的

U

UHF(Ultra High frequency)			超高频
ultrasound	['ʌltrə,saund]	*n.*	超声波
ultraviolet	['ʌltrə'vaiəlit]	*adj.*	紫外线的，紫外的
		n.	紫外线辐射
underlie	[ʌndə'lai]	*vt.*	支撑；构成(理论，政策，行为等)
			的基础；位于……之下
underlying	['ʌndə'laiiŋ]	*adj.*	根本的
UNI(User-Network Interface)			用户网络接口
UNICODE			统一的字符编码标准，采用双
			字节
			对字符进行编码
uniform	['ju:nifɔ:m]	*adj.*	均匀的

Uniform distribution			均匀分布
upgrade	['ʌpgreid]	n.	升级
uplink	['ʌp,liŋk]	n.	[电信]向上传输，上行线，卫星上行链路

V

valence	['veiləns]	n.	[化](化合)价，原子价
variable	['vɛəriəbl]	n.	变量
variance	['vɛəriəns]	n.	方差
varicap	['væri'kæp]	n.	变容二极管 (=variable-capacitance diode)
VCO(voltage controlled oscillator)			压控振荡器
VDSL(Very High Bit-Rate Digital Subscriber Line)			甚高比特率数字用户线
vector	['vektə]	n.	矢量，向量
vector quantification			矢量量化
verification	['verifi'keiʃən]	n.	确认，查证
versatile	['və:sətail]	adj.	通用的，万能的
vertical	['və:tikəl]	adj.	垂直的
VHF(Very High frequency)			甚高频
via	['vaiə, 'vi:ə]	prep.	经由，取道
vibratory	['vaibrətəri]	adj.	振动的，振动性的
videophone	['vidiəufəun]	n.	电视电话
videotex video			可视图文电视
visualization	['vizjuəlai'zeiʃən, -ʒuə-; -li'z-]	n.	显像
VLC(Variable length coding)			可变长编码
VOD(Video on Demand)			视频点播
vocal	['vəukl]	adj.	发嗓音的，声音的，有声的，歌唱的
VOIP(Voice over IP)			IP 语音
volume	['vɔlju:m; (US) -jəm]	n.	体积，量，大量，音量
VPN(Virtual Private Network)			虚拟专用网
vulnerable	['vʌlnərəb(ə)l]	adj.	易受攻击的，易受……的攻击

W

waveform	['weivfɔ:m]	n.	波形
wave-guide			波导
wavelength	['weivleŋθ]	n.	波长

wavelet	['weivlit]	n.	小波，微波
WCDMA(Wideband CDMA)			宽带码分多址接入
WDM(wavelength division multiplexing)			波分复用
weight	[weit]	n.	加权
wire line			金属线路，有线线路
WLAN(wireless local area network)			无线局域网
WPAN(wireless personal area network)			无线个域网

X

| xDSL(A,H,I,S,V-DSL) | | 数字用户线 |

附录 2 科技论文写作常用句型

科技论文一般由摘要(Abstract)、正文(Body)、结论(Conclusion)、致谢(Acknowledgement)、参考文献(References)等组成。以下将按照这几个组成部分分别总结一下常用的句型。

一、摘要

1. 摘要的第一句常常是直接介绍文章的主要内容，通常有以下几种写法。

This paper describes…(本文描述了……)

This paper presents…(本文提出了……)

This paper discusses…(本文讨论了……)

This paper analyses…(本文分析了……)

This paper reports on…(本文报告了……)

This paper investigates…(本文调查了……)

This paper examines…(本文检验了……)

This paper deals with…(本文论述了……)

This paper researches into…(本文探讨了……)

This paper gives…(本文给出了……)

This paper points out…(本文指出了……)

This paper reviews…(本文总结了……)

This paper makes a study of…(本文研究了……)

This paper makes investigations on…(本文研究了……)

在以上各句中，也可用 The author 做主语，但一般不用 I 或 We 做主语。

在科技论文中一般使用被动语态用来强调所论述的客观性，因此，以上句子也可以采用被动语态的形式：

Information (regarding… or concerning…) is described.

Information (regarding… or concerning…) is presented.

Information (regarding… or concerning…) is discussed.

Information (regarding… or concerning…) is analyzed.

Information (regarding… or concerning…) is reported.

Information (regarding… or concerning…) is investigated.

Information (regarding… or concerning…) is examined.

Information (regarding… or concerning…) is dealt with.

Information (regarding… or concerning…) is given.

Information (regarding… or concerning…) is pointed out.

除此以外，还可以用以下的句型作为开始。

In this paper a new method of …is introduced. 本文介绍了一种新的……方法。

In this paper a new approach of …is recommended。本文推荐了一种新的……方法。

2. 第一句之后，是简述过程及论据，可以用以下几种方式。

An example of …is analyzed in detail.

An example of …is described in detail.

An example of …is discussed in detail.

An example of …is examined in detail.

An example of …is studied in detail.

3. 如果在论文中有图、表的话，可以用以下方式表达。

Data are displayed in graphs and tables. 数据显示在图表中。

4. 对于论文的主要结论，可以用以下方式。

Findings are presented.

Results are reported.

Findings are analyzed

Results are examined.

Findings are discussed.

5. 另外，摘要中常用的表达方式还有。

A series of experiments were made/carried out on …

对……进行了一系列实验。

Special mention is given here to (sth).

这里专门提到……

Examples of …demonstrate that…

……的例子表明……

Statistics confirm…

统计数字肯定了……

6. 摘要的末尾一般是用来表示论文所做工作的进一步意义及进一步研究方向，因此可以用以下方式表达。

These results also indicate that…　　　这些结果也指出……

These data also indicate that….　　　这些数据也指出……

These findings also indicate that…　　　这些发现也指出……

These experiments also indicate that…　这些实验也指出……

The findings imply that…　　　　　这些发现暗示……

Based on these conclusions…is discussed. 根据这些结论，讨论了……

The findings suggest that further research into … is called for.

这些发现提示要对……作进一步研究。

The results suggest that further research into…would be worthwhile.

这些发现提示对……进一步研究是值得的。

二、正文

1. 科技英语常用一般现在时态表示客观真理或客观规律。

High-speed digital design <u>studies</u> how passive circuit elements affect signal propagation(ringing and reflections), interaction between signals (crosstalk), and interactions with the natural world (electromagnetic interference).

高速数字设计研究无源电路元件如何影响信号的传播(环绕和反射)，信号间的互相作用(交调失真)，以及信号与自然界的互相作用(电磁干扰)。

2. 科技英语常用被动语态强调所论述的客观事物。

Revolutionary changes <u>have already been made</u> in a broad range of fields: communications, medical imaging, radar & sonar and high fidelity music.

在通信、医学图像、雷达和声呐以及高质量音乐等很多领域发生了革命性的改变。

3. 普遍使用名词词组及名词化结构，强调客观存在的事实而非某一行为，常用表示动作或状态的抽象名词。

Television is the <u>transmission and reception</u> of images of moving objects by radio waves.
电视是通过无线电波对运动物体的图像传送和接收。

4. 科技英语中常会提出一些假设、推理或判断，内容与事实相反，或不大可能实现，为了同客观实际相区别，常使用虚拟语气。

<u>If there were</u> no attraction between the proton and the electron, the electron <u>would fly away</u> from the proton in a straight line.

如果质子和电子之间没有引力，电子会沿直线飞离质子。

5. 常使用添加强调词、或采用强调句型 It is(was)+....+that(which, who, whom)，及改变句子成分的结构位置来强调某些成分。

Beta is approximately constant for an individual transistor, although it <u>does</u> vary with temperature and slightly with the collector current.　　(加强调动词 does)

对于某个单独的晶体管来说，β几乎是恒定不变的，尽管它确实会随着温度及集电极电流有微弱的变化。

<u>It was Bell himself who</u> invented one of the earliest light-wave communications devices in 1880. (It 引导强调句型)

是贝尔自己在 1880 年发明了最早的光通信设备。

6. 在正文中常用图表来帮助说明论据、事实等。最常有附图(Figure)和表(Table)，另外还有简图(Diagram)，曲线图或流程图(Graph)，视图(View)，剖面图(Profile)，图案(Pattern)等。在文中提到时通常表达法如下。

As (is) shown in Fig.4，　　如图 4 所示。

As (is) shown in Tab.1，　　如表 1 所示。

7. "由于……"的表达，可以用以下短语表示。

Because of sth…

On account of sth…

As a result of sth…

Due to sth…

Owing to sth…

In view of sth…

例：An object has dynamic energy because of its motion.

物体由于运动而具有动能。

也可用从句的形式表示"由于……这样……"的因果关系。

because +从句

as+从句

since+从句

now that+从句

in that+从句

例：Now that they have electronic computers, mathematicians are solving problems they would not have dared tackle a few years ago.

由于有了计算机，数学家正在解决若干年前还不敢着手去解决的问题。

8．可以用 cause，bring about，give rise to，produce (sth.)来表示"引起……"，"产生……"。

In the past 50 years new technologies have brought about many changes in everyday life.

近50年来，新技术在日常生活中引起了很多变化。

9．可以用 attribute sth. to sth. 或 ascribe sth. to sth. 来表示"归因于……"，"归功于……"。

The invention of television has been ascribed to a number of scientists.

电视的发明归功于许多科学家。

10．可以用 result from sth. 或 originate in/from sth. 来表示"起源于……"。

Most scientific progress originates in careful consideration of work that has already been done.

大多数科学进步均起源于对已经完成的工作的认真思考。

11．可用 result in sth. 或 lead to sth.表示"导致"。

Such observations lead to the discovery that there can be rapid corrosion when a metal is non-homogeneous.

这样的观察使人们发现，当金属是非均质金属时，就可能很快生锈。

12．可用"so/such … that +从句"或"so that+从句"或"with the result that+从句"表示"以至于……"。

In the magnet, the atoms are lined up in such a way that their electrons are circling in the same direction.

在磁铁中，原子的排列方式使得它们的电子按相同的环绕方向在轨道上运行。

13．可用"too…to"表示"太……以致不能……"。

Atoms are too small to be seen even through the most powerful microscope.

原子太小，以至于用放大倍数最大的显微镜也看不到。

14．可用"enough to do sth.…."表示"足以……"。

These solar batteries supply enough electricity to drive a car.

这些太阳能电池组提供的电力足以驱动一辆汽车。

15. 常用"therefore, hence, thus, consequently, as a result, for this reason"表示"因此……"。

Copper losses are proportional to the load being supplied by the transformer and <u>for this reason</u> are sometimes called the load losses.

铜损耗与变压器提供的负荷成比例，因此有时称为负荷耗损。

16. 用"be responsible for"表示"是……的原因"。

Electromagnetism <u>is responsible for</u> most of sensory experiences.

电磁对大多数的感知有影响。

17. 用"intend to do sth."或"mean to do sth."或"aim to do sth.",或"be going to do sth."或"plan to do sth."或"arrange to do sth."表示"打算做某事"。

Anyone who <u>means to advance science</u> must have a capacity for original thought.

无论是谁，如果想推动科学向前发展，都必须具备创造性思考的能力。

18. 用"to do …"或"in order to do…",或"so as to do …"或"in order that+从句"或"so that +从句"或"with view to sth."或"for the purpose of sth."或"for sth's sake"或"for the sake of sth"表示"为了……"。

The resistance must be reduced <u>so that</u> we can have a stronger current.

为了得到更强的电流必须减小电阻。

Bearings are lubricated <u>for the purpose of</u> reducing the friction.

为了减少摩擦要润滑轴承。

He argues <u>for the sake of</u> arguing.

他为辩论而辩论。

19. 用"lest+从句"或"for fear that+从句"或"in case+从句"表示"以免……"。

Isotopes of long half-lives must be handled with great care <u>in case they cause radiation damage.</u>

处置半衰期长的同位素必须十分小心，以免引起辐射伤害。

20. 用"be intended for sth."或"be meant for sth."表示"供……之用"。

This book <u>is intended for</u> beginners.

这本书供初学者使用。

21. 用"The purpose/aim/objective of …is sth./to do …"表示"……的目的是……"。

<u>One aim of</u> cybernetics <u>is</u> the investigation, design and construction of robots of various types.

控制论的一个目的是研究、设计和制造各种类型的机器人。

22. 可用"depend on/upon sth"或"rely on/upon sth."或"be dependent on/upon sth."表示"依靠……"。

Sweden is <u>dependent on</u> her hydro-electric resources for power.

瑞典依靠其水力资源作为动力。

23. 可用"dependent on sth"或"be dependent on sth"表示"取决于……"。

The value of a metal <u>depend on</u> whether it is rare or abundant.

金属的价值取决于它是稀有的还是丰富的。

24. 可用 "be based on sth." 表示 "以……为基础"。

His conclusion was based on experimental data.

他的结论是以实验数据为基础的。

25. 可用 "according to sth" 或 "in accordance with sth" 或 "depending on sth" 表示 "根据……"。

According to the reaction principle, there is also an equal force in the other direction.

根据反作用原理，在另一个方向也有相等的力。

26. 可用 "in accord with sth" 或 "in agreement with sth" 或 "in conformity with sth" 或 "agree with sth" 或 "accord with sth" 或 "correspond to/with sth" 表示 "与……一致"。

The actual production figures are in agreement/accord with the estimated figures.

实际的生产量和估计的数字一致。

The current impulses of the incoming signal correspond to the microphone electric impulses.

输入信号的电脉冲与麦克风的电脉冲相对应。

27. 可用 "compare …and/with …" 表示 "把……和……相比较"。

Compare vacuum tubes and/with transistors, and you will know the advantages of the latter.

把电子管和晶体管比较一下，就可以知道后者的优点了。

28. 可用 "compare…to…" 表示 "把……比作……"。

The tiny currents in the receiving antenna are very small and may be compared to the weak signal coming in over a long distance telephone line.

接收天线中的电流很小，可以和长途电话线路中传来的微弱信号相比。

29. 可用 "whereas" 或 "while" 表示 "而，然而"。

Radio waves go thorough clouds and fog quite well, whereas light waves do not.

无线电波可以很好地穿过云雾，而光波却不能。

30. 可用 "the same as sth." 或 "identical with sth" 表示 "与……相同"。

This machine is roughly the same as the other one in design.

这台机器的设计与另一台大致相同。

31. 可用 "similar to sth" 或 "analogous to sth" 表示 "与……相似"。

The curved reflector used for radar waves is similar in shape to the reflector of the flashlight.

雷达波用的曲面反射镜的形状与手电筒的反射镜相似。

32. 可以用 "differ from … in sth" 或 "be different from …in sth" 表示 "不同于……"。

Different kinds of radiation energy, such as light, X-rays and radio waves, seem to be quite different from one another.

各种不同的辐射能，如光、X射线、无线电波，看起来彼此很不相同。

33. 可以用 "differentiate …from sth" 或 "distinguish … from sth" 或 "tell …from sth" 表示 "区分……和……"。

We can tell low from high frequency light waves by the sensation of color they produce.

根据光波所产生的色感，我们能辨别低频光波和高频光波。

34. 可以用"by /in contrast"或"by comparison"表示"相形之下"。

The image-oriented remote sensing technology is older. <u>By comparison</u>, the technology of numerically oriented systems is still in its infancy.

图像遥感技术历史较长。相比之下，数字遥感系统还处于萌芽状态。

35. 可以用"形容词或副词比较级+than…"表示"比……(大，小，快等)"，可以用"less+形容词或副词原级＋than"表示"不如……"。

Digital computers are <u>much more</u> widely used <u>than</u> analog computer.
数字计算机的使用远比模拟计算机广泛。

Analog computers are <u>much less</u> widely used <u>than</u> digital computers.
模拟计算机的使用远不如数字计算机广泛。

36. 可以用"最高级+in+单数名词"或"最高级＋of/among+复数名词"表示"……中最……"。

The speed of light is <u>the greatest</u> speed <u>in</u> the universe.
光速是宇宙间最大的速度。

Uranium is <u>the most complicated of</u> the natural atoms.
铀是天然原子中最为复杂的。

37. 可以用"better than sth"或"superior to sth"表示"优于……"。

Radio telescopes are <u>better than</u> ordinary telescopes in that they can operate in all weather conditions.

无线电望远镜比普通望远镜好，因为它可以在一切气象条件下使用。

38. 可以用"have the advantage of th."或"have the advantage that+从句"表示"……的优点为……"。

Such a system <u>has the advantage of</u> eliminating the tremendous pollution of the environment.
这种体系的优点是消除了对环境的严重污染。

39. 可以用"either…or…"表示"不是…就是…"，可以用"neither…nor…"表法"不是……也不是……"。

The electronic switches in a computer have two states: they are <u>either</u> off <u>or</u> on.
计算机里的电子开关有两种状态，不是开就是关。

40. 可用"if+从句"或"in case +从句"或"in case of sth"或"in the event of sth"表示"如果……"。

<u>In the event of</u> neutron capture, the mass number of the nucleus will be raised, and it will thus become unstable and radioactive.

如果中子被俘获，原子核的质量数便提高，结果就会变得不稳定而且有放射性。

41. 用"on condition (that)+从句"表示"条件是……"。

The operation can proceed indefinitely <u>on condition that</u> the controls are pre-set correctly.
此操作可以无限地进行，条件是预先设定好操纵装置。

42. 可以用"unless+从句"表示"除非……，如果不……"。

Harmful radiation will result <u>unless</u> the isotopes are shielded properly.
如果同位素不加以适当屏蔽，就会产生有害的辐射。

43. 可以用 "make…do" 或 "have…do" 或 "let…do" 或 "enable … to do" 或 "allow… to do" 或 "permit … to do" 或 "cause … to do" 表示 "使……做某事"。

In the broadcasting station, the radio waves are made to correspond to each sound in turn.
广播电台使无线电波依次对每一个声音做出相应变化。

44. 可以用 "make …+过去分词" 或 "have …+过去分词" 或 "get…+过去分词" 表示 "使……被别人做"。

You should get everything prepared before you begin the experiment.
你必须在开始实验以前把一切准备好。

45. 可以用 "change…into sth" 或 "turn…into sth" 或 "transform…into sth" 或 "convert…into sth" 表示 "把……变成……"。

Electric lamps of various kinds change electric energy into light.
各种电灯把电能变为光。

46. 可以用 "vary with sth" 或 "vary according to sth" 表示 "随……而变"。

The internal energy of a gas varies with a rise in temperature.
气体的内能随温度升高而变化。

47. 可以用 "vary as sth" 或 "be proportional to sth" 表示 "与……成比例"。

The insulation resistance of a cable is inversely proportional to its length.
电缆的绝缘电阻与它的长度成反比。

48. 可以用 "The+比较级…，the+比较级…" 表示 "……越……，……就越……"。

The heavier the electric current, the stronger is the electromagnetism.

49. 可以用 "consist of sth" 或 "be made up of sth" 或 "be composed of sth" 或 "comprise sth" 表示 "(整体)由……组成"。

The tranceiver consists of a transmitter and a receiver.
收发信机是由发信机和收信机组成的。

50. 可以用 "form sth" 或 "constitute sth" 或 "make up sth" 或 "comprise sth" 表示 "(部分)组成(整体)"。

The sequence of procedures makes up the so-called scientific method.
这一系列程序就构成所谓的科学方法。

51. 可以用 "send out sth" 或 "emit sth" 或 "give off sth" 表示 "发出"。

The command computer sends out a series of impulses which the receiving computer then absorbs and makes use of.
下达指令的计算机发出一系列电脉冲，接收指令的计算机便加以吸收和利用。

52. 可以用 "supply A to B" 或 "supply B with A" 或 "provide A for B" 或 "provide B with A" 表示 "把 A 供给 B"。

Power plants provide electricity for industry.
发电厂为工业提供电力。

53. 可以用 "join…to sth" 或 "link … to sth" 或 "attach … to sth" 或 "connect … to sth" 或 "couple…to sth" 表示 "连接"。

The machine is linked to the motor by a driving belt or chain.
机器用传动皮带或链条与发动机相连。

54．可以用"have…to do with sth"或"be related to sth"或"be associated with sth"或"be connected with sth"或"be concerned with sth"表示"与……有关"。

In the past, the field of robotics has tended to <u>be associated with</u> fiction.
过去，机器人技术领域一直倾向于和幻想相联系。

55．可用"equip …with sth"或"be equipped with sth"表示"装备"。

If an airplane flying at night <u>is equipped with</u> radar, the pilot can see on the radar viewing screen a mountain peak miles away.
如果夜间飞行的飞机上装有雷达，飞行员就能在雷达荧光屏上看到几英里以外的山峰。

56．可以有用"dismantle sth"或"take …to pieces"表示"拆除"。

We had to <u>take</u> the whole engine <u>to pieces</u> to discover the cause of the trouble.
我们不得不把整个发动机拆开，看看故障的原因是什么。

57．可以用"prevent… from sth"或"keep …from sth"或"stop …from sth"来表示"防止……发生"。

Insulators are used to <u>prevent</u> electrical charges <u>from</u> going where they are not wanted.
绝缘体用来阻止电荷流到不需要电荷的地方。

58．可以用"keep…from sth"或"protect…from sth"来表示"保护……使免受……"。

In space, astronauts have to be <u>protected from</u> harmful radiations.
在太空中，宇航员要保护自己不受有害辐射的伤害。

59．可以用"utilize sth"或"exploit sth"或"make use of sth"或"take advantage of sth"表示"利用……"。

Scientists have worked out ways to <u>take advantage of</u> the rise and fall of the tides to generate electric current.
科学家们想出了利用潮汐的涨落来发电的方法。

60．可以用"make the best use of sth"或"make full use of sth"表示"充分利用"。

Such properties of semiconductors have been <u>made full use of</u> in microelectronics.
在微电子学中，半导体的这些特性得到了充分利用。

61．可以用"contract"或"shrink"或"constrict"表示"缩小"。

With the development of the transistor, electronic devices <u>shrank</u> tremendously.
随着晶体管的发展，电子器件的体积大为减小。

62．可以用"the function of …is to do"或"the duty of …is to do sth"来表示"……的用途为……"。

<u>The function of</u> a governor <u>is to</u> control the running speed under all conditions of load.
调速器的作用是在各种负荷条件下控制发动机的转速。

63．可以有"a way of sth."或"a means to do …"或"an approach to sh"或"a method of sth"表示"……的方法"。

<u>A common method of</u> feeding information into the computer is with the use of magnetic tape.
向计算机输入信息的一个常用方法是利用磁带。

64．可以用"by way of sth"或"with the help of sth"或"with the aid of sth"表示"借助于……，通过……"。

These robots have sent back to the earth, <u>by ways of</u> radio, such important information on space as temperature, radiation, and so on.

这些机器人通过无线电将宇宙中的温度、辐射等重要资料发回地球。

三、结论

1. 关于"结论"可有以下表达方式。

The following conclusions can be drawn from…　　由……可得如下结论……

It can be concluded that…　　可以得出结论……

We may conclude that…　　我们得出如下结论……

We come to the conclusion that…　　我们得出如下结论……

It is generally accepted (believed, held, acknowledged) that…一般认为……(用于表示肯定的结论)

We think (consider, believe, feel) that…我们认为……(用于表示留有商量余地的结论)

2. 关于"建议"可有以下表达方式。

It is advantageous to (do)….　　做……是有益的

It should be realized (emphasized, stressed, noted, pointed out) that…应该意识到(强调的，注意的，指出的，)的是……

It is suggested (proposed, recommended, desired) that…建议……

It would be better that…是比较好的

It would be helpful if…　如果……将会是有帮助的

It would be advisable when…建议……

四、致谢

在论文结束后，作者通常会以简短的谢词对曾给予支持与帮助或关心的人表示感谢，可用如下方式。

I am thankful (grateful, deeply indebted) to sb. for sth..

I would like to thank sb. for sth..

Thanks are due to sb. for sth..

The author wishes to express his sincere appreciation to sb. for sth..

The author wishes to acknowledge sb..

The author wishes to express his gratitude for sth..

参 考 文 献

[1] 翻译中国网站.

[2] 陶友兰，查国生. 研究生英语翻译[M]. 上海：复旦大学出版社，2002.

[3] 邓炎昌，刘润清. 语言与文化——英汉语言文化对比[M]. 北京：外语教学与语言研究出版社，1989.

[4] 胡文仲. 跨文化交际学概论[M]. 北京：外语教学与研究出版社，1999.

[5] 王德春，孙汝建，姚远. 社会心理语言学[M]. 上海：上海外语教育出版社，1995.

[6] 胥懋云. 二十一世纪大学英语教学改革[M]. 北京：外语教学与研究出版社，2000.

[7] 陈申. 语言文化教学策略研究[M]. 北京：北京语言文化大学出版社，2001.

[8] 陆国强. 现代英语词汇学[M]. 上海：上海外语教育出版社，1983.

[9] 高永照，程勇. 科技英语的文体写作与翻译[M]. 北京：学苑出版社，1998.

[10] www.51Test.net.

[11] 秦荻辉. 实用科技英语写作技巧[M]. 上海：上海外语教育出版社，2001.

[12] 丁往道，吴冰等. 英语写作手册[M]. 北京：外语教学与研究出版社，1994.

[13] [美]Liz Buffaz. 英语研究报告高手[M]. 长春：长春出版社，2003.

[14] [美]John Langan. 美国大学英语写作[M]. 北京：外语教学与研究出版社，2004.

[15] 辛书伟，王波. 英语科技论文写作[M]. 天津：天津大学出版社，2003.

[16] [Anonymous].Required and Optional Sections of a Thesis or Dissertation [online] 2005. Available from: http://www.fis.ncsu.edu/grad_publicns/thesdis/req.html.

[17] [Anonymous]. Quotation Marks [online] 2005. Available from: http://owl.english.purdue.edu/handouts/grammar/g_quote.html

[18] [Anonymous]. Writing Guides [online] 2005. Available from:http://writing.colostate.edu/guides/index.cfm.

[19] Gary Klass. Presenting Data: Tabular and graphic display of social indicators [online] 2005. Available from:http://lilt.ilstu.edu/gmklass/pos138/datadisplay/badchart.htm.

[20] [Anonymous]. [online] 2005. Available from:http://www.scit.wlv.ac.uk/~jphb/cp4040/rolandonotes/CSNDSP2002/Papers/K2/K2.1.pdf.

[21] http://www.dsptutor.freeuk.com.

[22] High-Speed Digital System Design.

[23] [美] Michael A. Miller. 数据与网络通信(英文影印版) [M]. 北京：科学出版社，2002.

[24] [美] Andrew S. Tanenbaum. 计算机网络(影印版) [M]. 北京：清华大学出版社，1997.

[25] 任开兴. 部分否定句型的多义及翻译[J]. 中国科技翻译，2002 年(2)，P38-41.

[26] 高丽. 电子信息专业英语课程中翻译技巧的教法研究[J]. 淮南职业技术学院学报，2004 年(2)，P103-105.

[27] 孙永强. 科技英语被动语态隐性因果关系及其转换[J]. 中国科技翻译，2004 年(11)，P4-7.

[28] 于建平. 科技英语长句的分析及翻译[J]. 中国科技翻译，2002 年(8)，14~16.

[29] 刘兰云，杜耀文. 科技英语抽象名词的特点及翻译[J]. 中国科技翻译，2000 年(11)，P17-18.

[30] 郭海平. 科技英语词汇的构词特点及翻译[J]. 武汉工业学院学报，2004 年(6)，P115-120.

[31] 李丙午，燕静敏. 科技英语的名词化结构及其翻译[J]. 中国科技翻译，2002 年(2)，P5-7.

[32] 谭力红. 科技英语的词汇特点及翻译中的选词[J]. 河北职业技术学院学报，2004 年(6)，P22-24.

[33] 朱小玲. 科技英语的翻译技巧[J]. 甘肃科技，2005 年(3)，P188-191.

[34] 贾晓云. 科技英语的句法特点及其翻译方法[J]. 太原理工大学学报(社会科学版). 2003 年(6)，P67-69.

[35] 任芬梅. 科技英语的特点及其翻译[J]. 焦作工学院学报(社会科学版)，2001 年(9)，P46-47.

[36] 周洪洁. 科技英语的语域特征与科技翻译的标准[J]. 重庆大学学报(社会科学版)，2002 年(5)，P85-87.

[37] 牛灵安. 科技英语翻译词义的确定[J]. 中国科技翻译，2004 年(2)，P14-16.

[38] 牛晓红. 科技英语翻译探析[J]. 山东煤炭科技，2004 年(3)，P51-52.

[39] 单献心. 科技英语翻译应重视的问题[J]. 浙江科技学院学报，2002 年(9)，P46-50.

[40] 倪传斌. 科技英语共轭结构的特点及汉译方法[J]. 中国科技翻译，2003 年(11)，P18-20.

[41] 黄湘. 科技英语汉译的词义引申[J]. 中国科技翻译，2001 年(2)，P19-21.

[42] 赵晴. 科技英语术语翻译中常见错误分析[J]. 鞍山科技大学学报，2003 年(12)，P478-480.

[43] 周振锋. 科技英语文体中动词形态的用法及翻译[J]. 周口师范学院学报，2003 年(9)，P122-124.

[44] 曹国英. 科技英语文献的翻译研究[J]. 中国科技翻译，2000 年(2)，P6-9.

[45] 刘红梅. 科技英语语篇翻译的语域制约性[J]. 佛山科学技术学院学报(社会科学版)，2004 年(3)，P29-32.

[46] 高秀丽. 科技英语中倍数的表达与翻译[J]. 黑龙江科技学院学报，2001 年(6)，P62-65.

[47] 朱俊松. 科技英语中隐含因果关系句的表达及其翻译[J]. 华东船舶工业学院学报(社会科学版)，2002 年(6)，P60-62.

[48] 周秋琴. 也谈科技文体与科技翻译[J]. 中国科技翻译，2000 年(2)，P41-43.

[49] 潘福燕. 英语科技文体的语词特点及翻译[J]. 中国科技翻译，2005 年(11)，P56-58.

[50] 钱旭中. 英语科技文献的特点及其翻译[J]. 中国科技翻译，1994 年(2)，P21-24.

[51] 宋德富，司爱侠. 计算机专业英语教程[M]. 北京：高等教育出版社，2005.

[52] http://www.GameDev.net.

[53] White Paper of Video Compression, released by Array Microsystems, Inc.

[54] http://www. dunxd.com/articles.php?show=44.

[55] 张筱华. 通信英语[M]. 北京：北京邮电大学出版社，2003.

[56] 陈枫艳. 计算机专业英语[M]. 北京：科学出版社，2006.

[57] 李霞等. 电子与通信专业英语[M]. 北京：电子工业出版社，2005.

[58] 李白萍等. 电子信息类专业英语[M]. 西安：西安电子科技大学出版社，2003.

[59] 吴娜达，李辉. 英汉信息通信技术缩略语词典[M]. 北京：人民邮电出版社，2004.

[60] http://www.51edu.com/waiyu/2008/1124/article_53149.html.

北京大学出版社电气信息类教材书目(已出版)
欢迎选订

序号	标准书号	书名	编著者	定价
1	978-7-301-10759-1	DSP 技术及应用	吴冬梅 张玉杰	26
2	978-7-301-10760-7	单片机原理与应用技术	魏立峰 王宝兴	25
3	978-7-301-10765-2	电工学	蒋 中 刘国林	29
4	978-7-301-19183-5	电工与电子技术(上册)(第2版)	吴舒辞	30
5	978-7-301-19229-0	电工与电子技术(下册)(第2版)	徐卓农 李士军	32
6	978-7-301-10699-0	电子工艺实习	周春阳	19
7	978-7-301-10744-7	电子工艺学教程	张立毅 王华奎	32
8	978-7-301-10915-6	电子线路 CAD	吕建平 梅军进	34
9	978-7-301-10764-1	数据通信技术教程	吴延海 陈光军	29
10	978-7-301-18784-5	数字信号处理(第2版)	阎 毅	32
11	978-7-301-18889-7	现代交换技术(第2版)	姚 军 李佳森	36
12	978-7-301-10761-4	信号与系统	华 容 隋晓红	33
13	978-7-301-10762-5	信息与通信工程专业英语	韩定定 赵菊敏	24
14	978-7-301-10757-7	自动控制原理	袁德成 王玉德	29
15	978-7-301-16520-1	高频电子线路(第2版)	宋树祥 周冬梅	35
16	978-7-301-11507-7	微机原理与接口技术	陈光军 傅越千	34
17	978-7-301-11442-1	MATLAB 基础及其应用教程	周开利 邓春晖	24
18	978-7-301-11508-4	计算机网络	郭银景 孙红雨 段 锦	31
19	978-7-301-12178-8	通信原理	隋晓红 钟晓玲	32
20	978-7-301-12175-7	电子系统综合设计	郭 勇 余小平	25
21	978-7-301-11503-9	EDA 技术基础	赵明富 李立军	22
22	978-7-301-12176-4	数字图像处理	曹茂永	23
23	978-7-301-12177-1	现代通信系统	李白萍 王志明	27
24	978-7-301-12340-9	模拟电子技术	陆秀令 韩清涛	28
25	978-7-301-13121-3	模拟电子技术实验教程	谭海曙	24
26	978-7-301-11502-2	移动通信	郭俊强 李 成	22
27	978-7-301-11504-6	数字电子技术	梅开乡 郭 颖	30
28	978-7-301-18860-6	运筹学(第2版)	吴亚丽 张俊敏	28
29	978-7-5038-44407-2	传感器与检测技术	祝诗平	30
30	978-7-5038-44413-3	单片机原理及应用	刘 刚 秦永左	24
31	978-7-5038-44409-6	电机与拖动	杨天明 陈 杰	27
32	978-7-5038-44411-9	电力电子技术	樊立萍 王忠庆	25
33	978-7-5038-4399-0	电力市场原理与实践	邹 斌	24
34	978-7-5038-4405-8	电力系统继电保护	马永翔 王世荣	27
35	978-7-5038-4397-6	电力系统自动化	孟祥忠 王 博	25
36	978-7-5038-44404-1	电气控制技术	韩顺杰 吕树清	22
37	978-7-5038-44403-4	电器与PLC控制技术	陈志新 宗学军	38
38	978-7-5038-44400-3	工厂供配电	王玉华 赵志英	34
39	978-7-5038-44410-2	控制系统仿真	郑恩让 聂诗良	26
40	978-7-5038-4398-3	数字电子技术	李 元 张兴旺	27
41	978-7-5038-44412-6	现代控制理论	刘永信 陈志梅	22
42	978-7-5038-44401-0	自动化仪表	齐志才 刘红丽	27
43	978-7-5038-44408-9	自动化专业英语	李国厚 王春阳	32
44	978-7-5038-44406-5	集散控制系统	刘翠玲 黄建兵	25
45	978-7-301-19174-3	传感器基础(第2版)	赵玉刚 邱 东	30
46	978-7-5038-4396-9	自动控制原理	潘 丰 张开如	32
47	978-7-301-10512-2	现代控制理论基础(国家级十一五规划教材)	侯媛彬	20
48	978-7-301-11151-2	电路基础学习指导与典型题解	公茂法 刘 宁	32
49	978-7-301-12326-3	过程控制与自动化仪表	张井岗	36
50	978-7-301-12327-0	计算机控制系统	徐文尚	28
51	978-7-5038-4414-0	微机原理与接口技术	赵志诚 段中兴	38

序号	标准书号	书名	编著者	定价
52	978-7-301-10465-1	单片机原理及应用教程	范立南	30
53	978-7-5038-4426-4	微型计算机原理与接口技术	刘彦文	26
54	978-7-301-12562-5	嵌入式基础实践教程	杨 刚	30
55	978-7-301-12530-4	嵌入式 ARM 系统原理与实例开发	杨宗德	25
56	978-7-301-13676-8	单片机原理与应用及 C51 程序设计	唐 颖	30
57	978-7-301-13577-8	电力电子技术及应用	张润和	38
58	978-7-301-12393-5	电磁场与电磁波	王善进 张涛	25
59	978-7-301-12179-5	电路分析	王艳红 蒋学华 戴纯春	38
60	978-7-301-12380-5	电子测量与传感技术	杨 雷 张建奇	35
61	978-7-301-14461-9	高电压技术	马永翔	28
62	978-7-301-14472-5	生物医学数据分析及其 MATLAB 实现	尚志刚 张建华	25
63	978-7-301-14460-2	电力系统分析	曹 娜	35
64	978-7-301-14459-6	DSP 技术与应用基础	俞一彪	34
65	978-7-301-14994-2	综合布线系统基础教程	吴达金	24
66	978-7-301-15168-6	信号处理 MATLAB 实验教程	李 杰 张 猛 邢笑雪	20
67	978-7-301-15440-3	电工电子实验教程	魏 伟 何仁平	26
68	978-7-301-15445-8	检测与控制实验教程	魏 伟	24
69	978-7-301-04595-4	电路与模拟电子技术	张绪光 刘在娥	35
70	978-7-301-15458-8	信号、系统与控制理论(上、下册)	邱德润 等	70
71	978-7-301-15786-2	通信网的信令系统	张云麟	24
72	978-7-301-16493-8	发电厂变电所电气部分	马永翔 李颖峰	35
73	978-7-301-16076-3	数字信号处理	王震宇 张培珍	32
74	978-7-301-16931-5	微机原理及接口技术	肖洪兵	32
75	978-7-301-16932-2	数字电子技术	刘金华	30
76	978-7-301-16933-9	自动控制原理	丁 红 李学军	32
77	978-7-301-17540-8	单片机原理及应用教程	周广兴 张子红	40
78	978-7-301-17614-6	微机原理及接口技术实验指导书	李干林 李 升	22
79	978-7-301-12379-9	光纤通信	卢志茂 冯进玫	28
80	978-7-301-17382-4	离散信息论基础	范九伦 谢 勰 张雪锋	25
81	978-7-301-17677-1	新能源与分布式发电技术	朱永强	32
82	978-7-301-17683-2	光纤通信	李丽君 徐文云	26
83	978-7-301-17700-6	模拟电子技术	张绪光 刘在娥	36
84	978-7-301-17318-3	ARM 嵌入式系统基础与开发教程	丁文龙 李志军	36
85	978-7-301-17797-6	PLC 原理及应用	缪志农 郭新年	26
86	978-7-301-17986-4	数字信号处理	王玉德	32
87	978-7-301-18131-7	集散控制系统	周荣富 陶文英	36
88	978-7-301-18285-7	电子线路 CAD	周荣富 曾 技	41
89	978-7-301-16739-7	MATLAB 基础及应用	李国朝	39
90	978-7-301-18352-6	信息论与编码	隋晓红 王艳营	24
91	978-7-301-18260-4	控制电机与特种电机及其控制系统	孙冠群 于少娟	42
92	978-7-301-18493-6	电工技术	张 莉 张绪光	26
93	978-7-301-18496-7	现代电子系统设计教程	宋晓梅	36
94	978-7-301-18672-5	太阳能电池原理与应用	靳瑞敏	25
95	978-7-301-18314-4	通信电子线路及仿真设计	王鲜芳	29
96	978-7-301-19175-0	单片机原理与接口技术	李 升	46
97	978-7-301-19320-4	移动通信	刘维超 时 颖	39
98	978-7-301-19447-8	电气信息类专业英语	缪志农 周荣富	40
99	978-7-301-19451-5	嵌入式系统设计及应用	邢吉生 周振雄 山传文	44

请登录 www.pup6.cn 免费下载本系列教材的电子书(PDF 版)、电子课件和相关教学资源。

欢迎免费索取样书,并欢迎到北京大学出版社来出版您的著作,可在 www.pup6.cn 在线申请样书和进行选题登记,也可下载相关表格填写后发到我们的邮箱,我们将及时与您取得联系并做好全方位的服务。

联系方式:010-62750667,pup6_czq@163.com,f105888339@163.com,linzhangbo@126.com,欢迎来电来信咨询。